MW01028366

CARL JUNG AND
MAXIMUS THE CONFESSOR
ON PSYCHIC DEVELOPMENT

In what ways does psychological development differ from spiritual development and psychological experience from spiritual experience?

Bringing together two disparate theories under a trans-disciplinary framework, G. C. Tympas presents a comparison of Carl Jung's theory of psychic development and Maximus the Confessor's model of spiritual progress. An 'evolutional' relationship between the 'psychological' and the 'spiritual' is proposed for a dynamic interpretation of spiritual experience.

Carl Jung and Maximus the Confessor on Psychic Development offers a creative synthesis of elements and directions from both theories and further explores:

- Jung's views on religion in a dialogue with Maximus' concepts;
- the different directions and goals of Jung's and Maximus' models;
- Jung's 'Answer to Job' in relation to Maximus' theory of 'final restoration'.

Tympas argues that a synthesis of Jung's and Maximus' models comprises a broader trans-disciplinary paradigm of development, which can serve as a pluralistic framework for considering the composite psycho-spiritual development.

Constructively combining strands of differing disciplines, this book will appeal to those looking to explore the dialogue between analytical psychology, early Christian theology and Greek philosophy.

G. C. Tympas has degrees in medicine and theological studies and a PhD in psychoanalytic studies from the University of Essex. His research focuses on the relationship between early psychic models and psychiatric nosology and he is currently a priest and pastoral counsellor of the Greek Orthodox Church in London.

CARL JUNG AND MAXIMUS THE CONFESSOR ON PSYCHIC DEVELOPMENT

The dynamics between the 'psychological' and the 'spiritual'

G.C. Tympas

Routledge
Taylor & Francis Group

LONDON AND NEW YORK

First published 2014
by Routledge
27 Church Road, Hove, East Sussex, BN3 2FA

and by Routledge
711 Third Avenue, New York, NY 10017

Routledge is an imprint of the Taylor & Francis Group, an informa business

British Library Cataloguing in Publication Data
A catalogue record for this book is available from the British Library

Library of Congress Cataloging-in-Publication Data

Tympas, G. C.
Carl Jung and Maximus the Confessor on psychic development : the dynamics between the "psychological" and the "spiritual" / G. C. Tympas. — First Edition.
   pages cm
 1. Psychology and religion.   2. Jung, C. G. (Carl Gustav), 1875–1961.
3. Maximus, Confessor, Saint, approximately 580–662. I. Title.
  BF51.T96 2014
  261.5′15—dc23
  2013040117

ISBN: 978-0-415-62516-6 (hbk)
ISBN: 978-0-415-62517-3 (pbk)
ISBN: 978-1-315-81298-4 (ebk)

Typeset in Times New Roman
by Apex CoVantage, LLC

TO MY FATHER POLYCARPOS

CONTENTS

CONTENTS

FIGURES

TABLES

FOREWORD

This book is unique in many respects and it needs to be approached with an appreciation that does justice to it.

First of all, thematically, it relates the psychology of Carl Gustav Jung with the writings of Maximus the Confessor, one of the foremost and eloquent authorities of early Christianity. This is important because Jung's knowledge of the Christian texts was limited, despite the breadth of his erudition. Undoubtedly, for a psychiatrist, Jung was extremely widely read and well versed with an astonishing range of cultures and traditions, including the Christian one. However, he certainly had some significant gaps that have affected negatively his understanding of Christianity, and one of these was his lack of knowledge of eastern Christian philosophy and the patristic tradition. Nobody would disagree with the claim that Jung was virtually completely ignorant of these traditions, of which Maximus is one of their most articulate representatives. It is called 'patristic' because it is associated with the early Church authors ('Church fathers') that lived and wrote well before the schism between the eastern and western churches. Although the patristic tradition is shared by both churches, it has been followed by and kept alive in the practices and outlook of the Eastern Orthodox Church much more than in its western counterpart.

Dr Tympas is uniquely qualified to address the inter-relationship between the Jungian and Maximian approaches because he is deeply rooted in both. Following his medical training, he obtained a PhD in psychoanalytic studies, having researched for several years Jungian and post–Jungian psychology at the Centre for Psychoanalytic Studies of the University of Essex. Not only is he a priest and a pastoral counsellor in the Eastern Orthodox Church, but his earlier book (in Greek) has been considered a classic for many years (*God the Logos and Human 'Logos'. Energies of the Psyche in Patristic Anthropology,* 1998) because of its astute treatment of psychic models in Maximus and other Church fathers.

Maximus' voice and message are, indeed, very eloquent, but this does not mean that his writings are easily comprehensible. One needs to have a sound grounding in the themes and styles of his time in order to be able to access this eloquence, and Dr Tympas succeeds in this task most admirably, differentiating lucidly the Maximian positions into graspable units.

Another substantial contribution of this book lies in the methodology that it adopts. Proper comparative studies are notoriously difficult, often resulting in examining the one perspective from the exclusive lens of the other perspective, thus not allowing for an accurate comparative investigation of both perspectives from a vantage point that can afford equal access to both. This book avoids this erroneous tendency and, instead, develops a masterly treatment of Jung and Maximus within a truly comparative framework, crafted meticulously.

This book will be invaluable for all serious scholars of Jung and Christianity but also for the wider public who are interested in familiarizing themselves with a specific comparison between a psychological and a spiritual discourse. There is no other serious study that investigates the relationship between Jungian psychology and Early Christian philosophy and theology, and focusing this comparison onto the opus of a person of the calibre of Maximus the Confessor is a most apt and brave choice. Despite the enormity and complexity of this task, Dr Tympas succeeds in offering us a book that constitutes a substantial contribution insofar as it combines (a) an authoritative comparative treatise, (b) a coherent and insightful examination of Maximus' ideas that are becoming increasingly influential in the western world (especially within the last couple of decades, when the translation of his books started appearing), culminating in (c) a creative synthesis of the two approaches by constructing an innovative framework of psychological and spiritual development using elements and directions from both the Jungian and Maximian perspectives.

It is for these reasons that I warmly welcome this book!

Renos K. Papadopoulos, PhD
Professor of Analytical Psychology
Centre for Psychoanalytic Studies
University of Essex

PREFACE

It was during my undergraduate medical studies that I became preoccupied with the question of psychic development as being distinct from the development and pathology of the human body. I soon realized that psychiatry and depth psychology approach the human *psyche* differently than ancient Greek philosophy and Christian theology do; but, as I hope to illustrate in this book, the profound insights of the latter might be of importance to the former.

I have been researching the subject of this book for a number of years. It began as an exploration of the significance of Maximus' concepts in patristic anthropology. The comparison between Jung and Maximus emerged during my postgraduate research at the University of Essex Centre for Psychoanalytic Studies. Further concerns arose when the thesis had to be transformed into a book, addressing the broader perspectives of the discussion between analytical psychology and Christian theology. The enormity of this task, which transcends the limits of psychology, still challenges me. This book forms part of my personal journey towards 'wholeness' – both in the spiritual and the psychological sense of the term. I hope that the reader will discover the motivation for a similar exploration.

ACKNOWLEDGEMENTS

I owe a debt of gratitude to those who explicitly or implicitly inspired, encouraged, and supported me during all the stages of the preparation of this book, but first and foremost to Renos Papadopoulos, my PhD supervisor, for his invaluable support and encouragement during and after the doctoral supervision.

Special thanks are due to the academic staff at the Centre for Psychoanalytic Studies, University of Essex, Andrew Samuels, Roderick Main, Matt Ffytche, Karl Figlio, Bob Hinselwood, and Susan Rowland, for their substantial help and valuable feedback during the years of my doctoral research; also I wish to thank Andrew Louth, Nicholas Sakharov, and Rene Gothoni for critical comments and constructive feedback on earlier drafts of this book. I would also like to thank the administrative staff of the Centre for Psychoanalytic Studies and the staff of the Albert Sloman Library as well as the staff at the British Library for their help in providing sources from a wide spectrum of disciplines.

This book would have not taken its current shape without insightful suggestions by Angie Voela, Iro Mylonakou-Keke, Demetrios Bathrellos, Nikolaos Loudovikos, Vasileios Thermos, Eustratios Papaioannou, Dimitri Conomos, Chloe Demetriou, Paul Brighton-Cross, Frank Garcia, Amanda Hon, and Theodore Veniamin, as well as without the editorial support of Kate Hawes and Kirsten Buchanan.

Finally, special thanks go to my late father Polycarpos, a priest, and my mother Maria. Without their support and solace, this study would have not been finished.

Permissions acknowledgements

Thankful acknowledgements for permission to reprint are made to Taylor & Francis Books and Princeton University Press, excerpts from JUNG, C. G., *Collected Works of C. G. Jung*, 1977, Princeton University Press; reprinted by permission of Princeton University Press. Excerpts from Maximus the Confessor ©1996 Andrew Louth, published by Routledge.

Material from published article G. C. Tympas, 'The psychological and the spiritual: an evolutionary relationship within an ontological framework. A brief comment on Jung's Self', published at www.tandfonline.com, in *International*

Journal of Jungian Studies 2013, DOI: 10.1080/19409052.2013.795181, was reprinted by permission of Taylor and Francis.

Excerpts from *Memories, Dreams, Reflections,* © 1963 by Random House, Inc.; *The Wisdom of Rilke,* trans. by Ulrich Baer, © 2005 by Ulrich Baer, published by Modern Library; *On the Cosmic Mystery of Jesus Christ. Selected Writings from St Maximus the Confessor* © 2003 St Vladimir's Seminary Press; *Philosophy and Social Science* © 2008 Westview Press; *Anthropology in Theory. Issues in Epistemology* © 2006 Blackwell Publishing Ltd.; *A Pluralistic Universe* © 1909 William James, published by Longmans, Green and Co.; *Hegel's Phenomenology of Spirit* © Oxford University Press 1977; *The Body and Society. Men, Women and Sexual Renunciation in Early Christianity* © 1988 Columbia University Press; *Cosmic Liturgy. The Universe According to Maximus the Confessor* © 1988 Johannes Verlag, Einsiedeln.

The photograph of Jung, Freud, and other figures in front of Clark University is included here by permission of The Marsh Agency on behalf of Sigmund Freud Copyrights.

ABBREVIATIONS

Works by Maximus the Confessor

Amb.	*Ambiguorum liber: Ambigua ad Thomam* 1–5: *CCSG* 48: 3–34. *Ambigua ad Ioannem* 6–71: *PG* 91: 1061–1417.
Cap.	*Capitum Quinquies Centenorum Centuria I–V: PG* 90: 1177–1391.
Char.	*Capitum de Charitate Centuria I–IV: ACW* 21 (*PG* 90: 960–1073).
Ep.	*Epistulae 1–45: PG* 91: 361–650.
L.Asc.	*Liber Asceticus: CCSG* 40 (trans. in *ACW* 21).
Myst.	*Mystagogia:* (Soteropoulos 1993); *PG* 91: 657–717.
Opusc.	*Opuscula theologica et polemica* 1–27: *PG* 91: 9–285.
Pyrr.	*Disputatio cum Pyrrho: PG* 91: 288–353.
Q.Dub.	*Quaestiones et dubia: CCSG* 10 (*PG* 90: 785A–856C).
Q.Thal.	*Quaestiones ad Thalassium* 1–55: *CCSG* 7; 56–65: *CCSG* 22.
Th.Oec.	*Capita theologica et oeconomica: PG* 90: 1084–1173.

Works by C. G. Jung and post–Jungians

CW	*Collected Works of Carl Gustav Jung.* Sir H. Read, M. Fordham, G. Adler and W. McGuire (eds.), trans. R. H. F. Hull, London: Routledge and Kegan Paul; Princeton, NJ: Princeton University Press, 1953–1983.
CDJA	Samuels, A., Shorter, B., and Plaut, F. (1986) *A Critical Dictionary of Jungian Analysis.* London and New York: Routledge.
HJP	Papadopoulos, R. K. (ed.) (2006) *The Handbook of Jungian Psychology. Theory, Practice and Applications.* London and New York: Routledge.
MDR	*Memories, Dreams, Reflections,* recorded and edited by A. Jaffé, trans. R. Winston and C. Winston. Vintage Books. New York, 1989 (originally published in 1961).

Other Abbreviations

ACW	*Ancient Christian Writers No 21:* St Maximus the Confessor, *The Ascetic Life, The Four Centuries, On Charity.* Pol. Sherwood (ed. and trans.). New York: The Newman Press, 1955.

CCSG	*Corpus Christianorum Series Graeca.* Turnhout: Brepols 1953ff.
Diels	Diels, H., *Die fragmente der Vorsokratiker.* W. Kranz (ed.). Berlin, 1934.
GNO	*Gregorii Nysseni, Opera.* Werner Jaeger (ed.). Leiden: E. J. Brill, 1958ff.
PG	J. P. Migne (ed.). *Patrologiae cursus completus. Series Craeca* (161 volumes) Paris, 1857ff.
PL	J. P. Migne (ed.). *Patrologiae cursus completus. Series Latina.* Paris, 1844–1864.
SC	*Sources Chrétiennes.* Paris: Les Éditions du Cerf, 1943ff.
SVF	*Stoicorum Veterum Fragmenta.* Collegit Hans Friedrich August von Arnim (ed.). In aedibus B. G. Tuebneri, Stutgardiae, 1964.

1

INTRODUCTION

This book brings together two dissimilar theories on psychic development and introduces a theoretical framework for a synthesis that integrates and, at the same time, exceeds both. Within this theoretical framework, we shall explore the interface between aspects of the developmental process (*individuation*) in Carl Jung's psychology in juxtaposition to and compared with Maximus the Confessor's theological insights (*deification* or *theosis*) on spiritual development.

Psychic development or '*the process of individuation*' – as a dynamic process in one's becoming an individuated personality by shaping self-formation as an integrated personal whole or Self-distinctive but not alienated from the collective – constitutes 'the central concept' of Jung's psychology (*MDR*: 209). Regardless of the interpretations concerning the concept of the Self, whether through an inelastic 'monotheistic' perspective or within a 'polytheistic' pluralism of Self-embodiments, psychic development remains the epicentre around which most of the contemporary Jungian academics and clinicians focus their interests and research. Individuation has been explored from numerous angles and compared with a range of equivalent concepts that stem from disciplines other than psychology. Nevertheless, to examine the individuation process as a concept of the 20th century beside the reference to the insights of Maximus (a 7th-century philosopher and theologian) would be a particularly arduous task to accomplish. A series of epistemological criteria must be introduced to build a methodology that can cope with the different conceptualisations of a psychic development that was cultivated in the entirely different philosophical and socio-cultural contexts in which the two thinkers lived.

The goal of this study is to overcome a reductive interpretation of Jung's and Maximus' theories on psychic and spiritual development – an interpretation that is reduced to solely psychological dimensions – while attempting a synthesis of both within a *trans-disciplinary* context. Some critical questions that this study attempts to answer are: Is psychological development distinct from spiritual progress/development? In what ways does psychological experience differ from spiritual experience? Is a 'psychologically' mature individual simultaneously 'spiritually' mature; does the multiplicity of factors that regulates psychic development towards 'wholeness' need a trans-disciplinary context to be understood?

1

And in which ways could professionals related to psychic development benefit from understanding the trans-disciplinary character and the epistemological challenges of a multifaceted development?

A fundamental line of investigation in this monograph is based upon the hypothesis that psychic-spiritual development as a complex phenomenon is composed of distinguished facets, perspectives, or dimensions of progression. Whilst these perspectives and directions may address dissimilar levels of life, a degree of convergence and complementarity amongst them enables common viewpoints. I specifically distinguish among five such levels that are involved in this process: the bodily, the psychic, the interpersonal-social, the cultural, and the metaphysical levels (see below, Chapter 2). I also introduce and further analyse, relative to the concepts addressing all stated levels, the notion of the 'spiritual' as an evolution, an emergent property from psychological and socio-cultural features, which nevertheless maintains its own potential in both phenomenological and ontological terms; this potential could span psychosomatic and metaphysical levels. The dynamic range of the overlapping perspectives, alongside their respective parameters that play a significant role in the developmental processes, constitute a spectrum within which the phenomenon of psychic development will be explored.

Through the prism of a multifaceted process on various levels, it is understood that in some cases, psychic development entails a progression on specific levels and directions alone, whereas other cases indicate a development corresponding to a maturation process that is imbalanced or even results in a degree of regression with regard to certain areas of psychic growth. Scientific disciplines have provided models of development in which the original potential is not completely achieved. Embryology, for instance, illustrates rigorously the perplexed physical development from the zygote to a complete human body, a process not always efficiently accomplished, which may culminate in inadequately developed organs or systems – analogously to the more or less developed perspectives/areas in the psychic sphere. Yet to conceptualise psychic development in all possible spheres is imperative to considering beyond the boundaries of psychology by introducing a trans-disciplinary context.

Inter-disciplinarity and trans-disciplinarity

In this study, psychic development inexorably has an *inter*-disciplinary character, inasmuch as the Jungian and Maximian models belong to different disciplines and contexts (psychology vis-à-vis philosophy-theology, modernity vis-à-vis early Christianity). The *inter*-disciplinary approach entails an engagement of at least two different scientific fields or discourses. However, I want to emphasize that this study has a rather *trans*-disciplinary character that embraces the interdisciplinary considerations and addresses further all possible developmental potentials. Trans-disciplinarity has emerged as a relatively new theory, which deals with the existence and dynamics of different 'levels of reality' and explores the specific 'logic' and 'laws' governing each of these levels to perceive the 'structure of the totality of all levels' as '*a complex structure*' (Nicolescu 2002, 2010: 24). The trans-disciplinary approach strongly suggests that for complex quests that attempt to understand phenomena of a greater scale, such as those dealing with human development on different levels (i.e. social, cultural, and/or metaphysical), collaboration amongst experts from various disciplines is imperative. Trans-disciplinarity also implies that theories stemming from a particular discipline or context have to expand their horizons and incorporate insights that address the same subject from different disciplines and angles in order to achieve 'wholeness'.

By overarching two different systems of thought by means of a trans-disciplinary understanding, we are able to introduce an approach that distinguishes Jung's and Maximus' logic and standpoints, allowing, thereby, a synthesis at a third level. A synthetic approach addresses the *spiritual* perspective as an 'emergent' property from elements belonging to different realms. This stance is an alternative to Aristotle's principle of wholeness, which affirms that 'the whole is something besides the parts' (*Metaphysics H*: 1045a 8–10). Discussion of all possible aspects of the spiritual, as construed by each theory, permits a profound understanding overall.

Trans-disciplinarity and emergence theory can interpret the perplexing functionality of the human body within a high level of 'complexity', which cannot be reduced to the parts that are engaged as such. Neurophysiology has long ago dealt with those holistic patterns that are applied to interpret the final outcome of the neurons' functions, which transcends any anatomical structure. Thus, by bringing together Jung and Maximus, we are inevitably led to consider more than two levels of 'reality' within their systems and their particular logic that co-acts within. By incorporating insights from interpersonal, social, and cultural realms, I intend to advance the elementary logic of this comparison between the psychological and the spiritual to the manifold dynamics of a trans-disciplinary system.

It is now possible to understand one of the main points that I wish to illustrate: psychic development cannot be thoroughly investigated within the principles and perspectives of development solely adopted by Jungian psychology. A fuller understanding of psychic development is a discourse that should engage rationales stemming from theories addressing the psyche from other than purely psychological viewpoints. Despite the fact that this method may engage in a degree of uncertainty, a clearer picture of the development may be attained. It was in early modernity when method, experiment, precision, and *certainty* determined the unchallenged, at first sight, boundaries of the scientific world, within the authenticity of the Cartesian 'thinking mind' (*cogito ergo sum*). However, since then, modern physics (specifically quantum theory) and postmodern threads of investigation have a tendency to assert that the only certainty that can be unchallenged is uncertainty. Within reason, science cannot explain everything, though it may speculate and corroborate possibilities.

In this vein, the limitations of those psychological concepts introduced to describe psychic development can be seen as a parallel to the limitations of the concepts that modern physics has proposed in order to describe the cosmos. The static Newtonian model of external planets/bodies interacting under the rules of gravity was long ago replaced by quantum theory, according to which even an infinitesimal particle 'somewhere out' in the vast universe definitely has an imperceptible interaction with the rest of the world – and possibly with our existence (Pauli's *exclusion principle*). However, this interaction cannot be measured accurately when referring to our daily scale. Furthermore, it is by *observation* that humans may cause an alteration to the observed phenomenon. This is known as the 'observer effect'.

In psychology, the subject matter is at the same time the object of observation, in which we experience and simultaneously 'know' our own psychological world, namely us. It is at this point that human knowledge and experience are subjected to limitations. Therefore, psychology is critically challenged to anticipate and consider an understanding of development that supersedes the boundaries of our perception within a merely psychosomatic perspective. This integration within the inner and outer worlds can be understood as an inter-disciplinary discourse between psychology and philosophy and/or theology through which a synthesis can advance to a trans-disciplinary perplexity via the lens of third part fields (such as sociology and the philosophy of science). The complexity of diverse levels of life demands scientific disciplines that can fully address and tackle such dissimilar levels. It is understood, therefore, that disciplines such as sociology and theology become important in integrating, respectively, social and metaphysical levels with psychological dimension.

Epistemological considerations on psychic-spiritual development

The critical difficulty underlying the endeavour to bring two different models of development under the same epistemological framework is to avoid reducing the perspectives of the one system against the other. Furthermore, a synthesis of two systems frequently exceeds a mere 'complementarity', as is suggested by the sophisticated and 'uncertain' solution through the 'principle of uncertainty-complementarity' by quantum physics (*Heisenberg principle*). However, although the same 'reality' appears to co-act within the microcosmic and macrocosmic scales, the 'reality' of the psychic facts inevitably engages the ontological question 'what is real' (or what is 'psychic' or 'spiritual'), as well as an epistemological theory that reveals how we can attain knowledge of this reality.

In the past, with questions on the ultimate point of human development, it sufficed for one to use an *ontological* assumption of what is real or what is the ultimate reality that permeates beings. Plato's eudemonistic ethics of human well-being (*eudaimonia*) and the Christian conception of human perfection in God's 'likeness' (*deification, theosis*) were, respectively, grounded in a cosmic/divine dimension of the reality of the *forms* – the true nature and pattern of all beings – or of *God* as the 'uncreated' source of life. The psyche was accordingly gifted with 'faculties' capable of reaching the 'divine', the metaphysical real. Epistemology as a theory of knowledge was thus principally aligned with the ontological perspective. Ontology is defined as a theory of Reality, a 'doctrine of the being and relations of all reality'.[1] Ontology could therefore be understood as a complex matrix of relations at all levels, a matrix implying that only a *trans-disciplinary* view could propose a hermeneutical line able to permeate all realms of life.

In theories which hold a prevailing ontological aspect, the degree of conscious participation in the 'real' was of secondary importance because self-consciousness, or the psyche, was lying in a different 'ontological' ground. In modernity, 'self-consciousness' has emerged as the fundamental dimension within the psyche, despite certain epistemological principles that set limits in psychic perception. Kantian transcendental apperception finds a heuristic balance between the *phenomena* and the *noumena,* leaving aside the unapproachable *thing-in-itself.* This was a decisive moment for modern epistemology, with a profound impact on depth psychology. Hegel also introduces an epistemology entirely different from the ontological – namely the *phenomenological.* The latter lays emphasis primarily on the emerging 'self-consciousness', evolving through history, science, arts, and religion. Existential philosophers, such as Kierkegaard and, later, those upholding particular strands within depth psychology, owe to the Hegelian system – of an 'evolving consciousness' – their openness to Christian narratives and positive views on religion. But the point of gravity was constantly moving towards the unexplored depths of human conscious and unconscious, highlighted by Nietzsche's goal of *Übermensch,* as an integration of both the *Apollonian* and *Dionysian* drives. The unconscious is now gradually emerging not only as the locus of psychological investigation but also as having imposed the limits of human knowledge, long before Freudian and Jungian psychology (Ellenberger 1970).

Freud heralded a new era with his understanding of the unconscious dynamics and their drives and instincts by contrasting them to socio-cultural associations. As an heir of the Enlightenment focusing on the human perspectives within nature, Freud highlighted the undermined primitive, inherited cultural features which could decisively shape psychic constructs, until then labelled as 'spiritual' or 'religious'. In *Totem and Taboo* (1913), Freud explored the primitives' narcissistic phase and the relationship between an animistic mode of thinking and the magic powers that are attributed by projections to the external world. Freud worked out an inter-disciplinary method that demonstrated an adaptation of these projections at the cultural level, which led him to the fundamental position that religion – and to a certain extent the 'spiritual' – is a mode of a collective illusion or 'a longing for the missing father' (*The Future of an Illusion,* 1927). By elaborating on the helplessness of childhood, Freud elevates the idea of the protecting father toward the notion of the God-as-father, construing the spiritual dimension reductively through the repressed history of the infantile life.

Freud noted the high degree of permeability of facts between the psychic level and the socio-cultural realm, namely amongst the vestiges of the suppressed forces propelled by social norms and psychic drives. Socio-cultural restrictions, standing for a censoring *superego,* now become decisive in shaping psychic development: it can be understood as a 'balance' between the ego's compulsive intentions and the unconscious primary drives that oscillate between eros and death. In his *The Civilisation and Its Discontents* (1930), Freud unveiled the roots of human behaviour and of the masks that cover and rule our crude nature and enthroned the cultural level as imposing its restrictions to the psychic motives and instincts which make people unhappy. However, this final point is not a trans-disciplinary synthesis but rather a reduction of all parameters to the principally decisive psychic drives.

Freud claimed himself that he had given the final of the three 'death blows' against *Genesis* by following the cosmological blow by Copernicus and the biological blow by Darwin.[2] Yet, despite this highlighted antipathy to religion, there have been reconsiderations that unravel Freud's deeper attitude to religious issues, related to his Hebrew inheritance, personal incidents, and contemporary socio-cultural dynamics (see Wallace 1984; Hoffman 2011), which are implicit in the works of post–Freudians such as Winnicot and Rizzuto. A reappraisal of Freudian viewpoints from a different angle could evoke a return to values of truth, honesty, and humility, not distant from the intimate values of the key Judaeo/Christian narratives (Hofmann 2011).

Carl Jung reversed Freud's reductionist view of religion and introduced a teleological approach. Alfred Adler had previously opened up the theoretical perspectives by reconsidering Freud's focus on psychic instincts alone and placing emphasis on the importance of social factors. Instead of repressed desires, Jung's intuitive view valued the potential of primordial images and particularly of the God-image(s) towards the restoration of the lost inner Self within the individuation process. Jung's archetypal figures (hero, wise man, great mother, etc.), developed further by the post–Jungians, ultimately become personal figures in particular socio-cultural contexts: the Freudian so-called 'universal psychology' now witnesses the emergence of Jungian culturally oriented psychology. Whilst both Freud and Jung considerably value the inherited/archetypal unconscious elements, Jung goes beyond the restrictions imposed by the socio-cultural norms and develops the archetypal images through the constructive impact of cultural symbols. But does this teleological and inter-disciplinary view of psychic progression ultimately address all possible perspectives of development? Jung's emphasis on phenomenological facts appears, like Freud's, to doubt the meta-psychological (ontological) nature of the spiritual. In fact, the Jungian epistemology and methodology, which we shall extensively examine, has proved to be rather slippery, inasmuch as it leaves the exact character and the ontological dimension of his key concepts, namely the Self and individuation, to remain ambiguous. Could this also mean that Jung's teleological approach is an incomplete holistic view?

Carl Jung and embedded Eastern constructs

Reading Jung is a captivating, although at times perplexing, encounter with diverse disciplines such as psychiatry, psychology, anthropology, sociology, philosophy, and theology. However, it is scarcely evident a systemic (trans-disciplinary) – or even a convincing inter-disciplinary methodology – which leaves room for principles that determine other than psychology disciplines. Despite the fact that Jung mobilized ideas from all these disciplines, his analysis leading to key concepts (such as the archetypes) is primarily based on psychological principles alone and thus does not engage a systemic (trans-disciplinary) method, one which respects the principles applied by disciplines other than psychology. At the heart of Jung's model lies the 'cardinal' principle of integration of opposites that addresses the ultimate potential of man, comprising dark and light, masculine and feminine, matter and spirit – a rather unacknowledged loan from Nietzsche's *superman* and Hegelian dialectics. In fact, Jung's most original and mature insights emanate from the Far East, especially those that refer to the 'fourth element' (body, feminine, evil), which are necessary in forming wholeness along with the psychologically interpreted 'trinity'. Despite this plurality of loan and insights, Jung is not absolutely clear as to which are the exact boundaries and the final (ontological) potential of psychic wholeness, that is to say the Self.

Jung lived in a transitional era, departing from the solid ground of certain values of Enlightenment and modernity to the subjectivity and pluralism of emerging post-modernity. Jung's motive for knowledge could be traced back in the discussions with his father, a Protestant pastor, who was irritated when his own child questioned him on faith, and who would answer: '. . . you always want to think. One ought not to think but to believe' (*MDR*: 43). In Jung's reply, 'No, one must experience and know' (ibid.), one can trace the two elements of his epistemology: knowledge and psychic experience. These are the two pillars of Jung's edifice, namely, a 'knowing' and 'experiencing' self-consciousness that draws upon psychic archetypal foundations. Jung thus understood at an early stage that the one-sided Western man and culture, which emerged from the industrial revolution in the 19th century, inevitably had to encounter and institute a deep dialogue with other traditions to extend the horizons and to experience profound spiritual 'knowledge'. For Jung, modern man 'abhors faith and the religions based upon it. He holds them valid only so far as their knowledge-content seems to accord with his own experience . . .' (Jung 1928/1931a: para. 171). It could therefore be argued that if the individuation process is the epitome of psychic development towards the unfathomable realms of the inner wholeness/Self, psychic experience, in all its aspects and perspectives, is the quintessence of individuation. Experience is both the essence of psychic life and the building blocks of psychic development.

Psychic experience, however, due to the 'endless' end of the individuation process, inevitably crosses the boundaries of the psyche itself and opens up to such realms as the spiritual and, potentially, the metaphysical. Jung was constantly delving into a worldwide range of cultural and historical sources, textual, visual, oral, pictorial: those ideas that ultimately led him to shape a model that, contrary to the Freudian one, would incorporate, in both theory and practice, a profound experiential and, ultimately a spiritual, dimension. Jung's positive view of religious and spiritual phenomena, propelled by W. James's (1902) pragmatic examination on religious experience, could be understood through a 'mediation' because 'the psyche (and psychic reality) function as an intermediate world between the physical and spiritual realms, which may meet and mingle therein' (*CDJA*: 118). By replacing the repressed psychic energy, the libido, with an '*energic concept of the libido*', in Palmer's interpretation (1997: 102), within a manifold of archetypal forces, Jung escaped from Freudian monism. But there is still room for criticism insofar as Jung's habit 'of personifying unconscious contents can be highly confusing to all but the uninitiated', whereas the therapeutic value of the alchemical *lapis philosophorum* discourses could be questioned as sliding to elitism (ibid.: 166).

Jung's entire life could be seen as a reflection of the unsaturated thirst for genuine psychic experience of a universal man who lived beyond the limitations of the Western culture. At an early stage, Jung demonstrated his interest in Eastern concepts (*Symbols of Transformation*, 1911), whereas in his maturity he turned to the Far East more vigorously. His autobiography narrates enthusiastically his experiences in the Far East, long after the transatlantic trip and break with Freud. It is in his trip to India (1938) that Jung appears to find a promising answer to the missing aspects of psychic 'wholeness'. The overwhelming dynamism of medieval alchemy had long before struck him, when admitting that this 'journey formed an intermezzo in the intensive study of alchemical philosophy on which I was engaged at the time' (*MDR*: 275). Despite the significance that Jung attached to alchemy, his encounter with Eastern philosophies appears to open a new chapter in the assimilation and development of fundamental aspects in his model – particularly of the integration of good and evil. This was a missing element in Christian theology, which 'often appeared to him as far too rationalistic', as Clarke avers (1995: 10). Jung writes:

> In a conversation with a cultivated Chinese I was also impressed, again and again, by the fact that these people are able to integrate so-called 'evil' without 'losing face'. In the West we cannot do this. . . To the Oriental, good and evil are meaningfully contained in nature, and are merely varying degrees of the same thing.
>
> (*MDR*: 275–6)

Whilst being accused of sliding towards elitism, occultism, and para-psychological phenomena, Jung, inspired by Eastern insights, worked out an integration of thorny accounts, particularly from a Christian perspective, such as the feminine and evil. These insights led him to 'the self-discovery and self-transformation . . . so appealed to him in Buddhism and yoga', which 'must have represented for him a powerful echo of the Gnostic inner path' (Clarke 1995: 11). This does not nevertheless mean that basic Christian ideas had less impact on Jung's model. Despite his anti-metaphysical methodology (Heisig 1979), Jung addressed the 'religious function' of the psyche, a loan from Tertullian's maxim of a soul *naturaliter religiosa*, and highlighted the psychic image(s) of *transcendence*, tracing the way to the *Self*. Jung also meticulously read Origen and Tertullian as paradigms of extra- and introverted psychological types (1921/1971). Origen was a distinguished figure of the 3rd century, but his works, seriously influenced by Neoplatonic ideas, quickly became controversial and received strong criticism, in particular by Maximus the Confessor, who later refuted their notions.

The Gnostics and the Neoplatonics, from whom Jung borrowed extensively, were the two main philosophical opponents of Christian doctrines that also influenced Origen profoundly. It is important to note that for Maximus, the Neoplatonism and Gnostic tenets were the initial motives for a critical restoration of certain of their elements. On the contrary, Jung incorporated Gnostic insights within the principle of opposites, the alchemical *coniunctio* and the *lapis philosophorum,* being, therewith, aligned with important Gnostic tenets (see Segal 1992). The question that nevertheless remains is: What is the final end, in both scientific and empirical terms, of these concepts? On the one hand, by embedding evil, body, and feminine into the 'rigid' Christian doctrines, Jung stepped on new territories, revaluating the Christian narratives and symbols within contemporary perspectives in a much broader sense than the classical Christian view; but on the other, it appears that just as Freud reduced psychic drives to the bodily functions, Jung's radical approach to religious/spiritual issues at bottom is a reductionistic treatment of the spiritual perspective, confined solely within the psyche.

Although Jung possessed a degree of familiarity with patristic writers (for instance, Origen and Augustine), his knowledge of the core of Christian theology, as it had been formulated in the first eight centuries (before the schism between the eastern and western church in 1054), appears limited. In the General Index (*CW* 20), the headword *Orthodox Church, Eastern* offers but one quotation, whereby Jung refers to the Church of Russia (in the 20th century) in not at all flattering terms: '. . . haze of an Orthodox Church . . . crowded out by a superfluity of sacred paraphernalia' (1936: para. 372). As we have said, Jung's indifference to Christian theology, concomitant with the underlying doubts towards his Protestant tradition, propelled his interest in the direction of the Far East. The Eastern impact was decisive to expand further the perspectives of the *imago dei,* upgrading it into a universal scale. But some critical questions emerge at this point. What would have been the final shape of Jung's 'teleology' and wholeness/Self should he have studied the Christian sources carefully rather than making a rather hasty evaluation of the potential of their originality? Could insights from early Christianity have improved Jung's ideology of the experiential dimension of a soul *naturaliter religiosa,* had he surveyed and profoundly investigated the mind of the Christian Middle East? Could a hypothetical retrospective interplay between Jung and an Eastern Christian philosopher have reshaped the Jungian model on development in both ontological and phenomenological/experiential terms?

Carl Jung's 'retrospective' encounter with Maximus the Confessor

Jung attempted to restore Freud's reduction of spiritual/religious domains as a regression of the infantile unconscious fixations to a pre-rational state by considering psychic images by means of cultural symbols and myths as unconditionally con-veying trans-rational meanings. Wilber (2000) has considered these ideologies as examples of the *pre/trans fallacy*.[3] Jung's visit to the Far East was an incentive to resolve the conflict between the rational and irrational, but the lack of a trans-disciplinary framework resulted in an ontological ambiguity. Centuries ago, Neo-platonic tradition and Maximus the Confessor followed a different, hierarchical approach and reached a point that might have provided Jung with a constructive way to bridge these opposites through an inter-disciplinary understanding. It is important to stress here that in the wider context of the Middle East, the rhetoric on human life and purpose was perpetual, constantly leaving the necessary flexibility for an inter-disciplinary discourse among theology, philosophy, and psychology. Hann and Goltz, searching the anthropological perspectives of Eastern Christi-anity, have aptly put it: 'What the West rediscovered with the help of the Ger-man Jews Martin Buber and Franz Rosensweig – namely, the dialogical nature of human existence – the Orthodox had never forgotten' (2010: 14). This is a generic but important statement that stresses the perennial interaction among disciplines in the Eastern thought, in which Jung would undoubtedly be interested.

Owing to a lack of primary sources, Jung had never encountered Maximus' writings. Retrospectively, it could nonetheless be said that Maximus' cosmologi-cal and anthropological insights, linked with his pluralistic and multifunctional psychic model, might have appeared thought provoking to Jung's investigative mind. The dynamics between Eastern and Western strands and philosophies, so vigorous in Jung's life, also appear, as we shall see, as critical in Maximus' thinking. The latter ultimately resorted to the West to support his positions. Maxi-mus' work, viewed as 'a symphony of experience' (Florovsky 1931: 213), could function as a volatile ferment to Jung's priority on psychic experience and could have led to a reappraisal of the rigid and, for him, far 'too rationalistic' Christian insights. The vivid phenomenological perspective of early Christianity, linked with a clearly ontological stance, as it unfolds in Maximus' concepts, could feasi-bly act as a bridge between a leading scientific figure of the 20th century, namely, the self-declared 'empiricist' Carl Jung, and a prominent Christian thinker of the 7th century, at a new meeting point between Christian narratives and developmen-tal processes.

It still remains questionable whether Maximus' vision of psychic develop-ment is based on a religious model-as-institution, such as the 'Church', in a view that echoes merely 'systems' of 'beliefs' in a contemporary understanding. Moreover, it is very difficult to know whether Maximus' insights have been fully incorporated by the Christian Church throughout its history, either in the East or in the West. Religion as a system of faith and worship, or as 'inherently socio-psychological phenomena' (Hill *et al.* 2000), as it is broadly construed nowadays, does not ideally apply to Maximus' vision of church and faith, which is a 'syner-gic union' between the divine and the whole cosmos in terms of spiritual love. In Maximus' *Mystagogy,* cosmos and God, human and divine are found within the church in a mutual exchange of spiritual gifts and experiences. This would be a relevant point that would certainly challenge Jung's understanding of the church merely as a system of doctrines, drained from any experiential dimension. On the other hand, the perspectives whereby Jung develops the 'fourth element' within God's eternal wisdom (*Sapientia dei*) openly challenges the degree of the Christian implementation of these elements (the body and the feminine) – while not completely absent from Maximus' system. Attaining wholeness, by incorporating dark nature as well as the body and the feminine, in one's life, is still not fully welcome in traditional circles. As discussed below, both Jungian 'wholeness' and the 'one-sidedness' of certain Christian practices may constantly challenge each other. The resulting exchange of insights, with their respective, specific affiliation to the socio-cultural and metaphysical realms, may prove to be invaluable.

Maximus considers psychological development principally as a spiritual progression from the psychological state of 'God-image' to the status of becoming a person 'after God's likeness' (see *Genesis* 1: 26), wholly deified, in the love of God towards all of his creation. Spiritual progress in fact is a double movement: 'Seen from below, the spiritual life seems to be an incessant combat, an "invisible struggle" . . . Seen from above, it is the acquisition of the gifts of the Holy Spirit' (Evdokimov 1998: 167). However, the concept that accurately depicts spiritual maturity, wholeness, and perfection in Maximus' era is *theosis* (deification), a term-watermark with a long history extending back to Neoplatonism.[4] Deification goes beyond mere salvation or redemption (Nellas 1997: 39) and targets the 'innermost longing of man's existence' (Mantzaridis 1984: 12), which could enrich a solely redemptive vision of Christianity.

Maximus attained his vision of psychic and spiritual development by contesting tenets that influenced Jung: what Jung espoused, namely Gnostic ideas as well as Neoplatonic tenets, Maximus opposed by refuting Origen's thesis of a psyche fallen and trapped into matter. Whilst Jung principally focused on psychological experience and cultural symbols via his archetypes – in a horizontal perspective from personal history to socio-cultural impacts of symbols – Maximus considers development as bearing principally a vertical dimension: it advances from the psychological to the divine level, from fragmentation of the self-centred personality to the deified person within the all-embracing 'love', mutually shared by God and man.

This study can thus best be seen as an attempt to make a retrospective journey of Jung to the Middle East and early Christianity on his way back from the Far East and encounter with Buddhism, Hindu, and Tao. In the Middle East, Jung might have found in the Maximian insights an alternative conception of his *unus mundus,* a united 'one world', through Maximus' view of the essential principles (the *logoi*) of beings spread in the universe and at once gathered under God's ultimate principle of love. While Maximus is not, strictly speaking, considered to belong to the circle classified as mystics in the Christian East, his insights and processes of a constant development towards perfection, such as those of Symeon the New Theologian, could have been read by Jung like a Christian 'mystical' or 'alchemical' process mingling matter and spirit, body and soul in search for the *lapis* of an 'all-in-one' spiritual status. Jung's Protestant understanding of a 'remote' God might have ultimately been reshaped by redressing further the principal idea of a 'dying God', through his encounter with Maximus' God – a God mutually in love with the cosmos, the principles of which, like Jung's symbols, constantly 'call' for integration.

This constructive synthesis could of course stretch much further. Jung's concept of 'synchronicity', in collaboration with the 20th-century physicist W. Pauli, while still challenging our understanding of the natural and psychical world as a 'meaningful coincidence', might appeal to an alternative theoretical framework, including metaphysics – within Maximus' vision of the interrelated physical-outer and spiritual-inner world via the spiritual principles of all living creatures. This inter-disciplinary framework, which Jung wittingly applied to the notion of synchronicity, is missing from other Jungian insights. The introduction of Maximus' concepts through a trans-disciplinary perspective could provide the ontological ground for the unclear metaphysical potential of Jung's central notions of the Self and individuation.

Viewed within the principles of trans-disciplinarity that respects the logic of different theories, the hermeneutical approach of this book – in line with Gadamer's method of seeking the 'metaphysics of finitude'[5] – will progressively delve into the fuller potential of Jungian and Maximian models through a comparison at many levels. It will also reveal an emergent complementarity that may enhance both. An integrated *trans-disciplinary paradigm* of development can accordingly emerge at the end of this study. Jungian archetypes, in their unconscious dimension, and the Christian virtues, as principles stemming from the divine, could ultimately be understood as not exclusive each other essential elements of psychological development, since both mark a perspective of advance and maturation. Maximian and Jungian insights may be synthesised to bridge the gulf between psychologically grounded development and the Christian conception of spiritual development towards God's likeness within the multiple levels of union. Jung's intuitive reasoning and logical process of *coniunctio oppositorum* may help modern Christian thinkers to understand how internal objects and unconscious complexes function, facing *imago dei* perspectives towards a psychic pluralism that prevents one-sidedness. Furthermore, Christian insights on the 'hidden person of the heart' (1 *Peter* 3, 4), could link the individuation process towards a new understanding, whereby psychological experience can advance on the levels of spiritual knowledge of a personal all-embracing God.

Apart from assessing both thinkers, this book ultimately proposes an interface between basic psychological insights and manifestations of the numinous within a spiritual framework too broad to formulate a restrained religious system that seeks validation in the spirit of the words: 'the wind blows where it wills, and you hear the sound thereof, but can not tell from where it came [from the unconscious or the heart?]' (*John* 3, 8): it is here that Jung is deeply convinced that '[t]he knowledge of the heart is in no book and is not to be found in the mouth of any teacher, but grows out of you like the green seed from the dark earth' (Jung 2009: 233).

What, therefore, is being suggested is an innovative experiential approach through a rebirth out of our 'dark side', which engages archetypal imagery and contemporary socio-cultural constructs and which challenges the rather undeveloped contemporary spiritual/religious systems – based on symbols and practices alone – being at pains to embed what Jung suggested as the 'fourth element'. But it is also at this point that Maximus' focus and elaboration of the 'hidden' inner aspects of the psychic centre, the 'heart', follows a different process that leads, in a parallel way with individuation and psychological pluralism, to the wholeness of spiritual love. Experiencing both perspectives appears to be challenging, but it promises a deeper knowledge of psychic development.

The structure and the chapters

This monograph is formed of two parts. The first, comprising four theoretical chapters, acts as an introduction to the second part, in which psychic development is examined extensively. The inter-disciplinary methodology implemented to conduct a comparison between the two theories, which involves a discussion of concepts drawing upon different levels (the bodily, psychic, social, cultural, and spiritual-metaphysical), is the theme of Chapter 2; it is here that an 'evolutional' conceptualisation of the 'spiritual' as a *spiritual continuum* is introduced. This multilevel framework is intrinsic to understanding in depth the unfolding trans-disciplinary exploration of the complex phenomenon of development.

Chapter 3 investigates Jung's approach to the main points of religion from an analytical context; it commences by discussing Jung's 'complex' reflections on religion from his childhood and advances towards a resolution of this 'complex' by a re-evaluation of religious narratives in later maturity. These points are: (a) the fact that dogmatic/religious principles are to be understood not only as religious doctrines but also in psychological terms and the equivalents (further discussed in Chapter 5); (b) the necessity of the psychological experience that shapes any authentic spiritual/religious perspective (investigated in Chapter 6); and (c) the issue of the *fourth element,* which consists of bodily, feminine, and shadow/evil aspects, along with their importance and implications for the integration of spiritual experience (more in Chapters 7 and 8). Correspondingly, these points will also be the basis for a critical analysis of the equivalent Maximian positions and, by extension, Christian viewpoints.

Chapter 4 introduces Maximus' life and philosophical background that shaped his anthropological views, both cataphatic and apophatic. Maximus' key concept and clear ontological position is the essential principles of creation (*logoi of beings*), which will be discussed in contrast with Jung's *archetypal theory,* grounded in a rather 'ambiguous ontology'. Maximus' theology as a 'symphony of experience' and not simply an unbending system of doctrines provides reasonable scope to interrelate Jung's fundamental issue of psychic experience and to enlighten religious perspective. Jung's phenomenological reduction of the 'spiritual' to a psychological dimension that revolves around the dynamics of the 'God-image' is juxtaposed with the establishment of the Maximian ontological *logoi* through one's free will that is manifested in the transfiguration as 'in God-likeness'. This contrast between 'image' and 'likeness' is the starting point of comparison that stimulates further discussion on development.

Chapter 5 emphasizes in detail the specific directions and stages of psychic development according to both Jung and Maximus. Psychic development towards the Self is explored within specific levels by discussing the impact of certain archetypes – for instance, of 'mother' and 'shadow' on the interpersonal and social levels, or of the 'hero' and 'wise man' on the cultural level. This chapter continues with a search for the factors that play a significant part in development according to Maximus, who provides abundant processes-as-metaphors to describe different stages of progress. Furthermore, discussions on attitudes and practices engaged in both systems are presented. Attention is drawn to the issue of the 'other' as approached differently by Jungian and Maximian concepts: the former draws on the dynamics of the other within the inner Self and the 'transference', whereas the latter draws on the attitude of 'renunciation' that involves spiritual guidance. In spite of some striking similarities, the Jungian model emphasizes the unconscious archetypal and socio-cultural elements contributing to a diversity of potentialities/ directions of psychic development, whereas Maximus focuses on the spiritual principles-as-*virtues,* the source of metaphysical potentialities that ultimately lead to the love of the Other-God. Both approaches encompass practices that challenge the individuality and loneliness of modern man, thereby creating new paths towards encountering either a deeper Self or the experience of a personal God, respectively.

Chapter 6 addresses the foundations of Jung's typology of the 'four functions'. Analyses of these are based on Plato and Aristotle's equivalent notions that illustrate psychic faculties and functions. These functions are subsequently compared with the functions of Maximus' psychic model. The degree of engagement of the functions in spiritual experience is further investigated by bringing into the equation 'active imagination' and 'prayer'. Psychological types and functions are further seen through Maximus' stance, revealing how these functions play a role by encountering the archetype of the Self and by experiencing the numinous. Active imagination and prayer, in terms of manifestations of psychic functionality, can challenge the myopic view of our inner potential with the possibility of broadening an esoteric experience.

Chapter 7, subtitled 'A Question of Wholeness or Holiness?', is central to this study; it explores the final goals of the two systems by examining and highlighting their differences. Whilst Jung's model aims to justify the multifaceted *Self* by embracing as many human potentialities as possible at all levels of life (addressing the body, the feminine, and the shadow/evil aspects), Maximus seeks an eschatological union with God and the *logoi-as-virtues* (the state of man's deification) according to the paradigm of the archetypal incarnate Logos and his 'deified body'. The degree to which religious systems encompass the body and the feminine, as prevailing themes of today's culture, become a challenging issue.

The embodiment of these elements also determines the sustainability of these systems in contemporary societies overall.

Finally, Chapter 8 escalates the comparison and deals with a challenging theme in Jung's corpus, the *Answer to Job*. The dark and evil sides in Jung's understanding of wholeness are perceived as issues of time and *perspectivism,* whereby he attempts to resolve the problem of the 'wholeness' in God. Maximus, on the other side, conceives time differently, namely eschatologically, by suggesting a transfiguration of the dark side into the eschatological light. The limitations and the mutual complementarity between the archetypal dualities in Jung – manifesting key aspects of the fourth element – and the eschatological perfection in Maximus are extensively discussed.

The concluding Chapter discusses the synthesis of a compound view of psychological-spiritual development beyond theoretical reductions and psychic one-sidedness. The potentialities of each system could complement each other, but at the same time they could seriously challenge the feasibility of the attainment of all possible goals. However, there is sufficient evidence that the experiential-therapeutic perspective through discovering and experiencing our inner Self, as viewed and practised by Jung as a psychotherapist, could be complementary to the eschatological perspective as seen by Maximus the Confessor of a personal God embracing all beings through their *logoi* and spiritual meanings that the human soul is endowed with. Within these mutually interrelated conceptions, the *trans-disciplinary paradigm* of psychic development is introduced, which proposes a potential integration of all possible directions of development that overcomes the problem of psychic one-sidedness.

Having read this book, the reader, I trust, will have come to appreciate that there is additional scope remaining for improvement of both models by addressing the fuller perspectives of psychological development: it is a development that must follow the suggested trans-disciplinary framework within the range from the psychological level to the socio-cultural level and ultimately to metaphysical realms. In this respect, Jungian and Maximian models could be further elaborated and expanded, accordingly, towards readdressing their aims to reach both psychic and spiritual 'wholeness' – namely, by avoiding 'one-sidedness' whether it is a psychological or a spiritual partiality. A new developmental model is therefore proposed, the 'trans-disciplinary paradigm of development': one which emerges from critiques of Jung and Maximus, ultimately aiming at a constructive treatment of problems relative to psychic and/or spiritual one-sidedness. Analogous proposals of contemporary 'paradigms' that depart from classical mono-dimensional interpretations enrich the complexity of theory of modern science, such as Kuhn's 'paradigm shift' of basic epistemological and scientific assumptions (1970) as well as Aziz's 'syndetic paradigm' (2007), both of which go beyond the Freudian and Jungian models of development.

It is then reasonable to anticipate that modern religious practices and perspectives could be challenged on the highlighted three Jungian viewpoints, namely (a) in which ways psychological experience has to function as a pivotal point of religious life, (b) how doctrines must be interpreted through psychological terms, and (c) how shadow/evil aspects may be a source of 'incalculable potential' in human life, as Jung suggested. Nevertheless, it is a matter of personal choice as to whether one appreciates and acknowledges that Jung's theory of psychic wholeness or individuation evidently opens new paths to understanding how Christian love and other spiritual goals must embrace body, shadow, and the feminine as essential parts of human life and development in contemporary contexts. It can also indicate serious gaps in what spiritual love might mean in contemporary religious circles.

On the other hand, the individuation process is challenged with respect to its ontological ground and perspectives, both of which Jung mostly reduced to a merely psychological level. Maximian insights could function as an incalculable source of perspectives for development in that they are able to convey a combination of a robust ontology with an embedded epistemology that incorporates vital phenomenological and experiential dimensions. This could thus be an uncommon sound of a 'symphony of experience', which opens up to experience of a personal God within a mutual interexchange of life, understanding, suffering, and, ultimately, unconditional love.

Notes

1. See B. Bosanquet, Metaphysics 22 (1884), cited in *Oxford English Dictionary online* (www.oed.com), accessed on 14.12.2012.
2. Commenting on Freud's final blow, Palmer's query is whether this was 'not just a devastating critique of religion but a terminal one' (Palmer 1997: 60).
3. We will discuss this issue further in Chapter 2.
4. Beyond the ontological affirmation of a metaphysical God, the developmental and experiential dimensions of *theosis* are manifold, as illustrated in classic treatises of Christian literature, such as John Climacus' *The Ladder of Divine Ascent* (7th century AD) and John of the Cross' *Ascent of Mount Carmel* (16th century).
5. In Grondin's interpretation (2003: 154), see Chapter 2.

2

THE 'PSYCHOLOGICAL' AND THE 'SPIRITUAL'

An evolutional relationship

The relationship between the psychological and the spiritual dimensions of psychic life is of prime importance for an inquiry on psychic development. Depending on the angle through which this relationship is considered, the dynamics between the psychological and the spiritual – and by extension the religious – could be construed in different and often antithetical ways. The range of these considerations could accordingly lead to contradictory interpretations of psychic development. Modern theory has extensively explored and conceptualised the spiritual and/or the religious attitude and adopted diverse approaches to the spiritual/religious perspective. Evolutionary psychology, for instance, re-evaluating Freud's characterisation of religion as an *illusion,* considers religion as a social adaptation or a *by-product* – placing emphasis on the social dimension. However, a deeper understanding of the dynamics between the psychological and the spiritual perspectives has to be drawn from insights emanating from other than psychological fields and rather focus on a broader framework, which extends beyond solely psychological context.

We may have a profounder understanding of the psychological-spiritual relationship through an investigation of these two notions via the lenses of third-party disciplines, such as sociology and philosophy. This approach could address not only the phenomenological aspects but also the ontological potential of the psychological-spiritual relationship. It is for this reason that philosophy of mind, when concerned with metaphysical enquiries, points out the significance of a 'clear conception of an underlying ontology' (Heil 2004: 191) for advancing an empirical theory of mind. In the next paragraphs, we shall follow an exploration of the dynamics between the psychological and spiritual dimensions through an inquiry on their ontological and phenomenological aspects in both ancient and modern contexts, which could lead to a new understanding of the evolutionary dynamics between these two entities.

Since the early 20th century, when William James (1902) embarked upon a systematic investigation of religious phenomena from a psychological viewpoint, there have been pioneering contributions to the interface between psychology and religion. Challenging Sigmund Freud's reductionist approach to religion as 'illusion' (1927), Carl G. Jung highlighted the immanent 'religious function' of the psyche (1944: para. 14), which becomes part of the process of *individua-tion* and the *Self* – elaborated by post–Jungians mainly from the classical and archetypal schools (e.g. Edinger 1972; Stein 1985, 2004; Corbett 1996; Dour-ley 2008). Alfred Adler addressed religion as propelling activities that encom-pass both personal goals and social achievements (see Adler & Jahn 1933). A similar 'multilevel' approach to religion is further implied by Gordon W. Allport that distinguished between 'intrinsically' and 'extrinsically' religiously oriented individuals (1950, 1959). Early engagement with psychology of religion was followed by a decline of interest, as psychology sought a more 'solid' scientific ground for its projects (see Paloutzian 1996: 42–47; Belzen 2012: 16). The last quarter century has, nevertheless, witnessed an unparalleled interest in the psy-chology of religion (see Emmons & Paloutzian, 2003; Belzen 2012). However, despite progress in conceptualising religion and spirituality (Wulff 1997; Hill *et al.* 2000; Emmons & Paloutzian 2003: 381), the question of a holistic-multilevel understanding of the religious/spiritual dimension by psychology remains open, since the latter 'has paid only sporadic attention to the psychological processes underlying human religiousness' (Paloutzian & Park 2005: 3). In spite of con-structive insights on religion from various disciplines (I shall refer to philosophy, sociology, sociology of religion, and theology), what appears to be missing is a holistic approach to the religious/spiritual dimension, one that could overcome the assumed polarity of the internal (psychic) and external (socio-cultural and/or metaphysical) perspectives.

Therefore, such a holistic approach can be subsequently introduced via the lens of concepts stemming from different than psychology fields, such as sociology, philosophy, and theology. This approach develops an *evolutionary* viewpoint to interpret the dynamics between the 'psychological' and the 'spiritual' that leads from the former to the latter. For this purpose, a framework consisting of five 'ontological' levels – namely the bodily, the psychic, the interpersonal-social, the cultural, and the metaphysical – is introduced.[1] This multilevel framework suggests that the spiritual can be considered as a dynamic, constantly evolving multi-faceted property that might 'emerge' from elements stemming from all these realms while maintaining its own potential. Within this framework, the dis-tinct aspects of this multi-faceted property of the spiritual (i.e. its psychological, social, cultural, and metaphysical features) can be explored and evaluated more systematically.

This approach possibly could enhance 'the *multilevel inter-disciplinary para-digm*' that the psychology of religion needs as a model, proposed by Emmons and Paloutzian (2003: 395) – aligned to the paradigm and methodology of trans-disciplinarity that presupposes 'different levels of Reality' as well as their distinct underlying laws as 'a part of the totality of laws governing all levels' (Nico-lescu 2010: 19). The proposed evolutionary perspective overcomes the polarity of the internal-external factors – also projected by the phenomenological-ontological polarity – and sequentially elaborates concepts and methodologies stemming from other than psychology fields. But before exploring these concepts from different disciplines, we must follow certain critical moments in the history of the relationship between the psychological and the spiritual.

The 'spiritual' and the 'psychological' in context

The specific features of the 'religious' and the 'spiritual' will be discussed in the following paragraphs. It would, however, be necessary to begin with the basic definitions of 'religion' and the 'spiritual'. Despite the inevitable overlap between religion and the spiritual, the latter appears to bear a more 'human' perspective than the former, as being closer to the 'intellectual' psychic aspect. According to the Oxford English Dictionary (*OED*),[2] 'religion' is defined as 'the condition of belonging to a religious order' (OED, 1) or 'a particular system of faith and worship' (4a) or 'a pursuit, interest, or movement, followed with great devotion' (4b). Two elements can be identified here, one internal-psychological (devotion, faith) and another external (movement, system). The OED also defines the 'spiritual' as 'of or relating to, consisting of, spirit, regarded in either a religious or intellectual aspect; of the nature of a spirit or incorporeal supernatural essence; immaterial' (ibid.: 4a) or 'of or relating to, emanating from, the intellect or higher faculties of the mind; intellectual' (6). According to these definitions, it can be understood that the spiritual, emanating from 'higher faculties of the mind', can develop either independently of religious contexts or may follow a development aligned with devotion and faith within a religious movement or system. From a psychological standpoint, the spiritual appears to be a broader notion, since it encompasses a range of perspectives from the intellectual to the 'supernatural essence' (metaphysics). Yet religion overlaps with the psychic and/or spiritual aspect, since the 'dimensions of religious commitment', according to Paloutzian, span from the 'experiential' and the 'intellectual' to the 'ritualistic' and the 'ideological' – of which the latter two are aligned with the external system of faith (1996: 12–21).

Contemporary interpretative methods and epistemologies that endeavour to understand 'how and to what degree we may know what is real' are found on entirely different grounds, compared to previous equivalent theories. It is widely acknowledged that modernity caused significant shifts from antiquated 'ontological' to modern 'phenomenological' considerations, namely, from the question 'what is real?' to 'what can be experienced?', and from a theoretical but rather unapproachable 'reality' towards an epistemology of 'know-how' through the experience of self-consciousness perceiving things as they 'appear'.[3] It is thus noteworthy to briefly follow historically how the spiritual was subjected to evolution, resulting in 'emancipation' from the psychosomatic bond as well as from its engagement with religious contexts.

In the ancient world, human existence was not entirely dissociated from the spiritual. According to Lévy-Bruhl, primitive humans have 'no conception of matter, or of a body, whence *some* mystic force, which we should term spiritual, does not emanate' (Lévy-Bruhl 1965: 113). Similarly, referring to the Homeric period, Snell states that 'Homer has no one word to characterise the mind or the soul . . . For Homer, *psyche* [ψυχή] is the force [the vital spirit], which keeps the human being alive' (Snell 1960: 8). Although the spiritual is distinguished here from the body, it is also identified with the soul/psyche. In Greek philosophy and in Christian tradition, the discourse of the 'spiritual' was related principally to a specific *ontology,* or a *religion,* incorporating a strong metaphysical aspect. Ontology is defined as a 'doctrine of the being and relations of all reality'; it has been given precedence 'over Cosmology and Psychology, the two branches of enquiry which follow the reality into its opposite distinctive forms' (see Bosanquet, *Metaphysics* 22, 1884, cited in OED, B). In ancient/classical Greek discourses, the spiritual was thus considered an 'ontological' aspect of such an eternal reality. Although the term 'ontology' first appeared as a philosophical term in the 17th century,[4] it was the pre–Socratic philosophers that first posed the question concerning the eternal form of the being(s) (ὄντων) to answer 'what is real?' or 'what is the true form of reality?'.

The pre–Socratics emphatically conceptualised the question over the first principle, which was identified with the boundless, the divine, as Anaximander held.[5] The dynamics of different qualities within the psyche, still not clearly defined, were also present in Heraclitus' thought, in his dictum that 'the psyche has *logos* which increases itself' (*Diels* B115). *Logos* could also be a counterpart of the spiritual, a psychic aspect that constantly develops and expands. Similar to this was the Stoics' view of a psyche attuned to its internal 'logos', which is a spiritual state of life (*SVF* 3: 473).

Plato's conceptualisation of the spiritual related to the ideal *Forms* in the 'divine' realm but at the same time to the highest part of the soul (such as the nous, a counterpart of the function of the intellect): 'God gave the sovereign part of the human soul to be the divinity of each one . . . [being] a plant not of an earthly but of a heavenly growth' (*Timaeus* 90a).[6] A dipole between the spiritual and the non-spiritual psychic part is thus introduced. Insofar as 'Plato's epistemology expressed a deeply religious belief in transcendent and permanent values' (Nagy 1991: 49), the spiritual strongly implies a world beyond the psyche, 'the region above the heaven' (*topos hyperouranios,* in *Phaedrus* 247C). The unresolved tension between these two poles, namely between the psychic and the spiritual/ divine, is more apparent in the Gnostic myth, according to which the 'psyche' (from Greek *psychesthai,* to be cool) fell from heaven, because the ardour of rational beings for contemplating God spiritually was cooled, from where all psyches derive (Origen, *Principles* II, 8.3: *SC* 252: 343–9). The visible world and bodies were created afterwards in order to cover and protect the soul's nakedness.

Aristotle follows a more materialistic approach in an attempt to bridge the distance between the body and the psyche and also between the psyche and the divine. Aristotle applies the term '*pneuma*' (spirit), a 'peculiar kind of body' (very close to *ether*), aligned with the *entelecheia* or a kind of 'completeness' of the body–soul bond (*soul* seen defined as the final potential, the *telos* of the body).[7] On the other hand, Aristotle is not clear enough on the distinction between the functions of the 'passive intelligence/nous' and 'active intelligence/nous';[8] the latter is immortal and seems to enter the soul from *without*.[9] An agent 'from without' strongly indicates the spiritual/metaphysical area, of which Aristotle himself, as Guthrie states, 'was aware that it was for him a kind of religious conception, and difficult to keep within the bounds of a philosophy that was intended to be purely rational' (Guthrie 1967: 159). Despite these ambiguous points, both Plato and Aristotle articulated a spiritual dimension beyond what can be understood within the merely psychological functions and perception.

Neoplatonics develop analogous ideas within the three hypostases, the *One,* the *Nous,* and the *Soul.* Plotinus asserts that the divine 'light' is essential for the life of beings, or 'nous is dead until it receives the light of The Good [One]' (*Enneads* VI: 7.22), but this is 'the most clearly un-Hellenic thing', according to Armstrong (1940: 32). In fact, Plotinus supports the idea of the ontological continuity of divine and human (*Enneads* V: 2.1) – insofar as both Nous and Soul proceed from a spontaneous efflux of One's life and power. For Plotinus, the light and power of the One is an *external* extra-psychic agent that illumines its derivatives, Nous and Soul. However, due to the fact that no specific ontological distinction between God(s) and the cosmos existed in either Platonic or Neoplatonic philosophy, the spiritual remained indistinguishable from the metaphysical 'real' world.

Christianity introduced the belief that man was created 'in the image and likeness of God' (*Genesis* 1, 26), with respect to both the inherited spiritual dimension of the psyche (image) and the path towards the acquisition of God's metaphysical qualities (likeness). A new ontological feature is now attributed to the spiritual, because for the Christian philosophers, 'it was necessary to find an ontology that avoided the monistic Greek philosophy as much as the "gulf" between God and the world taught by the gnostic systems' (Zizioulas 1985: 16). Paul the apostle also stressed the critical ontological difference between the 'soul' and the 'spirit': the spirit no longer belongs to human nature as an inherent component but is rather identified with the Holy Spirit (1 *Corinthians* 2, 12–14). Philo's statement that 'pneuma' is the highest part, and thus a component, of the soul, the inbreathed divine pneuma-image of God in man (see Armstrong 1947: 163), is superseded by Christian teaching that man is a composite nature of body and soul that receives the Spirit from an extra-psychic realm.

Although modern theory considered the prevailing aspect of Christian theories as a system of purely ontological doctrines, the psychic/experiential dimension was not eliminated, based on the belief that man can experience the qualities of God through spiritual life.[10] For Maximus the Confessor, ontology clearly incorporates a vivid experiential aspect:

> For the union between Creator and creation, rest and motion . . . has been manifested in Logos the Christ . . . and in itself brings God's foreknowledge to fulfilment, in order that naturally mobile creatures might secure themselves around God's total and essential immobility . . . so that they might also acquire an active knowledge of him.
>
> (*Q.Thal.* 60: 79)[11]

21

According to Maximus, the 'naturally mobile' man, with his body and soul/psyche (ψυχή), is able to evolve through the knowledge stemming from the energies and love of God. It is a process in which the inherited 'image of God' is transfigured into the 'likeness' and qualities of God not only within the psychic boundaries but also beyond them, as in a metaphysical dimension. Thus, a new 'epistemology' is clearly introduced that allows humans to 'experience' knowledge of the divine.

The Christian view of the spiritual, which seeks a balance between the phenomenological aspect and the ontological potential, is located in the middle of two antithetical approaches: at the one pole stands Heraclitus' maxim, 'human nature has no knowledge, but the divine nature has' (*Diels* B78), whereby ontology dominates; at the other pole, and 23 centuries later, lies Nietzsche's standpoint that, '[k]nowledge for its own sake – this is the last snare set by morality . . .' (*Maxims and Interludes* 64, 1886: 72), where the ontological aspect is eliminated. In modernity, the centre of gravity is about to move toward the phenomenological aspect in terms of what can be experienced and up to the limits of human knowledge within the psychic boundaries.

Not until Descartes' verification of reality through the thinking mind (*cogito ergo sum*) did modern philosophy examine non-material entities with a more systematic and rational approach. In the pre–Kantian epoch, the spiritual is treated with scepticism, and concepts such as Leibniz's *monad* generated a lot of later criticism, especially from Kant. In *Religion within the Boundaries of Mere Reason Only,* Kant frames spiritual/religious issues within the concept of two homocentric spheres: 'the wider sphere of faith', aligned with the unknowable *thing in itself,* and a narrower one of 'religion of reason' (1793: 40) – as it is appropriate to expect from the philosophical viewpoint. Concepts such as Schopenhauer's *Will,* a potential 'thing in itself' (Schopenhauer 1819: 87f), and axioms that, 'there are no moral phenomena at all, only a moral interpretations of phenomena . . .' (Nietzsche 1886: 78) put human experience in contradistinction with metaphysics. Consequently, after the dominance of nominalism and the ensuing trajectory of modern philosophical thought – either towards the Kantian compromise between rationalism and empiricism or towards German idealism – the spiritual, and by extension, the religious discourse was approached from a basis entirely different from the ontological, namely, the phenomenological. The phenomenological approach emphasizes primarily an emerging 'self-consciousness' that perceives nature-cosmos 'as it appears', contrary to the axioms suggested by ontology or religion(s).

As a result, amongst other epistemological criteria of this time (e.g. reason or physical senses), consciousness and psychic experience are predominantly applied to validate the 'truth' of spiritual concepts. Hegel introduced the concept of *geist* (a spiritual dimension within the cosmos), a quality that animates all beings in general, and the mind in particular, towards the development of all possible forms of consciousness:

> In pressing forward to its true form of existence, consciousness will
> come to a point at which it lays aside its semblance of being hampered

with what is alien to it, with what is only *for* it and exists as an other, where appearance becomes identified with essence . . . and finally, when it grasps this its own essence, it will denote the nature of absolute knowledge itself.

(Hegel 1807/1931: 145)

By attributing the attainment of 'absolute knowledge' to the constantly evolving self-consciousness (through history, science, the arts), Hegel opposed the unknowable Kantian 'thing-in-itself' and established a consciousness-based new epistemology. In the ensuing philosophical movement known as existentialism, the spiritual dimension is similarly located within 'consciousness' as man's own place in the world (see, for instance, Heidegger's *dasein*).[12] Not only did phenomenology begin to function as a ground-breaking philosophical movement, but it also established an objective basis for the emerging self-consciousness. The concept of self-consciousness, under the influence of the French materialists (e.g. Cabanis in the 18th century), was also related to the brain's functions, and contemporary advances in neurophysiology validated the materialistic aspect of consciousness as a higher mental activity. With the rising importance of 'consciousness' in modern philosophy, the spiritual was confined within human apperception.

Hans-George Gadamer introduced a fresh dimension of the 'spiritual' perspective of the human mind, through the 'hermeneutics of understanding', by developing or modifying concepts of Hegel and Heidegger. Gadamer drew a sharp distinction between experience as a 'state of mind' (*Erlebnis*), a mode of aesthetic experience Kant obviously narrowly viewed as sensibility, and experience within the Hegelian sense (*Erfahrung*), which presents us with the challenge that we should 'change our minds' – as Heidegger worked on his *Hegel's Phenomenology of Spirit*.[13] Experience as *Erlebnis* is connected with *Verstand,* a word Kant mostly used for 'understanding' (in a narrow and objectifying sense), whereas experience as *Erfahrung* is related to *Verstehen,* an ontological 'understanding', non-objectifying, in Hegel's perspective of a subject's very being in the world that 'expands' our experience by a new knowledge.[14] Gadamer places emphasis on the hermeneutical process of an aesthetic event:

The event of the beautiful and the hermeneutical process both presuppose the finiteness of human life. We might even ask whether the beautiful can be experienced by an infinite mind . . . Can this mind see anything other than the beauty of the whole that lies before it? The 'radiance' of the beautiful seems to be something reserved to finite human experience.

(Gadamer 1975: 480)

Gadamer's approach reveals a new perspective on the *finite* human mind-consciousness and the limits of its knowledge. All classical and medieval thought,

Gadamer remarks, presupposes that this knowledge 'is incorporated in being. . . . In this thinking there is no question of a self-conscious spirit without world which would have to find its way to worldly being' (Gadamer 1975: 454–5). Commending these points, Grondin notes that, '[i]n fact, Gadamer intends to prepare, not new thoughts about infinity, but a metaphysics of finitude' (Grondin 2003: 154). There is little room, obviously, for any mediation through a third point 'from without'.

On the other hand, the state of deeper experience/*Erfahrung,* as an external impact that 'changes' our mind-understanding, challenges once more the boundaries of the conscious potential towards something beyond the regular functions of sensibility and reason. This state of mind might indicate a deeper function of intuition or 'inner seeing', the direct impact of which could transform our understanding; such a function appears to be in line with the Homeric 'noos' (nous/intellect), 'a type of seeing', and 'the mental act which goes with the vision' (Snell 1960: 13). It is about this perspective that both Plato and Aristotle speak, as we saw above, indicating the unique potential of the intellect/ nous. Contrary to the Hegelian idealism of a 'permanent beyond', Gadamer's understanding stresses an 'ontology' of 'here and now', framing the 'spiritual' through what could drastically 'change' our experience. By so doing, he opens an encouraging perspective that finite beings have the potential to reach and experience knowledge beyond any pre-established belief, affirming to an ontological potential towards metaphysics of the 'finite' self-consciousness and experience.

It can therefore be understood that the spiritual, either in the sense of Heidegger's search for the *Dasein* or in Gadamer's perspective of the 'metaphysics of finitude' experience, aspires to be grounded in the depths of the consciousness, whose boundaries strive constantly to expand by activating the internal insight, understanding, or vision. These strands, open to new perspectives beyond the limits of ordinary experience, are, nevertheless, challenged by postmodern tenets, through which classical ideas are seen as merely 'narratives' exposed to subjective views and evaluations. The spiritual or 'theological' meaning(s) delivered by authors' texts or theories have been 'replaced by a negation to assign a "secret" or a spiritual meaning to this text: it is an antitheological activity', as stated in Burthes' *The Death of the Author* (cited in Butler 2002: 23–4).

From all these we may conclude that historically, the conceptualisation of the spiritual has changed positions between two opposite poles, the psychosomatic and the metaphysical, finding in modern times a more appropriate 'accommodation' within an experiencing 'consciousness'. Despite these philosophical challenges spanning a flux of reductions and subjectivities, the fundamental epistemological concern that occupies contemporary theory can be expressed with the following questions: Does the 'spiritual' exist in any aspect of human existence *beyond* what can be grasped by bodily senses or psychic functions? Accordingly, does the 'spiritual' possess a more advanced, larger, higher, or deeper *nature* than the 'psychosomatic', or is it of a lower, insignificant quality and possibly an *illusion?* To answer these questions, epistemology must address the limits of self-consciousness and, in turn, phenomenology to relate adequately to ontology – and consequently to reflect on the questions that ontology raises.

'Genres' for relating psychology to religion

Before exploring further the multilevel ontological factors that may play a role in shaping the spiritual, it is important to take a closer look at the dynamics between the spiritual/spirituality and religion in modernity. Following Nietzsche's declaration of 'God's death', or the death of metaphysics after the decline of institutional religion, the quest for the spiritual has had to contend with Freud's fundamental position that religion, and by extension the spiritual, is a mode of collective illusion, or an unconscious 'longing for the missing father' (Freud 1927). Thus, the 'spiritual-as-religion', the prevailing theoretical position in the past, was gradually replaced by the 'spiritual-as-psychological', which now seeks to analyse its subject matter within the psychic boundaries of conscious and unconscious processes. The promise of a new life, in terms of 'New Age' movements, replaces the classical spiritual approach of a 'life-as-spiritual growth' with the spirituality of the 'holistic milieu', whereby seeking 'a source of significance which lies within the process of life itself' (Heelas & Woodhead 2005: 31). Despite the criticism that the 'New Age' movement has received, its affiliation with systems such as atheism, polytheism, holistic theories, motivational psychology, and astrology reveals an archetypal and thus inherited dimension of spiritual development that seeks psychological validity and understanding that does not fit within classical religious boundaries (e.g. see Crowley 2003).

However, other thinkers leave more room for the notion of transcendence and avoid a sharp reduction of the *trans*-rational to the *pre*-rational or to the psychological. This view reduces the potential of the spiritual and denies a genuine *post*- or *trans*-rational perspective (an authentic spiritual dimension), a misconception that Kenneth Wilber (2000) has described as a *pre/trans fallacy.* In addition, Kuhn's description of 'paradigm shift' notes the subjective and transitional character of the ways we validate knowledge 'selectively', which is in itself a criticism of Freud's reductive view of religion (Kuhn 1970). At first sight, both Freud and Jung seemingly slipped into the pre/trans fallacy. The primitive and infantile unconscious fixations alongside the myths, which allegedly convey supernatural, divine meanings, are examples of Freudian and Jungian interpretations, respectively, within this misconception. This does not mean, however, that Freud and Jung are entirely subject to this fallacy. Post–Freudians certainly leave some room for the 'trans-rational' by reconsidering Freud's positions on religion (Rizzuto, Winnicot, Horney, Bion, for instance; see Wallace 1984; Black 2006: 7–15). Thus, some psychoanalysts are now positively disposed towards the relevance of religion (such as Eigen 2001).

The religious dimension is currently discussed seriously within psychoanalytic schools, and, as Nathan Fields notes, 'thanks to the late work of the most radical of the post–Kleinian analysts, W. R. Bion, psychoanalysts are presented with the prospect that by following the true path of psychoanalysis, they will come closer to the mystical knowledge of God' (Field 2005: xvii). A degree of emancipation from the initial rigidity of 'religion-as-illusion' towards a constructive dialogue is also evident. In the same vein, David Black argues that 'psychoanalysis can help religion by its insights into the formation and functioning of internal objects, and religion can help psychoanalysis by its understanding of the nature of faith or conviction' (2006: 7). Psychology and psychoanalysis are emerging as full counterparts to religion and, by extension, to spirituality (see Stein & Black 1999). As a result, scholars do not speak simply in terms of the psychology *of* religion but also in terms of psychology *and* or *as* a religion. Similar trends are also apparent in Jung's treatment of religion, which is discussed below.

These debates that investigate the degree of influence of religion on psychology and on psychoanalysis, and vice versa, have generated specific articulations describing the dynamic relationship between the two parts. Thus, in Jonte-Pace and Parsons's formulation (2001), we can speak of psychology 'and', 'of', or 'in dialogue with' religion. Consistent with this perspective, theorists have created specific *genres* of research and scholarship on this subject. Chris Schlauch considers three such genres: (a) psychology *of* religion, (b) psychology *and* religion, and (c) psychology *as* religion (2007: 203). The repercussions of such distinctions indicate that the psychological, and by extension the spiritual as an emergent from the psychological, could be explored independently of religious contexts. Scholars currently adopt the position that religion and spirituality are distinct issues. For instance, Heelas and Woodhead argue that 'religion is giving way to spirituality' and they distinguish between 'life-as-religion and the normativization of subjectivities' and 'subjective-life and the sacralisation of the unique subjectivities' (2005: 31). Religiousness and spirituality nevertheless are intertwined within one's psychological ground, since spirituality is understood as working through an 'affective basis' and as 'a return to virtue' (i.e. gratitude, forgiveness, and humility) – a common basis for major religions (Emmons & Paloutzian 2003: 384–390). It is also suggested that the spiritual is usually contextualised within religious contexts but can also evolve independently (see Emmons & Paloutzian 2003: 382; Elkins 2001; Hill *et al.* 2000). We thus live in an era in which the spiritual may constitute an independent feature within other socio-cultural parameters and in which 'psychology as religion is a cultural reality' (Jonte-Pace & Parsons 2001: 6).

Analytical psychology has also shown a strong interest in the religious/spiritual dimensions through either the concept of the Self or the individuation process. Influenced by James's systematic exploration of religious-spiritual phenomena on a pragmatic basis of inner experience,[15] Jung understands the spiritual (or religious) as an amalgam of gnostic ideas (*philosophical stone*), theosophical approaches (such as Jakob Böhme's approach), alchemical processes (*coniunctio*), and patterns of Eastern cultures. The psyche's religious function, anchored in the God-image, has been addressed and investigated specifically by E. Edinger (1972), J. Heisig (1979), L. Corbett (1996), and more generally by M. Stein (1985, 2004). Meckel and Moore (1990), R. Moore (1988), A. Ulanov (1999), R. Main (2004, 2006), and others. These studies primarily place Jungian concepts next to and in comparison 'with' religion. Thus, they advance the discourse of 'psychology *and* religion' and, to a lesser extent, the discourse of 'psychology *of* religion'. Attempts have also been made to examine analytical psychology based on the perspective of 'psychology *as* religion' (see Noll 1996; Shamdasani 1999). Beyond constructive comparisons of key Jungian concepts (such as individuation and the Self) with other theories (see Chapter 3) and despite the fact that in many cases the spiritual is understood *next to* or *as* the psychological, as a distinct property, the prevailing psychological viewpoint does not address the ultimate ontological potential of these concepts, a potential that exceeds psychic boundaries.

In an attempt to formulate a multilevel exploration of the spiritual, we may extend the three formulations of psychology 'and', 'of', or 'in dialogue with' religion and Schlauch's *genres* by suggesting three areas of investigation: (a) the spiritual/religious from psychological viewpoints (e.g. psychology of religion, aspects of Jungian psychology), (b) the psychological from spiritual and religious perspectives (as in comparative religion, philosophy of religion, and theology), and (c) the spiritual/religious through the exploration of links with, and impact on, social, cultural, and political life, that is via sociology.[16]

A multilevel approach to the spiritual should take into account all these areas of investigation so as not to endorse a causal or reductionist interpretation restricted to a certain field alone. Theories stemming from different disciplines and realms must be mobilised and engaged constructively in order to more profoundly comprehend the dynamics between the psychological and the spiritual. It could thus be argued that the spiritual, as an event or an experience, is a possible 'form' of an evolutional development (either in a positive or in a negative sense) of the psychological experience, which can further develop by interacting with factors belonging to realms other than the psychological (i.e. social, cultural, metaphysical). Whereas the connotations of the term 'evolutional' are linked to Darwinian evolution, I aim to differentiate this term from the biological or the psychological evolution of A to B. Hence, I adopt a thesis that considers the spiritual as a property that initially emerges from psychic facts (parallel to Hartmann's 'emergence'), a property that may not only incorporate and thus evolve from psychic, socio-cultural, and possibly metaphysical features but could also maintain and develop its own potential – in both phenomenological and ontological terms.

It is understood from the discussion so far that the spiritual may evolve further into the religious. Once spiritual experience is embraced under a system of faith, it becomes, to a greater or a lesser extent, religious, entrenched in this particular environment or system. This process demonstrates the precedence of the spiritual over the religious, which also could be explained anthropologically (for instance, see Lévy-Bruhl 1965). As discussed previously, the spiritual bears its roots in the intellectual psychic aspect, whereas religion requires in addition a movement or system of faith. A sufficiently developed spiritual aspect could manifest itself within a pluralism of forms outside religion, but this does not mean that it could substantially differ from a mature religious attitude, and vice versa.

A consideration of the features of the spiritual at all possible levels could suggest a line of investigation that avoids the pre/trans fallacy in relation to depth psychology as discussed earlier. We can now explore the spiritual as a distinct emergent property from facts belonging to certain levels that may yield different ontological properties. Given these acquired qualities, it could be argued that the spiritual is not fully reducible to psychic dimensions but may constantly evolve and incorporate *trans*-rational features that are not traceable in the psyche as such; rather, these features must be explored and validated within principles that essentially differ from those regulating psychological facts. This evolutional perspective addresses the call for a multilevel inter-disciplinary paradigm as described by Emmons and Paloutzian (2003). Concepts and methodologies from modern sociology could critically serve towards this inter-disciplinary paradigm.

The framework of different ontological levels in modern sociology

So far we have introduced the spectrum of the parameters that might shape the relationship between the psychological and the spiritual (from the psychic, socio-cultural, and metaphysical realms). It is therefore worthwhile to more closely consider the extent to which factors from the socio-cultural level might give rise to spirituality as a 'product' of human life and culture.

Contemporary insights into psychic or social facts maintain a balance between the visible and the invisible. Max Weber, while announcing the 'disenchanted world', also highlighted the need for a meaning in life and tied it to the ontological dimension. By introducing the concept of 'ideal types', Weber applied an analytical tool to explain small but important aspects of the complex social world. The ideal type is 'an abstraction . . . a utopia . . . a mental construct . . . that cannot be found empirically anywhere in reality' (1949: 91). Weber also suggested that we all share some 'meta-empirical' faith in the validity of our supreme values (ibid.: 111). This *meta-empirical* faith might provide a starting point for a contemporary approach to the spiritual, the dynamics of which are not grounded in a specific ontology or metaphysics. As previously mentioned, ontology, as a 'doctrine of the being and relations of all reality', could be perceived as a complex matrix of relations at all levels of reality. Here, too, our 'meta-empirical' faith in the validity of our 'ultimate values', as suggested by Weber, can be understood as an ontological concern from both psychological and spiritual perspectives.

Anthony Giddens explores further the impact of ontological dimensions on human life by introducing the term 'ontological security' (1991: 35–69). Ontological security refers to the 'confidence' that certain systems, such as physical order and social norms, provide to individuals as well as to the feelings from and

28

towards others, which generate self-identity in 'continuity' with the individuals' environments (Giddens 1993: 374–7). According to Giddens, ontological security concerns continuity and trust in the external world, grounded in the feeling of security in the social order, a security that can further be understood as a mode of 'spiritual refuge'. Ontological security also suggests that people require more than an adequate shelter to live satisfactorily and to lead fulfilled lives or even to cope with their destructive psychic drives (i.e. in Freudian terms). The fact that, as R. Laing (1960) suggested, social conditions such as 'insecurity' may generate schizoid disorders reinforces the view that social and psychic levels are 'ontologically' linked. In contemporary social sciences, the inquiry into modes of human activities and interaction is pursued on different 'ontological' levels that also signify a hierarchy of spiritual potentialities. Durkheim, for instance, postulated that 'the determining cause of a social fact should be sought among the social facts preceding it and not among the states of the individual consciousness' (1895: 55). Moore and Sanders explain the significance of this formulation, which was:

> a widely accepted view involved a hierarchy of levels, based on the assumption that culture presupposes society, society is based on individuals and individuals have both minds and bodies. . . . The result was a four-'level' approach to the study of human beings based on body, psyche, society and culture.
>
> (Moore & Sanders 2006: 2)

This fourfold hierarchical approach (body, psyche, society, and culture) echoes, to a considerable extent, the ontological considerations articulated by Weber and Giddens that indicated a shift from a focus on Freudian psychic drives towards the socio-cultural dynamics. At stake now is how both primary and secondary psychic processes, such as death anxiety and, by extension, life anxiety, might be linked to socio-cultural accounts beyond the psychic level. In this respect, the implicit existential and 'spiritual' perspectives of 'ontological security' could enrich psychotherapeutic approaches, which address specifically death anxiety (e.g. Yalom's existential psychotherapy). As the body becomes the locus and the visible reality whereby the psychological life is revealed, so society could become the locus in which the psychological and cultural development is manifested. Thus, the interrelation between the psyche, society, and culture may signify the evolutionary dynamics of the spiritual as an emergent from psychic, social, and cultural constructs.

This hierarchical organisation is present in Karl Popper's thought, which introduces the concepts of 'world 1' (physical objects), 'world 2' (mental experiences), and 'world 3' (products of the human mind; 1994: 47). World 3, as an outcome of 'products' of mental activity, such as scientific theories, could shape the understanding and the progress of mankind (ibid.: 59–61). Following the 'multilevel inter-disciplinary paradigm', this progress might be interpreted here as an evolution of the psychological level (from worlds 1 and 2 to world 3), firmly anchored in the 'products' generated by conscious experience and manifested in culture.

The cultural dimension appears particularly challenging at this point, and the notion of 'cultural complex', possibly a by-product of Popper's world 3, that expresses the cultural – and in broader sense also the spiritual – progress of mankind, becomes significantly relevant. Thomas Singer elucidates the concept of cultural complexes as a diachronic accumulation of both inner and outer experiences that ultimately comprises an 'inner sociology':

> Cultural complexes can be defined as emotionally charged aggregates of ideas and images that tend to cluster around an archetypal core and are shared by individuals within an identified collective. They accumulate experiences that validate their point of view and create a store-house of self-affirming, ancestral memories which are based on historical experiences that have taken root in the collective psyche of a group . . . cultural complexes can be thought of as the fundamental building blocks of a truly inner sociology.
>
> (Singer 2010: 234)

These 'building blocks' that constitute our inner sociology may articulate more precisely the 'continuity' between the individual and society that ontological security entails. In this respect, ontological security, being 'a store-house of self-affirmation', can further provide a set of beyond merely psychological features as the foundations of an unceasingly evolved 'spiritual' perspective in modern life. Robert Torrance states that the spiritual quest today is the 'uncompletable endeavour to actualise, in some small part, the future . . .' (1994: 54), a 'future' that places importance onto the chronological, and thus evolutional, dimension that determines our existence. Inevitably, this evolutional dimension within time is also linked to the quest for transcendence and the idea of God(s). In a Jungian context, the spiritual emerges from the collective unconscious, the location of the Self/God-image archetype that preserves a zone of mystery; it is a zone that only time may reveal, a rather meta-physical realm, which could accommodate aspects of insights such as Lacan's order of the *real* and Bion's notion of 'O' (see Field 2005: 79).

The aforementioned concepts at the socio-cultural level may denote aspects of the evolution of the spiritual from elements stemming from the psychological and the socio-cultural realms; it is an evolution in different 'phenomenological' forms within the same ontological world. Consequently, these five levels, as the total of the four levels developed by Moore and Sanders (body, psyche, society, culture) and with the addition of the metaphysical level, comprise the multilevel ontological framework within which all the parameters that potentially shape the spiritual – as an emergent property from all possible spheres of life – could be investigated.

Methodological issues in modern sociology

Modern sociology has introduced certain methodological approaches in interpreting social phenomena that also are relevant when dealing with considerations linked with both the psychic and socio-cultural worlds – and, by extension, with the spiritual dimension. *Functionalism* considers the dynamics between the psychic and social facts through a particular 'function' of a social part, institution, or belief, whereby its impact on society is delivered. It has received a strong criticism and, amongst others, Root holds that 'the talk of functions is more a metaphysical article of faith than a statement of empirical fact' (1993: 83). On the other hand, Rosenberg argues more constructively:

> Functionalism is in some respects a far more appealing approach to deeper meanings than psychoanalytic theory. . . . Instead of investing unconscious psychological states with unrecognised purposes to explain action, one invests institutions with such purposes and then shows how the institutions constrain, overwhelm, or inform individual action with a deeper meaning, derived from their institutional function.
>
> (Rosenberg 2008: 164)

In this respect, functional analysis goes beyond psychoanalysis by bridging constructively – but not reductively – the socio-cultural and psychic levels and, in turn, providing a concrete basis on which both psychic and spiritual states can be explored within an inter-disciplinary logic. In addition, methodological approaches such as *reductionism, reciprocity, supervenience*, and *teleology* could serve to delineate the dynamics among all the different levels. Freud's statement that 'the superego fulfils the same function of protecting and saving what was fulfilled in earlier days by the father and later by Providence and Destiny' (Freud 1923: 58) suggests a *reductive* treatment of the 'spiritual': what previously was considered as higher or divine now belongs to the unconscious depths. Religion is addressed in the context of a 'return' of the forgotten historical past, and religious rituals are considered a sublimation of primitive 'biological' acts (see Quinodoz 2006: 268). By contrast, *supervenience*, a notion used in the social sciences, considers certain influences of superior on inferior levels as occurring *without* a strong dependency on physical laws (Zahle 2007). In simple terms, what exists at level A (e.g. the mind or the spiritual) does not necessarily exist at level B (e.g. the body or the psyche). Supervenience could be a useful tool for investigating the 'spiritual features' of a system that 'inexplicably' affects certain levels at which these features cannot be entirely understood through the classical reductive analysis.

Additionally, *reciprocity* draws on 'non-causal' effects between parts of the society; it is a model of non-exploitative social relations to overcome causality in which the 'capacity for freedom of agencies [is] a fundamental characteristic' (Gould 1983: 81). The moral and the spiritual could be two of these agencies (D'Andrade 1995/2006: 513). Finally, *teleology*, which examines the *telos*, the final consequences, is antithetical to the historical-reductive method – which endeavours to find the meaning of contemporary behaviour in the events of the patient's past. Teleology is more proximate to those effects of the spiritual that are not readily apparent within an existing psychic context and implies developmental processes engaged in the evolution towards the endless end of human existence. Supervenience and teleology could thus release the potential to interpreting psychic development within a pluralistic framework by means of introducing an approach that avoids epistemological fallacies.

The spiritual: an evolution from the psychological and the ontological potential

An evolutionary perspective of the spiritual, which suggests that spirituality emerges from certain features spanning from psychosomatic to metaphysical realms, stresses the impact of multilevel parameters whereby the spiritual is shaped. Both the fact that certain theories consider the spiritual as an innate quality of the psyche related to the potential for something higher, deeper, bigger, or future (eschatological) and the fact that aspects of the spiritual are manifested within the socio-cultural realm suggest, and to some extent verify, the evolutionary perspective of the spiritual. Just as the cognitive function is the unquestionable ground for the development of self-consciousness, so psychic facts are indispensable material and essential events for spiritual experience and evolution. However, as self-consciousness cannot be reduced to cognitive functions, as it incorporates dynamics from the external world, so can spiritual experience not be reduced to psychological facts insofar as it interrelates with the socio-cultural and the metaphysical.

In Figure 2.1, the spiritual quality (Sp) is understood as the result of the interaction between psychic experience (Ps) and another factor/agent C (or a sum

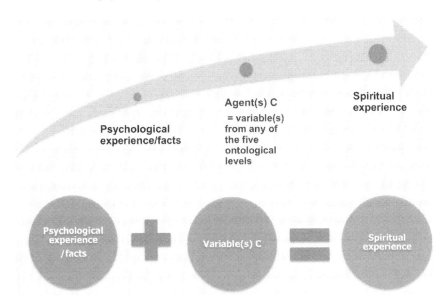

Figure 2.1 The Spiritual as synthesis of phenomenological and ontological elements

of factors/agents), which gain 'value' from the tank of concepts and dynamics within the mentioned five ontological levels – whereby the psychic experience is transformed into spiritual experience. Neither the psychic experience nor the agent C can stand for the spiritual; only their fusion can do so (i.e. Ps + C = Sp), where the variable 'C' could be, for instance, an archetype, such as a God-image, a cultural complex or product, or a metaphysical agent. This illustration could represent more emphatically the fact that the spiritual may constantly evolve through the impact of parameters spanning the framework of the five levels, thus having a dynamic form that cannot be easily conveyed by a specific scientific concept. It can be also understood that the equation may manifest different levels of evolution-development of the spiritual towards specific directions accordingly to the factors engaged. For instance, the spiritual, through cultural impacts, may be embedded in an artistic embodiment (as a spiritual symbol) or can further evolve in a metaphysical direction within a religious context. The Jungian Self, in its plethora of incarnations, provides an example of an immanent spiritual element that is embodied in numerous ways: from 'mandala' symbolism to Christ's figure. In any case, the spiritual maintains its own distinct character and potential.

The advantage of this holistic understanding is that while the conceptualisation of the spiritual departs from its traditional dependence on purely ontological and metaphysical considerations, it nevertheless maintains a dynamism that encompasses all possible levels of life and engages agents from different realms – frequently considered as opposites or irrelevant. It is therefore a model of the *spiritual continuum* that describes more precisely the holistic understanding of the spiritual as an emergent property (Figure 2.2). This approach allows a degree of interdependence between factors that might influence the formation of the spiritual. As discussed earlier, 'ontological security' provides strong links to the socio-cultural level that appears as decisive as other internal psychological factors in shaping one's cultural and spiritual background.

The spiritual continuum can be viewed as a spectrum analogous to the light spectrum, ranging from the infrared area (psychosomatic) to the ultraviolet (metaphysical), also containing intermediate scales (interpersonal, social, and cultural; see Preston 1990). Theories engaging the spiritual dimension can address different areas of this spectrum. Within the spiritual continuum both the psychological and the spiritual are subjected to mediation through the intra psychic (Z_1) factors or extra-psychic (Z_2) agencies. According to Figure 2.2, it is obvious that the spiritual continuum advances towards the socio-cultural level when intra-psychic agents (Z_1) are activated and further towards the metaphysical level (Y) by the intervention of extra-psychic factors (Z_2). In addition, it is also apparent that when psychic functions and processes (X_1, X_2, etc.) are reduced to biological laws, psychic development is viewed horizontally as bearing one dimension alone (the biological). On the contrary, teleology and supervenience provide reasonable freedom for viewing psychic processes as maintaining their own attributes and potential, regardless of the biological aspect.

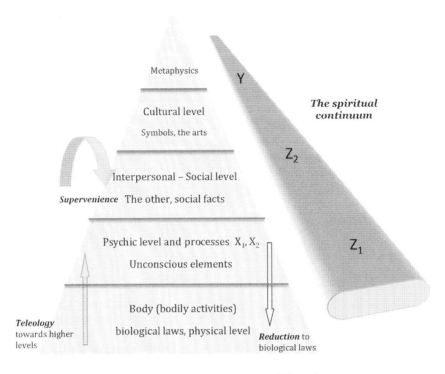

Figure 2.2 The spiritual continuum within the ontological hierarchy

The evolutionary relationship between the psychological and the spiritual within the multileveled framework, as manifested in the spiritual continuum, could further be implemented for an analysis of Jungian concepts. Jung's archetypal God-image is understood as approximately identical to the inherent potential towards psychic wholeness or the Self. However, the full potential of the Self/God-image is not revealed due to the fact that, as Jung states, the unconscious cannot be distinct from God as such: 'It is only through the psyche that we can establish that God acts upon us, but we are unable to distinguish whether these actions emanate from God or from the unconscious' (Jung 1952a: para. 757). Heisig attributes the ensuing epistemological ambiguity of the concept of God and, by extension, the God-image, to Jung's 'own defence against the charges of psychologism, Gnosticism, and mysticism', which resulted in Jung being 'not only non-metaphysical but actually *anti*metaphysical in his methodology' (Heisig 1979: 121). However, as we shall see in the following two chapters, Jung's archetypal theory, being enhanced through the post–Jungians' lens, clearly indicates meta-psychological perspectives. Jung investigated the archetypal manifestations of inherited archetypal patterns and formulated a clear view of the spiritual element of the psyche by reintroducing Tertullian's axiom: 'the soul is *naturaliter religiosa,* i.e., possesses a religious function' (1944: para. 14). The reality of one's spiritual experience is therefore affirmed within the concretized psychological experience, which manifests an obvious departure from the theoretical framework suggested by most religious circles. Considering the spectrum of the spiritual continuum, it could be argued that the principally psychological dimension of the Self addresses the lower levels, the 'infrared' of this spectrum: it corresponds to the more accessible psychological or socio-cultural elements that comprise the spiritual dimension of the psyche.

By contrast, Christian conceptualisations of the spiritual dynamics 'from the image of God to his likeness' could be interpreted as addressing the higher levels of the spiritual continuum, the 'ultraviolet area'. Certain insights may address the extra-psychic dimension. For instance, as previously mentioned, the philosopher Maximus the Confessor maintains that beings are endowed with their particular 'spiritual principles' (the *logoi*) but that their development depends on activating these principles through the co-operation of the human free will and God's intervention. According to this process, one's spiritual inheritance (God-image) can 'evolve' further through the acquisition of God's 'knowledge' – that is, toward God-likeness. In other words, the *intra*-psychic spiritual dimension (God-image) will reach its full ontological potential (*telos*) on an *extra*-psychic level (see *Amb.* 41: 1313AB). In this case, the soul and the body acquire new spiritual 'qualities' that cannot be construed reductively, that is to say in psychological terms. Applying the discussed earlier interpretative tool of *supervenience,* it could be said that these new spiritual qualities at the upper levels of the spiritual spectrum *supervene* in the psychological features. In other words, the ontological supervenes in, without becoming dependent on or being reduced to, the phenomenological.

From all these it is then understood that, despite the mainstream post-modern strands of subjectivism and scepticism, in contemporary philosophical thinking and sociological discourses the spiritual dimension retains its complexity in its distinct ontological and phenomenological dimensions. As previously discussed, the ontological dimensions of the spiritual continuum are not polarised at the level of the psyche or at the metaphysical level but are profoundly engaged within reality at all levels. Consequently, the fuller ontological perspectives of the spiritual must be sought beyond the psychological realms, namely within the socio-cultural and metaphysical realms, precisely because certain aspects of the psyche's spiritual dimension unfold in these levels. That the socio-cultural background could play a crucial role in formulating the spiritual or the religious perspectives is apparent in the tight bonds amongst the culture of a specific territory and its prevailing religion (e.g., Buddhistic or Muslim religion thrives in specific territories/ cultures). In many cases, therefore, the elements of the spiritual that stem from the socio-cultural background which characterizes traditional religions appear to prevail upon the ones addressing the psychic or the metaphysical realms. By distinguishing the parameters at those realms that shape spiritual development, we can obtain a much clearer picture of the manifestations and potentialities of the spiritual. Theories engaging an amalgam of ontological and phenomenological features, such as Maximus' understanding of psychic development through both intra- and extra-psychic perspectives, could substantially contribute to a holistic understanding of such concepts as Jung's Self – which could then reveal new potentialities through such an analysis.

Similar insights that challenge the reductionistic view of the spiritual dimension can also be found in contemporary contexts. For instance, Donald Winnicott's vision of a 'third area of existing which . . . has been difficult to fit into psycho-analytic theory' (1989: 57) and Popper's world 3 are both grounded in an ontological dimension that is missing from principally psychological concepts, such as the Self. The psychological and the spiritual are also deeply interrelated in applied psychology in the healing process. Commenting on the links between psychotherapy and spiritual direction, Susan DeHoff notes that both 'need not to be perceived as synonymous or competitive. There is a point at which psyche and spirit, psychotherapy and spiritual direction, meet: the place of healing' (1998: 333). Healing comprises a fascinating area, where ontological and religious doctrines have been set aside, but the spiritual and the psychological can act on a more common ground.

Healing is, however, not the only place where these two aspects intercept. As will be shown, psychological development encounters spiritual growth through a reciprocal interaction that could deepen and broaden self-awareness into depths in which hitherto only 'demons' and 'gods' reside. Although the spiritual is interacting with the psychological, it maintains its own features as an inherent aspect that may emerge and evolve from elements belonging to different realms, while its ontological character remains open to metaphysics. But before exploring further the interaction of these two elements, first we need to research the tensions between the psychological and the spiritual/religious dimensions in Jung's personal life.

Notes

1. The notion of metaphysics/metaphysical I use here is aligned with both the classical Platonic view of the supernatural *Ideas-Forms* of all things and the Kantian theorisation of the unknown 'thing-in-itself' (discussed below).
2. See *Oxford English Dictionary online* (www.oed.com), accessed on 14.12.2012.
3. For this account, see Carr (1994: especially in chapter 7; also 171–3); Nagy (1991: chapters 5 and 6); and Grondin (2003: 70–84).
4. For an account of the term *ontology* as used by Gideon Harvey and by Glauberg, 'who defines it as the part of philosophy which speculates on being *qua* being', see, respectively, the *Oxford English Dictionary online* and Zizioulas (2006: 99, note 1).
5. Jaeger writes: 'Therefore the first appearance of the expression "the Divine" is all the more noteworthy. We have already observed that while Hesiod's theology admits many kinds of gods, he has not yet inquired into their nature. But whoever first uses the general concept of the Divine must consider this question; and Anaximander does so. When he says the Boundless "encompasses all things and governs all things", he is satisfying the loftiest demands which religious thought has required of divinity from time immemorial' (Jaeger 1947: 31; see also ibid.: 206, note 45).
6. Plato, *Timaeus* 90a: 'And as regards the most lordly kind of our soul, we must conceive of it in this wise: we declare that God has given to each of us, as his daemon, that kind of soul which is housed in the top of our body and which raises us – seeing that

we are not an earthly but a heavenly plant up from earth towards our kindred in the heaven. And herein we speak most truly; for it is by suspending our head and root from that region whence the substance of our soul first came that the Divine Power keeps upright our whole body'. See *Plato in Twelve Volumes,* Vol. 9, trans. W. R. M. Lamb (1925) Cambridge, MA: Harvard University Press; London: William Heinemann Ltd.

7. See Armstrong (1967: 40): 'For Aristotle's cosmology, the ether theory is of prime importance'.

8. *De anima* I.4: 408b; II.2: 413b; III.5: 430a.

9. *De Degeneratione Animalium* II.3: 736b.

10. The Christian fathers signified the spiritual state by applying concepts of the Greek thought as an 'intellectual tool', but on a different basis, namely the revelation of the uncreated God on a human level. Gregory the Nazianzen, for example, reconsidered the classical Neoplatonic triad 'permanence (μονή), procession-fall (πρόοδος), reversion (επιστροφή)', through which the progress of being is signified. Instead, human nature now can be cleansed by its opacity, illumined by the divine light, and reach God's purity (*Orationes* 28, 31: *PG* 36, 72); it is exactly an establishment of 'order and law of the spiritual ascent' (*Orationes* 18, 25: *PG* 35, 532AB). The psychic development now is of a different spiritual quality compared to what was meant before: it is a spiritual 'transformation'.

11. Hereafter all the references in Maximus (unless otherwise stated) will be provided by citing the *abbreviation* of his specific work and the page (but not title and volume number) of the corresponding volume in which the quotation is found (e.g. *Amb.* 41: 1304A, instead of *Amb.* 41, *PG* 91: 1304A; *Q.Thal.* 60: 79, instead of *Q.Thal.* 60, *CCSG* 22: 79).

12. Heidegger appears to resort to people's own place in the world, their consciousness, or to what the world is for them (their *Dasein*), and 'that Dasein's Being towards an Other is its Being towards itself' (See Heidegger, *Being and Time* 26; 1927/1962: 162). In this respect, consciousness, in its collective dimension, is now one of the prime 'targets' of enquiries into the spiritual/transcendental origins of the world. As Mulhall puts it, 'the concept of the Other . . . is irreducible, an absolute basic component of our understanding of the world we inhabit, and so something from which our ontological investigations must begin' (2005: 63).

13. More on this subject in Heidegger 1994: 18–23.

14. For this account, see Wright 1998: 828; and Grondin 1999.

15. Jung writes to Virginia Payne (23.7.1949): 'Two personalities I met at the Clark Conference made a profound and lasting impression on me. One was Stanley Hall, the President, and the other was William James whom I met for the first time then' (Jung 1973: 531).

16. See, for instance, Davies, B. (2004) *An Introduction to the Philosophy of Religion,* 3rd edn, Oxford: Oxford University Press. Additionally, see the notion of *civil religion* and its impact on political discourse in Davie 2007: 154.

3

JUNG AND THE POST–JUNGIANS ON RELIGION

Breakthroughs and limitations

Jung's treatment of religion is the key to understanding the actual spiritual perspective of his central concepts such as the Self and individuation. The exploration of the spiritual and religious dimension in Jung's legacy is therefore essential for fathoming his theory on psychic development. Jung undoubtedly departed from Freud's approach to the religious discourse. However, certain aspects of Jung's approach to religion must be carefully explored before concluding the essential points of Jungian theory on religion – and in juxtaposition to the Freudian equivalent views. The post–Jungians, on the other hand, understood within a pluralistic framework Jung's spiritual/religious perspective. The discussion thus should engage different approaches to address more precisely Jung's set of religious ideas as well as the main viewpoints that could summarise his theory on religious and spiritual grounds.

Freud and Jung on religion: emancipation or interplay of opposites?

Carl Jung is widely renowned for having a rather 'positive' approach to religion contrasted to the basically 'negative' approach of Freud. These two polarised classifications, full of generalisations but nevertheless indicative of Freud and Jung's general attitudes respectively, could be challenged by a deeper analysis of Jung's theory on religion. The range of the spiritual continuum – shown earlier as spanning from psychosomatic to metaphysical realms – provides an idea of its complexity that transcends the psyche. At first sight, Jung's theory on religion is grounded in a psychic dimension that can be understood more precisely as a mode of oscillation between two psychic poles: the 'divine-numinous' and the 'sexual libido', the 'new numinous principle' that Freud, in Jung's words, promoted to a *deus absconditus*. This is because Jung in fact considers Yahweh and sexuality as 'two rationally incommensurable opposites', as manifestations of the same 'numinosity' or of a 'lost god':

> Just as the physically stronger agency is given 'divine' or 'daemonic' attributes, so the 'sexual libido' took over the role of a *deus absconditus,*

a hidden or concealed god. The advantage of this transformation for Freud was, apparently, that he was able to regard the new numinous principle as scientifically irreproachable and free from all religious taint.

(*MDR*: 151)

Jung' struggle to replace the Freudian religion/spiritual-as-illusion with the religion/spiritual-as-numinous, through the rich imagery of the God-image, is in fact a 'paradigm shift' in Kuhn's perspective (1970): a shift that can explain why two different scientists that follow similar criteria and search on an account (i.e. religion or the spiritual) would reach opposing conclusions. A set of reasons could explain this divergence: by means of different cultural and spiritual milieu, methodology, and philosophical influences. Looking deeper in Jung's life, however, at the heart of this shift one factor appears to be critically decisive, namely the relationship to his father, a minister of religion. Furthermore, it is intriguing to see how this relationship comprises elements that could suggest a formulation of a crippling psychological 'complex', which in fact indicates a 'complex' relation to the religious account.

Despite the criticism received on the Oedipus complex,[1] Freud applies psychoanalytic premises for justifying the illusionary character of religious beliefs – at bottom stemming from 'the feeling of infantile helplessness' (1930: 72).[2] In terms of scientific consistency, Freud remains to a great extent within the confidence of 'psychoanalytic' statements. The images of 'religion', as repressed contents from childhood, occupy the 'negative' pole of an unresolved father complex; and this accumulated energy of the unconscious contents, under the restriction of the cultural norms through the super-ego censorship, constantly seeks for sublimation through an unspeakable longing for a missing father, the projection of all gods.[3]

Jung's childhood, in particular his relationship to his father, had unsurprisingly a tremendous impact on his theory on religion. Certain of Jung's positions could be construed as stemming from events that engraved his early life. Analogous incidents, as in anti–Semitic attacks by Christians upon Freud's father (see Hoffman 2011: 6–7), had also detrimentally imprinted on Freud as a child, with critical impact on valuing religion. Despite the complexity of this rationale, we may consider to which extent Jung's fundamental positions on religion are closely related to his own personal history and experience. Deirdre Bair narrates succinctly the family context of the newly born Carl Gustav Jung in 1875 as 'the fourth-born but first-surviving child of Paul Achilles Jung, a poor country parson in the Swiss Reformed church, and Emilie Preiswerk, his unhappy and unstable wife' (2004: 7). The contradictory elements between his mother's 'natural unreliability' and father's 'reliability and powerlessness' (ibid.: 21) are distantly foretelling of Jung's theory of opposites as well as the ambiguity of the spiritual perspective.[4]

Jung's physical affection to his father soon ended up in a disillusion: he admits openly that, 'I understood the tragedy of his profession and of his life. He was struggling with a death whose existence he could not admit' (*MDR*: 55). In terms of suppressed aspirations in a Freudian sense, projected from his father's life, unexpressed disenchanted thoughts bothered Jung for a lifetime. The physical 'light' stemming from the father as a source of security and happiness became darkness for Jung and powerlessness of a dead world: this was the church, 'a place I should not go to. It is not life which is there, but death' (ibid.). Such vividly tragic words were rather conclusive and critical for Jung's later sentiment for religion. Implicitly, Jung embarked on his own *weltanschauung* to rectify, for his father's failure, his personal father complex. The desperate aspiration to find a way out of this dark side of religion must also have inspired the idea of the fourth-complementary element of psychic wholeness.

Jung never shared the frightening and shocking experience of a God befouling Basel's cathedral (*MDR*: 39ff) with his father, as the child Jung would never discuss important issues with him. Everything has to come to terms with his own subjective world, impelled by the desire to reconstruct his father's ignorance towards a rewarding knowledge. Watching him preaching at the church was an immediate disappointment: 'An abyss had opened between him and me' (ibid.: 55); even if Jung had asked anything on faith, his father had nothing to answer: 'One ought not to think, but believe'. Jung would think, 'No, one must experience and know', but he would prefer to say, 'Give me this belief', whereupon his father 'would shrug and turn resignedly away' (ibid.: 43).

All these feelings left Jung insecure in his own isolated world, in a sphere of struggling to transform illusions and paradoxes into genuine experience and solid knowledge. Agonising to resolve the 'complex' situation with his father's profession, belief, and poor communication, Jung was inexorably compelled to suppress, in a Freudian sense, all these conflicts. However, Jung presents himself to be subjectively free from any conflict and complex when he writes, '[Freud] is convinced that I am thinking under the domination of a father complex against him and this is all complete nonsense. . . . I liberated myself from the regard from the father' (*Letter to Jones* 5.12.1912, cited in Bair 2004: 233). Indeed, there is enough evidence that Jung wanted to liberate himself from a scientific paternalism; yet the implications of a traumatic childhood in some terms could justify the view that, although he appears to articulate a theory breaking away from the Freudian authority, in fact remains within the territory of a complex-archetypal dimension of an unresolved account: the poorly experienced and thus indeed suppressed religiosity.

Jung's overwhelming experience of his father's failure, his dark side, reveals the complex 'religious' impetus for his further development.[5] Inasmuch as the church 'became a place of torment' for Jung (*MDR*: 45), it was without doubt sensible for a child with such negative 'religious' experience to seek a 'legitimate faith' within his own individuation. But how easy was it for Jung to fully overcome these experiences and eventually to differentiate from the highly disillusioning network of the tormenting religious memories of his childhood?

In fact, Jung's passionate quest to reconcile and integrate the two opposites, of the sexual libido and the numinous, forced him to overlook his own psychological status. The adversities and dissolutions in the fragile soul of the child Jung could easily be suppressed into the unconscious. The unresolved experience in Basel's cathedral was not the only issue he concealed. His relationship with one of his female patients, Sabina Spielrein, was an experience that he also initially concealed from Freud.[6] Having thus a complex relation to both these two opposites, the reconciliation would come only through reductions that compromise the contextual with the actual personal material. Indeed, Jung is constantly striving with the issue of the 'other': his inner struggle commences with the division of his own psychological world between the personalities no. 1 and no. 2 (*MDR*: 45), faces the father-as-other, and afterwards breaks with Freud-as-other in anticipation of the spiritual/religious other – the one that could integrate all the fragmented aspects. In fact, Jung's struggle is 'a progression of reformulations of the problematic of the Other', as Papadopoulos notes when analysing Jung's 'break' with Freud and the ensuing 'breakdown' that led him to the 'breakthrough': it is the progression of the 'Other-as-Complex' towards the 'Other-as-Symbol', to eventually reach the 'Other-as-Archetype, the Self' (Papadopoulos 1991: 88).

The degree to which Jung strove to find an exodus and to come in terms with his personal conflicts is intriguing and debatable (for instance, see Adler 1979: 91–2; Bishop 2002: 164, 176; Giegerich 2011).[7] Giegerich openly challenges the 'integration' that supposedly lies at the heart of Jung's personal experience. Considering Jung's childhood through the 'disenchantment complex', arising from the Basel's cathedral vision, he notes that, '*Yes, truly,* I [C. Jung] live as an adult in the modern world, I am indeed disenchanted; *but still more truly,* namely "in my truest nature" I am "the age-old son of the mother"'. (Giegerich 2011: 15, italics original). Thus Jung 'had become unable to go all the way through it', that is 'the disenchantment was cut off from the soul's continuing life', which ended up 'into a *complex* that ruled *him*' (ibid.: 17). Should this be the case, is it not the situation of a man struggling within a complex never fully resolved, a complex that entails an oscillation between psychic opposites? In an attempt to avoid Freud's preoccupation with libido, did Jung entirely escape the tantalizing swing between his 'powerless' father and 'unreliable' mother as archetypal figures-complexes, and, further, between the psychic numinous and the untouchable area of God(s)?[8]

Accordingly, Jung's comments on Freud could naturally apply to himself, too: '[Freud] was blind towards the paradox and ambiguity of the contents of the unconscious. . . . He remained the victim of the one aspect he could recognize [sexuality], and for that reason I see him as a tragic figure' (*MDR*: 152–3). But was Jung entirely open-minded in front of the 'paradox' of religion with regard to the perspectives of the *numinosum* and not being 'in the grip of his daimon' (ibid.) – as he accused Freud? Provided Jung's confession that his 'entire youth can be understood in terms of this secret' (ibid.: 41; i.e. the vision at the cathedral), did he manage himself to escape from being a 'tragic figure' in Freud's lens with regard to a consistent theory on religion?

These questions will be further addressed throughout this monograph from different angles. What is important to be emphasized at this point is the fact that, whereas Jung seemingly departed from the grounds imposed by the Other (the religious other-father, first, and Freud later on), the Other-as-complex was a constantly inescapable and powerful force, ready to encase – and thus to reduce – the genuine quest for a spiritual/religious perspective within Jung's own subjective world. Ultimately, not only the child Jung but also the mature psychologist Jung was deeply and rather negatively affected by both the religious and father-complex experiences, which altogether may have comprised a kind of a 'religious complex' – ultimately transformed into the Self and the archetypal Other. The opposite of sexuality for Jung, the *numinosum,* was at bottom a psychological opposite and not, as we shall see, a genuine spiritual/religious point that could address a purely metaphysical potential. Regardless of the ways through which Jung ultimately differentiated from the Freudian one-sidedness on religion, he nevertheless did not entirely escape from being to some extent 'victim' of the 'Other-as-complex', which forced him to formulate a theory on religion that could fit to his personal psychological experience and needs.

Jung's 'complex' relation to and standpoints on religion

The foundations of Jung's theory on religion as directly related to the Other-as-complex and also drawing significance from the constantly changing contextual 'other' are important to understand his redressing view of modern religion(s). In the slippery grounds of a psychological 'complex', on the one hand Jung emancipated from the Freudian approach to religion, but on the other he remained within the psychic polarities. Seeking to integrate the opposites (sexuality versus Yahweh or manifestations of *numinosity*) without coming to terms with his personal spiritual inheritance, Jung had to confront his fragmented personalities 1 and 2. In his definition of psychological 'complex', Jung states that 'there is no difference in principle between a fragmentary personality and a complex' (1934b: para. 202). Including in their aetiology a 'trauma, an emotional shock . . . that splits off a bit of the psyche' (ibid.: para. 204), the complexes, or *'splinter psyches'* (ibid.: para. 203), function arbitrary and not in fully co-operation with the conscious. A set of strikingly similar ingredients, which hitherto have been described as concerning Jung's religious trauma, could not lead him but to a proclivity for developing a 'complex' relation to religion, with its negative and positive facets.

It was within the abilities of his exceptionally insightful nature that Jung early enough would pursue a way out of the oscillating religious considerations-as-complex between the two psychic polarities. From a psychological viewpoint, Jung's approach was of course a huge shift from a religion-as-an-illusion to a religion-as-an-experience within the psyche. But what precisely differentiates a psychic illusion from an authentic experience? Both could easily fall within the *pre/trans fallacy* (Wilber 2000), namely within the pre- and trans-rational states. Each side could challenge the other within an archetypal dipole between the phenomenal and the real. In fact, Jung's departure from a monotheistic interpretation within the complex/longing for the father towards a 'polytheistic' psychic wholeness, the Self, is a very large multi-faceted conception to be reduced to just an opposite of Freud's 'negative' view of religion. Yet this approach entails problematic points, as it is lacking the proper scientific epistemology for classifying 'trans-rational' experience as a genuine psychological entity.

On the other hand, from a meta-psychological lookout, Jung's innovative movement appears to lack the depth of an authentic religious perspective. The two rationally incommensurable opposites – Yahweh and sexuality (*MDR*: 151) – appear to fall within the psychological understanding of the 'numinosity', far from the concrete metaphysical perspective of the spiritual/religious fuller potential. Despite Jung's openness and positive understanding of religion, his theory could not be aligned to a systematic analysis or even an experiential approach of a religious context alone, such as Christianity or Buddhism. On the contrary, it is a psychological theory that integrates the immanent archetypal material with symbols of transcendence or wholeness (i.e. the mandala) – a theory nonetheless crucially inconclusive to convincingly address a particular religious perspective.

After his break with Freud, Jung was fully aware that part of the contemporary scientific community considered him 'a mystic' (*MDR*: 167). Jung was at a pains to prove that it was 'a widespread error to imagine that I do not see the value of sexuality' (ibid.: 168). Indeed, as we shall see, Jung develops the idea that sexuality is an expression of the entire psychic energy in general and of the chthonic spirit in particular that is the other face or God's dark side – as he notes in his *Mysterium Coniunctionis* (1955/1956). Paradoxically, in both Freud's and Jung's side, religion seems to play a decisive but at the same time undermining and dubious role. Freud needed Jung as a promising figure of psychoanalysis: 'I nearly said that it was only by his appearance on the scene that psycho-analysis escaped the danger of becoming a Jewish national affair' (*Letter to Abraham*, 6 May 1908, cited in Bair 2004: 133).[9] Yet it is also apparent that Jung would entirely avoid presenting himself as a religiously coloured figure and embarks on establishing his personal principles that could liberate him from any implications imposed by religious residues. Thus, *religion* is redefined as

> a peculiar attitude of mind which could be formulated in accordance with the original use of the word *religio,* which means a careful consideration and observation of certain dynamic factors that are conceived as 'powers' . . . or whatever name man has given to such factors in his world as he has found powerful, dangerous, or helpful enough to be taken into careful consideration, or grand, beautiful, and meaningful enough to be devoutly worshipped and loved.
>
> (Jung 1938/1940: para. 8)

Leaving aside any metaphysical perspective, Jung is now free to explore the religious elements more systematically within the psychic territory. This definition provided Jung the necessary space for a psychological evaluation of religion as well as for the critical points towards reconsidering the psychological foundations of religion. The fact that the 'mind' and the 'powers' of whatsoever kind are fused in one's 'psychic world' is the proper worldview of the psychological foundations that could shape anew a modern treatment of religion – which simultaneously could rectify the religious shock and trauma of Jung's childhood. For methodological reasons, we may consider three standpoints through which Jung's theory on religion can be explored in a concise way:

(a) Jung's 'primary concern to *understand* these religious ideas' (1938/1940: para. 339), that is the 'religious function' into the psyche; in other words, to construe comprehensively the religious doctrines and beliefs by relating them to a psychological 'process' and further to a 'psychological myth' or the inherent God(s)-image;
(b) The importance of psychic experience in religious faith: '"Legitimate" faith must always rest on experience' (Jung 1911/1956: para. 345); and
(c) The incorporation of the fourth element (conceptualized either as God's 'dark side' or the body, the feminine, and evil) into the concept of the Self-wholeness – much neglected by contemporary religion and particularly by Christianity.

A fuller exploration of these standpoints could reveal the most crucial points of Jung's theory of religion. More importantly, these three points could challenge modern religious systems on the significance of inner experience or of the feminine. An important clarification is needed here: Jung's 'critique' of modern religion is not at all 'a theological critique' – on the contrary, it receives its own criticism when compared to Maximus' theological insights, as will be discussed in the following chapter; rather, it can function as a *testing point system* towards expanding the boundaries of religious constructs, in particular of the ones projecting their practical implications on the socio-cultural dimension.

The first key Jungian position on religion is the insertion of an inner logic, namely of psychological character/value, in dealing with religious issues: 'My primary concern . . . is to *understand* these religious ideas, whose value I appreciate far too deeply to dispose of them within rationalistic arguments' (Jung 1911/1956: para. 339). Jung wants of course to depart from the rationalistic context of Enlightenment that hugely impacted Freud. Yet despite this promising announcement, Jung immediately after follows a rather rationalistic rationale when interpreting Christianity: whereas initially it 'was accepted as a means of escape from the brutality . . .', due to the regression into the unconscious, in modern times Christianity 'is bound to be confronted with the age-old problem of brutality' (ibid.: para. 341) – hence the historical roots of 'evil'. The dynamics of opposites, following the opposites of the inner religious complex, is also projected both to his constructs on religion and the notion of evil, which Jung develops further in his *Answer to Job* (1952a). By failing to address the metaphysical dimension, at least in the case of Christianity, and by entering the God-image as an ultimate replacement of Freud's father figure – also a remote adumbration of the missing father figure in his childhood – Jung fuses the psychic level with the metaphysical level and introduces an epistemology of ambiguity.[10] Christian religion, drained from certain vital spiritual aspects, is now confronted, in Jung's view, with the old-as-new brutality. Hence, Jung's concern on 'evil' becomes increasingly important, as we shall see in the discussion of his second and third points on religion.

It was a little before the break with Freud that Jung, to his colleague's strong approval, wrote his *Symbols of Transformation* (1911/1956), which was later massively revised in the years 1952 to 1956. The unfortunate religious experience in his childhood is now compensated by the dictum that 'legitimate' faith 'must always rest on experience' (Jung 1911/1956: para. 345). By introducing this second main point, Jung's concern was against the kind of faith 'of mere habit' that 'threatens stagnation and cultural regression' (ibid.). Despite his openness to all religions, Jung's concerns apply here mainly to his experience of a dying Christian church and its tradition, drained of the vivid knowledge and true experience of a personal God. Later on, during the two world wars, the brutal actions 'in the name of God' would propel Jung to seek the hidden dark side of God and his images. Ultimately, not too distant from the Freudian charges on religions and cultures and their censoring dark roles upon societies, Jung interprets Christian fundamental pursuit as a movement to depart from 'nature and the instincts in general, and, through its asceticism, from sex in particular' (ibid.: para. 339). Interestingly, and despite certain common points, Jung eventually departs from a Freudian understanding of libido by broadening this notion to embrace unconscious 'transformations' within opposites such as 'good' and 'evil' within the process of individuation. These transformations may also include faith: 'mere faith cannot be counted as an ethical ideal either, because it too is an unconscious transformation of libido' (ibid.: para. 342). Having understood sexuality as a manifestation of numinosum, the *psychological value* of the latter[11] is now what matters more for Jung – which reinforces his reductive perception and interpretation of the religious dimension.

Jung introduced the term 'religious function' in 1921 in order to provide the space needed for the integration of conscious with unconscious elements, and of course the dark/evil side. In fact, his purpose was 'to liberate the religious function from the cramping limitations of intellectual criticism', thus addressing beyond a merely intellectual function (Jung 1921/1971: para. 411). It was William James (1902) that first challenged human esteem in logical facts versus religiousness. Jung considers religiousness from a slightly different angle, because 'the empiricist has an almost religious belief in facts'; and 'we also know from the psychology of primitives that the religious function is an essential component of the psyche and is found always and everywhere' (ibid.: para. 529). The religious function is essential for linking consciousness with the God-image in the psychic territory and, hence, with inner experience.[12] In later advances, as we saw earlier, Jung reintroduces this idea by using Tertullian's axiom that 'the soul is *naturaliter religiosa,* i.e. possesses a religious function' (1944: para. 14). Jung's intention, however, is not to follow the traditional Christian approach to this function. Instead, he states:

> Not having any theological knowledge worth mentioning, I must rely in this respect on the texts available to every layman. But since I have

no intention of involving myself in the metaphysics of the Trinity, I am free to accept the church's own formulation of the dogma, without having to enter into all the complicated metaphysical speculations that have gathered round it in the course of history.

(Jung 1942/1948: para. 171)

It is an important statement whereby Jung feels permitted to apply subsequently his own principles to the psychological interpretation of the Trinity. This interpretation is grounded in the archetypal dualities of good and bad, father and son, and so forth, clearly echoing the opposites of his personal religious complex experience: a negative past towards a compensating and fulfilling future. This is the reason Jung's personal dark side must also reflect on the central Christian image, the Christ. According to Jung's principle of opposites, 'even the Christ-figure is not a totality, for it lacks the nocturnal side of the psyche's nature, the darkness of the spirit . . .' (ibid.: para. 232). The fact that Jung's indefinite approach to Christianity is oscillating within the ambiguous personal-complex dynamics – that is to say between the explicit value of God-images/figures and his inner subjectivity – inevitably forces him to redress the traditional Christian insights within the dynamics of the archetypal dualities. This is central in Jung's interpretation of Christian doctrines, which merit closer attention in the next paragraphs.

Jung and doctrines, dualities, and metaphysics: the fourth element

Choosing to construe the Christian doctrines without considering 'all the complicated metaphysical speculations', Jung proceeds to unfold his vision of quaternity:

The development of the Trinity into a quaternity can be represented in projection on metaphysical figures, and at the same time the exposition gains in plasticity. But any statements of this kind can – and for scientific reasons, must – be reduced to man and his psychology, since they are mental products which cannot be presumed to have any metaphysical validity . . . nobody really knows what they are 'in themselves'. . . At any rate, science ought not to treat them as anything other than projections.

(Jung 1942/1948: para. 268)

Statements of this kind manifest the core of Jung's treatment of religion in general and of Christian doctrines, such as of the Trinity, in particular. The reduction of the Trinity to 'man's psychology' is nothing more than the reduction to the archetypal polarities of good and evil, personal and collective – and of any other form of opposites. It is clear, according to Jung, that the history of the Trinity 'presents itself as the gradual crystallization of an archetype that moulds the anthropomorphic conceptions . . . of different persons into an archetypal and numinous figure, the "Most Holy Three-in-One"'. (ibid.: para. 224). To connect the archetypal manifestations of God-Trinity with other psychic elements through the religious function is the next logical step in Jung's reductive rationale. The ultimate purpose of such links between the conscious and the unconscious is to incorporate into one's psychic wholeness the fourth element (evil/shadow, feminine, body). As an incarnation of the Gnostic *Sophia,* 'who corresponds to the archetypal mother' (1955/1956: para. 498, 401–3), the fourth element functions, in Jung's theory, as an integration of the psychologically 'incomplete' Trinity. Therefore, Jung's reduction ultimately suggests that any doctrinal 'statement', as a merely psychological conception, should have an equivalent psychological resemblance.

These psychological interpretations of projections or God(s) are treated in such a way that God-symbols, and by extension God-images, claim priority against God-as-such or God's actions – like Christ's passion. This is extremely essential for Jung' view of man's wholeness; hence, even Christ needs man's dark side and evil to be vividly engaged in the psychological process of the psychic maturation process. According to this understanding, Christ's passion 'signifies God's suffering on account of the injustice of the world and the darkness of man. The human and the divine suffering set up a relationship of complementarity with compensating effects' (Jung 1942/1948: para. 233). The human and the divine (metaphysical) levels are fused within the psychological domain insofar as there is no perception, in Jung's epistemology, for a different logic – namely a transdisciplinary logic – that could solve the interface of the psychic and the divine levels under a set of different principles other than reductive.

In fact, this 'relationship of complementarity' is, for Jung, the inner principle for understanding man's psychological growth, namely the process of individuation from the ego-conscious to the Self. It is also here that the divine and the human/psychic levels encounter and complement each other. This encounter is not only an allegory but also a parallel process that leads to self-realisation: 'since man knows himself only as an ego, and the self, as a totality, is indescribable and indistinguishable from a God-image, self-realisation – to put it in religious or metaphysical terms – amounts to God's incarnation' (Jung 1942/1948: para. 233). Hence, if the first person of the Trinity, the Father, stands for the undifferentiated unconscious, the Son is consequently the psychological equivalent of one's self-realisation, whereas the Holy Ghost is the hidden life, the power and a 'function' that fuels this process: 'a process of human reflection that irrationally creates the uniting "third" is itself connected with the nature of the drama of redemption, whereby God descends into the human realm and man mounts up to the realm of divinity' (ibid.: para. 241). This is the *transcendent function* that Jung later develops further and subsequently to the abovementioned 'religious function'.[13]

As already shown, in Jung's understanding, 'even the Christ-figure is not a totality' and needs the evil or dark aspect to become wholeness, the Self.[14] Due to the fact that the Father must have his opposite, that is the Spirit, in a similar way, the Son, as a human figure, must have his own opposite, the devil. This is an 'innovative' new element that Jung constantly applies to his vision of psychic totality, a vital engagement for which he writes, 'because individuation is an heroic and often tragic task, the most difficult of all, it involves suffering, a passion of the ego . . .' (Jung 1942/1948: para. 233) – in an imitation of Christ's passion and confrontation with evil. The end of this process is the acquisition of the divine wisdom that is hidden in the figure of Mother, because the Holy Spirit and Logos eventually 'merge in the Gnostic idea of Sophia': it is the *Sapienta Dei*, insofar as 'in gremio matris sedet sapientia patris (the wisdom of the father lies in the lap of the mother)' (ibid.: para. 240). For Jung, the incommensurable 'third', the Spirit that bears the life and the potential to integrate all in one, the *Sapienta*, opens the way for the engagement and incorporation of the fourth element. The originally archetypal dimension of the Spirit is, however, 'an ambivalent dualistic figure' (Jung 1951/1959: para. 141), because Christ needs a chthonic counterpart, the spirit-Mercurius, to liberate and enlighten the souls to reach the *lapis,* the philosophical stone. This is the end of both man's and God's parallel individuation process.

Despite Jung's 'friendly' approach to religion and acknowledgements of the kind that 'psychological truth does not exclude the metaphysical truth',[15] there is actually little space for essentially metaphysical 'truth' in Jung's system. This is because Jung utterly rejects the Archimedean-as-metaphysical point of view within the psyche (see 1911/1956: para. 344). The fact that ultimately Jung never distinguished, but rather identified, the God-image with the inner Self/wholeness has immense implications. Could this God-image not be an evolution of the father-image in a Freudian sense, bespeaking a lost father image in Jung's childhood? The implicit ambiguity of God-image is in fact a strong indication that Jung, despite redressing the spiritual/religious dimension, did not depart thoroughly from the Freudian perspective – that is from the purely psychological implications of religious experience, in either negative or positive terms. The strong evidence that Jung never resolved entirely his own father-complex that was further developed as a 'complex relation' to religion – not distant from a 'religious complex' – provides the ground for a profounder understanding of the exact reasons of his ambiguous and 'complex' treatment of religion. Both Freud and Jung ultimately view religion within principally psychological perspectives (negative or positive). However, whilst Jung appears not to address the fuller potential of the religious dimension, it was he that innovatively explored the religious truths, doctrines, and insights linking them to certain psychological processes, thus highlighting the indispensable psychological foundations of the spiritual experience.

The post–Jungians on religion and the Christian perspective

In general, psychoanalysis evaluates the spiritual perspective as 'metaphors from the pre-Galilean world-view' (Black 2005: 32). However, basic Freudian ideas on religion have witnessed a worth-noting redressing by certain psychoanalytic strands (see Black 2006). Marie Hoffman, amongst others, elaborating perspectives addressed by Winnicott, Klein, Bion, Kohut, and Horney, explores the advances in the psychoanalytic account and its connections with Christian narratives; she concludes that 'incarnation, crucifixion, and resurrection as a cycle of "eternal return" are reflected in a psychoanalysis matured by a plurality of narratives including the ones that Freud contemplated but rejected' (2011: 219). On the Jungian side, the post–Jungians responded to Jung's theory on religion in different ways, following the main viewpoints of the different schools of analytical psychology. Amongst these revaluations of a particular interest are the advances concerning the dialogue on Christian perspectives.

Victor White, with whom Jung held a long correspondence,[16] made an important statement that 'Jung's psychology . . . brings modern science to the very frontiers of the realm traditionally held by theology' (White 1952: 81). It is then not surprising that the 'religiousness' of this psychology 'has alarmed many of the religious-minded hardly less than it has alarmed the sceptic' (ibid.: 83). However, Jung's underlying ambiguity on religion generates responses either contradictory or open to a plurality of interpretations.

In his critique of Jung, Palmer signifies a kind of 'tautology that stands at the heart of Jung's method' based on the principle that '*all Self-images are religious*' (1997: 193). Palmer is aligned with White's restraint about accepting Jung as a 'friend' of religion, insofar as ultimately 'Jung opens himself up to the charge of "psychologism", namely, that God has been reduced to nothing more than a subjective experience' (ibid.: 195). The impact of Freud's blow on religion, in spite of certain constructive lines developed by his colleague Jung, appears to also have an impact on Jung's rather inconclusive position on religion. Attempting to find the bottom line of Jung's problematic approach, Heisig also criticises Jung's methodology when interpreting the *imago-Dei*. For the latter, Jung applies 'two logically distinct sorts of datum': one by the patient description and another by the analyst evaluation of the patient's psychic state. This fluctuation results in a 'subjectively conditioned perception as an objective datum of observation, without recognising the serious epistemological problems such a view involved' (Heisig 1979: 119). Apparently, this antithesis follows Jung's problematic epistemology regarding the ultimate potential of the spiritual/numinosity with ambivalent results.

On the other hand, Jung's subjectivism and epistemological reduction of the spiritual allows the religious function of the psyche to engage Christian narratives more vividly and directly to one's subjectivity. Edward Edinger, exploring the developmental perspective within his 'ego-self axis', considers the crucifixion, a central image for the western culture, as the culminating point of Christ's individuation: it is where 'Jesus as ego and Christ as Self merge. The human being (ego) and the cross (mandala) become one' (Edinger 1972: 150). Within this psychological understanding of the spiritual, *crucifixion* and *resurrection* are the equivalents of the individuation crisis followed by a rebirth of a new and more individuated personality.

In this respect, Jung's theory is now open to relate to other theories of spirituality. Aside from non-specific comparisons with other schools of psychoanalysis (see, e.g. Fordham 1995) or with other theorists, such as with Kohut's *Self* (Jacoby 1990), Jungian psychology has been juxtaposed to diverse paradigms of psychological and/or spiritual development spanning from Christian traditions to postmodernism. Becker's critical comparison between *individuation* and Loyola's *Spiritual Exercises* (2001) unravels parallel and thus potentially complementary processes that signify psychological and spiritual development.[17] In a similar perspective, Avis Clendenen compares individuation with spiritual life, noting that 'Hildegard's unique approach to examining virtues/vices as imprints or images within the soul resonates with Jung's notion of archetypes' (2009: 38). Within such 'resonances' between Jungian archetypes and Christian virtues, the question of the exact dimensions of the spiritual, echoing the 'ontology' of man's archetypal foundations, becomes more critical.

Leaving aside at the moment the epistemological clarity, Jung's theory on religion, on the other hand, has been considered a criticism of mainstream Western Christianity. It is because, in John Dourley's view, 'it endorses an extraverted literalism that would understand God as beyond the psyche intervening in human historical events in dramatic revelations made from a position wholly transcendent to the human and its historical maturation' (2008: 172). Jung does not recommend a God above criticism and without a 'dark side' or a church drained of *experiential* knowledge of God. It is therefore the inner life that must be renovated in a spiritual dimension, which Jung found more robust in Eastern contexts. These innovations must be understood as a way of 'exploring and redirecting the West's neglected inner psychic life' (Clarke 1995: 2). In addition, this exploration has also a serious therapeutic perspective, for which Jung was clear: 'the main interest of my work is not concerned with the treatment of neurosis but rather with the approach to the numinous . . . [which] is the real therapy' (Jung 1973: 377)

Indisputably, Jung's pluralistic approach to the numinosity, distant from any 'theological restraints', is opened to a 'polytheistic' interpretation, beyond the 'monotheistic' Self. In this respect, Andrew Samuels speaks of new aspects of spirituality, actually a new 'anatomy' of spirituality, consisting of 'social spirituality, democratic spirituality, craft spirituality, profane spirituality and spiritual sociality' – related to politics (2005: 122ff). It is when the spiritual perspective in a Jungian sense does not function as a doctrinal datum but allows the dogma to bridge the numinous with both the inner world and the outer life. The consequences of such liberal implementation can thus challenge the whole spectrum of human morality and values.

Jungian perspectives on religion have been explored not only through their relationship to Christian ideas but also to Buddhism (by Meckel & Moore 1990), to Shamanism (Smith 1997), and to the New Age (Main 2004: 152ff). In the long catalogue, one must also include contemporary discourses, such as Jung's relationship with feminism (Rowland 2002), or with post-modernity (Jugler 1990;

Hauke 2000). The fact that Jung's psychology sustains a constructive dialogue with a variety of systems of religion or spirituality 'is testimony to how deeply and insightfully it has penetrated into this perennially significant area of human experience' (Main 2006: 317).

It is then apparent that aside from the criticism that Jungian psychology has received on its problematic methodology and epistemology, the post–Jungians reinforce the understanding that the main territory that Jung's theory on religion addresses is the encounter of the psychic inherited potential, the immanent, with the numinous within the archetypal polarities (good-evil, personal-collective, conscious-unconscious, etc.) – engaging religious insights and symbols in a pluralistic embodiment. Beyond thus the confrontational implications of Jung's inconclusive theory on religion, the realization that, as Murray Stein notes, '[t]heology for Jung is, rather, a transformation from psychology' (1990: 13), is precisely the conducive and versatile ground for further developments and revaluations of both religious ideas and spiritual insights in the modern man's psychic territory – seriously neglected from the institutional Western religion. The discussion and constructive interface is further intriguing when Jungian viewpoints are juxtaposed to positions and insights from the Eastern Orthodox Christian perspective, for which we allocate the following section.

Jungian psychology and Eastern Christian thought

The interface between Jungian psychology of religion and theological insights from the Eastern Orthodoxy commenced when Jung, well versed in the literature of medieval times, was citing writers from the early Christian world. For instance, he extensively cited Origen (whose influence on Maximus is widely acknowledged as significant) and the earlier-mentioned Tertullian as characteristic examples of *introverted* and *extraverted* personalities (1921/1971: para. 17–30). However, there is absolutely no evidence that Jung had come across Maximus' theological treatises. Whereas the works of Origen and Tertullian were already published in the 19th century, the rare publications of early Christian authors at the time compelled Jung to overlook poring over the thought of one of the greatest minds of Christianity.[18]

Maximus' corpus has recently received a remarkable amount of academic interest from scholars, especially from the West.[19] Maximus' work has been received as belonging to the mature age of Christian theology and philosophy. This perception nevertheless does not fully concur with contemporary understanding of an 'institutional' Christian system and teaching. Indeed, as the discussion further unfolds, aside from different ontological priorities, certain views from Maximus would fall in line with Jungian equivalents: the importance of the inner experience and the metaphors of doctrinal statements at the psychological level are also present in Maximus' theory.

Since I. Kornarakis (1958) first introduced Jungian concepts into Eastern Orthodox theology, later studies (such as by Thermos 1999; Stauropoulos 2000;

and Yiannaras 2003) open the discussion between 'psychotherapy' and Orthodox Christian theology in a manner understandable to both the Eastern and the Western reader. N. Loudovikos, for instance, discusses the issue of the will/desire in both the Eastern and Western Christianity while emphasising the potential convergence between the Lacanian concept of the Other with the key Maximian notion of will/desire (2003: 107). Loudovikos also identifies as a potential-towards-an-'orthodox interpretation' Jung's emphasis on 'fundamental human need for meaning, ultimately for spiritual meaning' (ibid.: 110).[20]

Critically, J. Moran examines Maximus' theology and his binary concept of 'pleasure and pain' and parallels it with Freudian fundamental concepts of pleasure principle and death instinct: 'you can almost substitute the literal words of one for the other' (2000: 136). It is also argued that Maximus and Freud seem to be in agreement about fantasy 'as a background psychic process, exerting the utmost power against reason and any self-control allied with reason' (ibid.: 137). Referring to Jung, Moran concedes that both Jung and Maximus agree that 'symbols' stand for a source carrying the energy for formulating and interpreting the depths and origins of human life. On the other hand, he criticises 'Jung's fatal misunderstanding of symbols [which] allows him to use them to avoid making this commitment of our inner selves to that Giver' (ibid.: 144). Moran resonates Buber's view that 'Jung divinizes the soul without first sanctifying it' (ibid.). Here once again becomes obvious the necessity of a systematic analysis and methodology to understand thoroughly the exact dimensions of the role of the symbols as well as the degree to which numinosity is engaged in actions such as 'divinization' or 'sanctification'. The psychological limitation and the ontological potential of the spiritual in Jung's theory once again call for meticulous investigation.

Apart from the dissimilar understanding of the spiritual, another significant issue is the concept of the unconscious, playing a key role in Jung's understanding of development. Despite the fact that in Maximus' era the term 'unconscious' was not applicable in philosophy or theology, possibly equivalent concepts, such as *heart,* the hidden parts of the soul, are used more extensively.[21] Contemporary attempts to connect the unconscious with aspects such as psychic 'inactivity' or the 'demonic' are rather problematic, to the extent to which they are referring only to the 'passive' or negative psychic elements and not to the 'deeper' as well as very energetic archetypal material as sources of the psychic energy. For instance, G. Varvatsioulias[22] takes the view that '[t]he psychology of the unconscious is develness), a notion that St. Maximus links with the idea of the demonic' (2002: 293). It is obvious that an emphasis on 'demonization' of the unconscious could prevent a constructive view of the relationship between the equivalence of Maximian concepts with the immense potential of the unconscious realm. In a further attempt to link Orthodox theology and Analytical psychology, B. Gaist argues that Jungian psychology attempts to 'distil and elaborate' the existing religious dogmas.

rendering conscious the 'eternal' archetypes pertaining to universal human experiences through the psychology of the unconscious; whereas Orthodox Christianity tries to relate its faith and practice to these same archetypal foundations of the whole of the human existence and experience, rendering them conscious through its carefully formulated dogma of revealed eternal Truth.

(Gaist 2010: 132)

Despite this aspiration for an integrated vision of the two systems, it is unclear whether the 'same archetypal foundations' lay at the bottom of both Jung's approach and Orthodox Christian conceptions of human existence. Deification and individuation, as further analysis will demonstrate in the next chapter, do not at all share the same ontological and/or phenomenological 'foundations': what might be 'archetypes' for Jung, within the psychic boundaries, is for Maximus the metaphysical principles (*logoi*) of all the living beings.

Kenneth Becker's definition of 'Jung's psychology of individuation [as] a nontheological spirituality', in contrast with the 'theological spirituality' of Loyola's *Spiritual Exercises* (Becker 2001: 11), provides a more appropriate ground for understanding the difference that underpins 'individuation' in comparison with religious spiritualities. The question is once again what precisely constitutes the spiritual according to the two theories? – a spiritual which is rather a 'spiritual continuum' as shown in the previous chapter. Georg Nicolaus, comparing Jung's individuation and Berdyaev's concept of person, introduces an important hermeneutic distinction:

Jung's psychology tends to interpret the spiritual, that which transcends nature, in terms of the immanent. The implicit conceptual background does not allow for a sufficiently clear differentiation of the spiritual and the psychological. In Berdyaev's philosophy the transcendent dimension is secured by his notion of the super-conscious. The 'super-conscious' denotes the dimension of the spirit, which . . . becomes present in a non-objectifiable experience that goes right to the core of the person, to its existential centre.

(Nicolaus 2011: 80)

This is an important hermeneutic shift that allows different epistemologies to deal with the psychological and spiritual perspectives in a non-reductive way that reduces the one dimension to the other – obviously aligned with trans-disciplinarity. This is a critical distinction, which, when applied to Jung's theory on religion, could shed light on the inherent ambiguity of his thought. In this fashion, it may allow other conceptions like Maximus' insights to be juxtaposed to the Jungian views without confusing the different underlying epistemologies and ontologies.

The Jungian standpoints on religion discussed above can now be explored systematically within both Jung's and Maximus' corpus in the following chapters and some initial conclusions can be drawn. It is apparent that beyond Jung's psychological conception of the *numinous*, there are different conceptualisations of the spiritual dimension – within the *spiritual continuum*, based on unlike ontologies linked with the experience of man's existential centre. At man's *heart*, which expands beyond psychological limits, Jung's 'complex' relation to religion could be addressed further and potentially be resolved. This 'complex' analysis of the religious account at many levels may trigger a challenging reconsideration of traditional conceptions and doctrines in old and modern eras. In this respect, Maximus' theory and practice, unfolding its own insights and perspectives, can also be challenged by Jung's standpoints on religion while simultaneously challenging the ontological potential of the archetypal theory – in an interplay that could improve our understanding of both sides.

Notes

1. Soon after Freud's theory broke the ground on depth psychology, eminent scientific figures raised serious oppositions to his theory. Malinowski, for instance, contested from an anthropological viewpoint the universal application of the Oedipus complex on the *matrilineal* families: see Malinowski, B. (1927) *Sex and Repression in Savage Society,* London: Routledge and Kegan Paul.
2. Freud writes, 'The derivation of religious needs from the infant's helplessness and the longing for the father aroused by it seems to me incontrovertible, especially since the feeling is not simply prolonged from childhood days, but is permanently sustained by fear of the superior power of Fate' (Freud 1930: 72).
3. It could be argued that Freud was not specifically against religion as such in absolute terms, since he admits that to 'assess the truth-value of religious doctrines does not lie within the scope of the present inquiry' (1927: 33), as confined to psychoanalytic considerations alone. Freud saw religion next to civilisation as two systems holding a sway on 'these dangerous masses', for which reason 'the relationship between civilization and religion should undergo a fundamental revision' (ibid.: 39).
4. Jung himself narrates in detail many incidents of his early life that shaped his initially negative experience related to faith, church, and religion. The question whether he gave himself a persuasive and fuller answer to his numerous queries from his youth cannot perhaps be answered completely. After many decades, he also inconclusively answered in his famous interview by Freeman (see McGuire & Hull 1977) whether he believed in God that 'I do not need to believe, I know'.
5. It was again the 'death' and the 'dark' since 'all religious talk bored [him] to death', especially after his father's blunt acknowledgment that he understood nothing as regards the Trinity's doctrine: 'We now come to the Trinity, but we'll skip that, for I really understand nothing of it myself' (*MDR*: 53).
6. See Kerr (1993); also Lothane (1996).
7. Gerhard Adler discusses his encounter with Jung in 1934 as an attendee of Jung's seminars. 'One morning', he narrates, 'I arrived in Jung's house and found him in a bad temper. With indignation he told me that he had been made the scapegoat for the breakdown of a patrician Swiss marriage, the partners of which he did not even know. But was this accusation not perhaps justified in a certain sense? Could it not have been than Jung's thoughts about human relationships in their authentic meaning . . . Jung himself felt this loneliness as a heavy burden. . . .' (Adler 1979: 91–2).
8. Jung writes in his autobiography: 'I had a strong intuition that for him [Freud] sexuality was a sort of *numinosum*. This was confirmed by a conversation that took place some three years later (in 1910), again in Vienna: I can still recall vividly how Freud

said to me, "My dear Jung, promise me never to abandon the sexual theory. That is the most essential thing of all. You see, we must make a dogma of it, an unshakable bulwark". He said that to me with great emotion, in the tone of a father saying, "And promise me this one thing, my dear son: that you will go to the church every Sunday". In some astonishment I asked him, "A bulwark – against what?" To which he replied, "Against the black tide of mud" and . . . then added "of occultism".' (*MDR*: 150). The connections between the two poles in Jung's mind and the projections of his own father-complex (my dear son . . .) are astonishing.

9. It is important at this point to envisage Jung's anti–Freudian approach within his subsequent – well-known nowadays – anti–Semitic attitude. Jung thus wanted to emphasize the rather religious/spiritual unconscious foundations of his entire movement in order to differentiate himself from Freud in scientific, religious, and, by extension, cultural terms – based on his undeniable Christian background versus Freud's Semitism.

10. Papadopoulos (2006) introduces an interpretation of Jung's epistemology as a bipolar oscillation within 'Socratic ignorance and Gnostic knowledge' and points out: 'Jung's ambivalent stance towards philosophy seems to have prevented him from acknowledging fully the implications of his own epistemological sensitivity' (ibid.: 47).

11. At a latter stage, Jung reintroduces libido as the whole psychic energy: 'By libido I mean psychic *energy* . . . the *intensity* of a psychic process, its *psychological value*' (1921/1971: para. 778).

12. Connecting the function of thinking with the symbols of God-images, Jung writes, 'Humanity came to its gods by accepting the reality of the symbol, that is, it came to the *reality of thought*, which has made man lord of the earth. Devotion, as Schiller correctly conceived it, is a regressive movement of libido towards the primordial, a diving down into the source of the first beginning. Out of this there rises, as an image of the incipient progressive movement, the symbol, which is a condensation of all the operative unconscious factors – "living form" as Schiller says, and a God-image, as history proves' (Jung 1921/1971: para. 202).

13. See Jung (1916/1957). We will discuss further the *transcendent function* in Chapter 5.

14. Victor White wrote to Jung on this account, arguing that 'If Christ is no longer an adequate symbol of the Self . . . then must one not choose – at whatever the cost? Faith in him, it seems to me, must be unconditional; once one "criticizes Christ" one as lost faith in him . . .' (Lammers & Cunningham 2007: 216).

15. Logical interpretation of the symbols and doctrines is a psychological process which, for Jung, lies within an ambivalence, insofar as '[p]sychological truth by no means excludes metaphysical truth, though psychology, as a science, has to hold aloof from all metaphysical assertions' (Jung 1911/1956: para. 344)

16. See Lammers and Cunningham (2007).

17. In fact, Jung 'wanted to examine the images functioning in other systems of spirituality, be they the *SE* [Spiritual Exercises], or yoga, or alchemy, or I Ching . . .' (Becker 2001: 65). However, Jung admitted that he 'relies on his imagination for any realisation of what the experience of the *SE* may be' (ibid.: 64), which renders Jung's approach subjective and weakens the essentially spiritual dimension of Loyola's *SE*.

18. Maximus' work was made available in volumes 90 and 91 of *Patrologiae Graeca Series* by J. P. Migne, 1895, in Paris, but this is even today a relatively rare collection: Migne, J. P. (1857–1904) *Patrologiae Cursus Completus, Series Graeca*. Paris.

19. Such as Balthasar (1947, 1988), Thunberg (1985, 1995), Louth (1996, 1997), Blowers (1991, 1992, 1996), Bathrellos (2004), Cooper (2005), Törönen (2007), and Loudovikos (2010).

20. Another interesting study between the two fields explores similarities and differences on 'personhood' in the theology of John Zizioulas and the archetypal psychology of James Hillman, a well-known post–Jungian (see Melissaris 2002).

21. More on this issue in Chapter 5.
22. Varvatsioulias's thesis (2002) compares the basic concepts of Horney, a post–Freudian psychoanalyst, with Maximus' equivalent notions. In spite of lacking a third overarching system through which the two models should be contrasted with each other, it is the first systematic comparison between Maximus and a modern psychologist. The investigation focuses *inter alia* on contrasting basic psychic elements, such as real-self, conscience, self-love, or suppressed emotions in Horney with the notions of deification, self-dispassion, and passions in Maximus. Apart from similarities, divergences also exist: 'Karen Horney [is] "struggling" to making the neurotic persons aware of what they need to do against neurosis in general . . . only interested in *healing* from neurosis . . . Maximus reflects on his aspects of integrity through the prism of man's *deification,* i.e. *unification* with God' (2002: 120). Thus, the metaphysical element and 'deification' in Maximus are emphasized as striking differences between the two models.

4

MAXIMUS THE CONFESSOR AND CARL JUNG ON THE FOUNDATIONS OF THE PSYCHE

In the previous chapter, it was shown that Jung understands the foundations of the psyche within his archetypal theory, namely the archetypal polarities between dualities such as personal and collective, masculine and feminine, good and evil. The image of God(s), the prevailing spiritual/religious dimension within the psyche that progressively leads to the manifestation of the unconscious Self, is the core around which Jung considers his 'complex' understanding of the religious aspect. Maximus the Confessor discusses the foundations of the psyche through a different perspective: the dynamics between the inherent God-image towards the also immanent potential of God-likeness. Maximus' positions constitute an alternative proposition to Jung's main points on religion that address primarily the psychological level. In other words, the potential of God-likeness towards a metaphysical dimension, or God as such, challenges the Jungian religious dimension reduced to the psychological dimension. However, prior to unfolding Maximus' ontology vis-à-vis Jung's archetypal theory, we need to encounter Maximus' life and era.

Maximus' life and philosophical background

Honoured as 'one of the outstanding thinkers of all time' (Thunberg 1985: 7), St Maximus the Confessor was renowned as one of the greatest philosophers and theologians of early Christian times (580–662 AD). Maximus' work is drawing a considerable body of contemporary academic theological research because his concepts provide a challenging synthetic view of the inner/psychic sphere and the outer/cosmic world, all ontologically linked to the divine level through the 'one Logos'. The fact that Maximus' work is becoming increasingly influential in the West is already evident, in a prefigurative way, in his own lifetime: mostly the Western state and church granted the support Maximus was seeking for his ideas. What is more, the vicissitudes of his life paradoxically form a sort of reconciliation between current 'Eastern' and 'Western' strands of thinking, an integration that Jung so extensively considered and advocated.

Maximus attained his vision of an *unus mundus,* one world, though different than Jung's one, being the successor of a great philosophical and theological legacy; in particular, Neoplatonics, Origen, Evagrius, Gregory of Nazianzus,

Gregory of Nyssa, and Dionysius the Areopagite all exerted a significant influence on his work. Following the fourth ecumenical Synod (451 AD), which formulated the Christological doctrine (two distinct natures, divine and human, *united without confusion* in one hypostasis-person of Christ), Maximus established a new 'beginning' for theology, focusing more on the inner experience and less on the systematic/doctrinal enunciations (Louth 1997: 344).[1] Not only thus did Maximus open a path to an experiential theology and by extension to an experiential psychology – aligned to Jungian points – but he also stood, as Jung many centuries after, at a decisive crossroad: the former between antiquity and Middle Ages, the latter between modernity and post-modernity. In this respect,

> [t]he vision of the world, which Maximus the Confessor has left us in his writings is, from more than one point of view, the completion and full maturity of Greek mystical, theological, and philosophical thought. It appears at that happy and fugitive moment, which unites for a last time, before an already close decomposition, the richness patiently acquired and developed through the effort of a whole culture . . .
> (Balthasar 1947: 11, cited in Berthold 1985: xi–xii)

Maximus was born in 580 AD in Constantinople[2] at a time when the Roman Empire was enjoying ascendancy.[3] Notwithstanding the contemporary security and prosperity, the inhabitants rather began to feel the transition to a new era, 'where a sense of identity (or of identities) needed to be fashioned afresh' (Louth 1997: 334). The earliest traces of the decay of Christian medieval society had begun to appear on the horizon. Scholars have highlighted the fact that Maximus' theological vision 'also addressed the concrete context of a culture still undergoing redefinition, a culture rocked by the emergence of a whole new religious and political entity on its immediate horizon: Islam' (Blowers & Wilken 2003: 19). Maximus' epoch could distantly mirror Jung's milieu and the radical changes of the 20th century, with its cultural, social, and scientific evolutions that inspired Jung's innovative view of the psychic world in a constant development.

Being of noble descent, Maximus received a sound education and showed a remarkable understanding of philosophical issues, sufficient enough to secure the post of first secretary to Emperor Heraclius (c. 575–641; see *PG* 90: 72BC). Later on, Maximus abandoned this post and the comforts of the palace and lived peacefully as a monk in various places, studying theological and philosophical works, particularly by Origen. Regardless of the influence by the Neoplatonic Origenistic views, his most important work, *Ambigua (Difficulties)*, constitutes a refutation of Origenism: he redresses and restores in an orthodox Christian approach the old issue of the initial 'satiety' and 'rest' of the rational beings contemplating the Godhead – from whence they fell and were captured into the sensible cosmos.[4]

Between the years 632 and 638, Maximus develops a more concrete theological response to the heresies of *monothelitism* and *monenergism*.[5] In a public debate in 645, Maximus defeated the monothelite Pyrrhus at a time when the Patriarch

of Constantinople and many of his officers were favouring the heretic monothe-
lites. This antithesis was a 'full tragedy of this religious and political integralism'
(Balthasar 1988: 31), which aimed to maintain occupation of crucial Eastern territories.[6] It was not until 649, during the Lateran Council in Rome, that Maximus
reinforced his relationship with the 'non–Eastern' West,[7] which later cost him exile.
In 655, Maximus returned to Constantinople as an enemy of the state, together with
Pope Martin I, archbishop of Rome. After a series of stressful events, he was exiled
a second time, publicly mutilated, and finally abandoned to die in 662 at a fortress
in Lazica (on the Black Sea). For his torments, the title 'Confessor' was honour-
ably conferred on him. The final vindication came in the sixth ecumenical Synod in
681, which renounced the *monothelitism* and *monenergism,* even though the name
of Maximus was nowhere mentioned in the Synod transcripts.

Maximus' spiritual descendants added rather little: indeed, he was used to
enrich what was already accepted and not to boost innovating thoughts, and thus
he was characterised as 'perhaps the last independent theologian' (Beck 1959:
436, cited in Geanakoplos 1969: 162). It must be emphasized that not only did
Maximus construct a Christian philosophical theory addressing the complexity
of a synthesis at all levels (physical, psychic, divine), but he also successfully
'bridged' the psychological and spiritual experience, 'speaking both the language
of spirituality and the language of theology' (Berthold 1985: 11). Thus, the fact
that Maximus highlighted the inherent ability of the psyche to relate to the spiritual principles (*logoi*) and meanings of all beings (see below) – as a vast sponge
absorbing knowledge and experiencing union with God – can promote him to a
bilingual mediator between psychology and religion.

The ability of Maximus to combine experience at the psychic level with the
spiritual principles at the divine level through an experiential dimension could
constructively resolve Jung's 'complex' relationship to religion by proposing
a holistic understanding of the metaphysical perspectives of the inherent God-
image. Despite the fact that Maximus' system cannot be considered as 'religious'
in modern terms – it is rather an *experience* of the church as the communion
between God and man in the space-time continuum – his standpoints could be
further elaborated to bridge the vacuum that Jung appears to have left on the non-
psychological implications of the God-image. This is due to the fact that Maximus
addressed the fuller range of the spiritual continuum without reducing the anthropological framework within the solely archetypal psychological dimensions.

Maximus on man: a 'cataphatic' or an 'apophatic' anthropology?

Maximus and Jung address the human 'psyche' under different principles; it is
therefore necessary to clarify further their subject matter. In theological texts,
psyche (ψυχή) is typically translated as 'soul', but the latter does not convey
the depth and the 'weight' of the original term in *Genesis* (see Ware 1997: 90f).
For Maximus, the soul/psyche is the invisible part of man, the 'living being',

inextricably entwined with the body, as 'the whole soul permeates the whole body and gives it life and motion' (*Amb.* 7: 1100A). Both the soul and the body bear the 'image' and 'likeness' after God (*Genesis* 1, 26), drawing their true existence and potential to the divine level, as we will discuss below. Although the soul/psyche is principally a human 'portion', it cannot exist without being related to a person and of course to a body: because 'it is only as they [body and soul] come together to form a particular person that they exist' (*Amb.* 7: 1101C).

According to Jung, the psyche is the 'totality of all psychic processes, conscious as well as unconscious', plainly distinguished from the 'soul', which he views as 'personality' or as a 'functional complex' (1921/1971: para. 797). However, Jung also connects personality with 'wholeness' as an achievement of integration of conscious and unconscious elements: he writes, '[i]n so far as every individual has the law of his life inborn in him, it is theoretically possible for any man to follow this law and to become a personality, that is, to achieve wholeness' (1934a: para. 307). In a post–Jungian further clarification, psyche as a term is closely associated with 'the word "soul" . . . in connection with such a depth perspective that Jung uses it, rather than in a conventionally Christian manner' (*CDJA*: 115). This 'depth perspective' is aligned to the archetypal dimension, which is different from the 'conventional Christian manner' – namely the religious/divine dimension traditionally attached to the psyche. Despite the dissimilar perspectives that the two approaches attribute to the soul/psyche, it would not be far from the truth to assume that 'psyche', 'soul', and 'person(ality)' correspond to overlapping areas of a constantly developing individual and thus potentially could represent psychic wholeness.

Due to the entirely different philosophical background, Maximus' view of the psyche is based on a ground different from Jung's archetypal theory. While Jung's key notion is the God-image and the Self, Maximus unfolds his vision of man as a 'composite nature' of body and soul in 'the image of God', simultaneously bearing the potential to attain 'God's likeness'. Maximus does not blindly support a doctrinal system remote from the psyche, something that Jung wanted to avoid as well, but applies an anthropological view open to a metaphysical perspective, or more precisely to a personal God, whose characteristics are imprinted in the human soul.

Maximus' ultimate vision of man's development is the state of *theosis*, deification, which, according to Thunberg, is '*a summary of his whole theological anthropology*' (1995: 430, italics original). Anthropology for Maximus is not a research for the origins and cultural manifestations of human beings throughout history; it is, instead, inextricably intertwined with his ontology and theology; it could also be named a 'theological anthropology', whose origins stem from antiquity. It was the period when philosophy and theology shared a nearly identical remit, embracing not only metaphysics or moral issues but also 'critical philosophy, including logic and epistemology' (Guthrie 1967: 17). Furthermore, Maximus applies both affirmative, cataphatic, and apophatic, by negation, approaches, since affirmation and negation in relation to each other display opposition but in relation to God display the affinity of meeting extremes (*Amb.* 34: 1288C). Apophatic definitions were used since Plotinus: '[g]enerative of all, the Unity is none of all; neither thing nor quality nor quantity nor intellect nor soul' (*Enneads* VI: 9, 3). In *Mystical Theology,* Dionysius the Areopagite follows the tradition that God is beyond any positive definition and knowledge (*PG* 3, 997AB). It is, without doubt, within the Christian tradition that 'in our talk about humans, as well as our talk about God, there needs to be an apophatic dimension; our negative theology demands as counterpart a "negative anthropology"'. (Ware 1987: 198). This bipolar dynamic approach avoids the fallacies of 'anthropological reduction' applied by Jung – as G. Nicolaus has characterised the reduction of the spiritual or religious dimension to the solely psychic world (Nicolaus 2011: 41).

Maximus' anthropology emanates from his ontology and cosmology. Classical theories in antiquity viewed both cosmos and man 'as mutually-reflecting images' (Louth 1996: 63), whereas pre–Socratics and Plato introduced notions such as *microcosm,* a small cosmos.[8] Maximus too thinks of the human being as 'micros cosmos' (*Ep.* 6: 429D), inasmuch as both cosmos and man consist of sensible and intelligible realms in a reciprocal relationship: 'for the entire intelligible world appears mystically imprinted on the sensible one within symbolic forms . . . and the entire sensible world cognitively exists within the intelligible through the logoi' (*Myst.* 2: 669C).[9] Thus, Maximus considers man as a repetition of the cosmos on a smaller scale, who has to develop a dialogue with the spiritual meanings and qualities of all the creatures, the principles/*logoi,* in order to enhance his knowledge about the origins of the cosmos. We shall further explore these principles or *logoi* in the next section.

Maximus employs further fundamental binary terms to delineate the dimensions of the human person: 'Person, namely hypostasis; nature, namely essence. Consequently, essence [is] the [making] "in the image", the logos, whereas hypostasis is the "in the likeness", the [mode of] existence, by which together, the virtue is completed' (*Opusc.* 1: 37BC). Whereas essence and nature define the universal characteristics of the beings, person or hypostasis determines the unique, the particular. Hypostasis as a concept – borrowed from the Cappadocian theologians that applied three 'hypostases' to God[10] – brings together the simultaneous unity and difference, the particular and the universal, the distinct and the unified.

Maximus adopts the biblical tradition that man is a 'composite nature' of body and soul (*Amb.* 53: 1373C; 42: 1341D, 1345AB). According to *Genesis,* man was made in God's image and likeness,[11] which means that uniqueness and communion are present in both God and man. Man acquired not only a direct resemblance to God's image but also the potentiality to become 'God's likeness'. In Lossky's words, man's creation 'demands not solitude but communion, the wholesome diversity of love' (1978: 69, cited in Staniloae 1978: 79). Contrary to the prevailing interpretation in the West by Tertullian or Augustine, the Eastern patristic tradition in its conception and interpretation of 'image' emphasizes the fact that man as a whole – and not a particular part of the soul or body – is endowed with this 'image'.[12] The predominant Eastern tradition is that 'image' refers to the whole man's composite nature. However, a fundamental distinction is

introduced between the 'being', as image in nature, and 'ever-being', in the state
of 'likeness' and grace – the latter displaying the apophatic perspective of man:

> [Man] is said to be made to God's image and likeness; to the image of
> His being by being, of His ever being by ever-being (though it has begin-
> ning, yet it is without end); to the likeness of His goodness by goodness,
> of His wisdom by wisdom. The one is by nature, the other by grace.
>
> (*Char.* III, 25: *ACW* 177)

Man is able to attain this resemblance, because Christ, man's original Archetype, 'took on himself our human nature in deed and in truth and united it to
himself hypostatically – without change, alteration, diminution or division' (*Amb.*
42: 1320C, see Garrigues 1976). By so doing, Christ opened to man the pathway
to become a 'man deified to God' (*Amb.* 10: 1113B), which is man's ultimate goal
and purpose 'without end': '[t]he plan was for him to mingle, without change on
his part, with human nature by true hypostatic union . . . so that he might become
a man . . . and so that he might deify humanity in union with himself' (*Q.Thal.* 22:
137; Blowers & Wilken 2003: 115). Deification is a result of Christ's incarnation
(the hypostatic union of God and man) and thoroughly alters the dynamics of
human nature, which now acquires the characteristics of a 'loving God'.

Maximus goes much deeper than a merely inner psychosomatic bond; he expands
it, precisely because the sensible and intelligible psyche 'does not cease acting
within both the body and its own physical energies' (*Ep.* 7: 436D).[13] Here Maximus follows Gregory of Nyssa, stating that the psychic energy pervades the body
and acts in accordance with the inherent ability of each bodily organ in receiv-
ing it.[14] Aligned with mainstream modern theories of psychosomatic disorders and
with certain views of depth psychology, Maximus clearly describes the reciprocal
relation of the two parts and denotes: 'the body is an instrument of the intellectual
soul of man and the whole soul permeates the whole body and gives it life and
motion' (*Amb.* 7: 1100A); and every bodily part absorbs the psychic energy in
accordance with its inherent potency that is responsive to the soul's activity (ibid.:
1100B). Body as an *organ* of the soul, aligned to Jung's conception of the archetypes as 'organs' of the psyche,[15] clearly derives from a holistic approach, which,
while bearing a metaphysical potential, is also affirmative to the visible reality.

Maximus' vision of man is certainly well balanced between the 'world-
affirming'/*cataphatic* approach and metaphysical/*apophatic* dynamics of deification. Maximus in fact adds this metaphysical dimension to man's perspectives,
which can be sufficiently defined only by negations. As Nellas remarks, '[s]ince
man is an image, his real *being* is not defined by the created element . . . but by his
uncreated Archetype' (1997: 33). In order to fill the gulf between affirmations and
negations, Maximus applies an extensive usage of the allegoric method introduced
earlier by the Alexandrian school of Origen's hermeneutics by using metaphors in
the interpretation of the scriptures, similar to Christ's narratives or parables. There
is thus a balance between apophasis and cataphatic in Maximus's thought: 'the

words of the holy Scripture are said to be garments, and the concepts understood to be flesh of the Word . . . and thus in the former case we reveal, and in the latter we conceal' (*Amb.* 10: 1129B, trans. Louth).

We might now be able to understand that Maximus' vision of man, being created according to God's image and likeness, is eventually interpreted in full terms apophatically: it is a union of body and soul having, nevertheless, immanent the potential to develop towards God-likeness. This is the stage at which both body and soul are transformed into God's divine qualities, the *logoi*-as-virtues. However, Maximus is still considered as 'the most world-affirming thinker of all the Greek Fathers' (Balthasar 1988: 61) because the human person of body and soul, in spite of their transformation on the divine level, retains its wholeness and integrity. Within this spiritual perspective in which both body and soul are participating in God's 'likeness' and divine qualities, we can investigate now in which ways Maximus allows a strong experiential aspect to complement his ontological

Figure 4.1 Maximus the Confessor interrogated by the Emperor in Constantinople. Section of *Maximus the Confessor and His Miracles,* 17th-century Stroganov school icon from Solvychegodsk.

63

vision of man's development – a system that Florovsky has characterised as 'a symphony of spiritual experience' (1931: 213).

Jung's archetypes and Maximus' '*logoi*' of beings: exploring the foundations of the psyche

Modernity attached prime importance to the experiential-phenomenological dimension of human existence by laying emphasis on 'self-consciousness' as antithetical to the ontological, the non-experienced 'real'. Jung addressed this challenge by laying more emphasis on the experiential dimension than the ontological. Maximus integrates these opposites: whereas he affirms the real on a metaphysical/divine level as the source of true knowledge, he simultaneously views the human psyche as endowed with functions able to experience this supreme knowledge. According to Maximus, the 'illumination' of the psychic functions (intellect/mind, logos/reason, and spirit, as images of the archetypal Trinity) is essential to reach God's likeness, towards which the functions are teleologically orientated (*Amb.* 7: 1088A). The divine realm is no longer outside human boundaries but is *within*, because it is available to psychic experience through the *logoi of beings,* the fundamental principles of the existence and development of all the created entities. We need to explore further this central concept within Maximus' ontological theory.

Maximus' ontological divisions and the 'logoi' of beings

Central to Maximus' view of the entire cosmos is the different levels of ontological reality, the five 'divisions' that he introduces – each comprising a pair of opposites – which are between (a) the uncreated nature (the Creator) and the created (the world); (b) the created beings perceived by the mind/intellect (intelligible realm) and those perceived by the senses (sensible realm); (c) (division of sensible things into) heaven and earth; (d) (division of the earth into) paradise and 'inhabited world' (translation of the Greek world *oikoumenê*); and (e) (human being divided by sex into) male and female. Christ, by his incarnation, resurrection, and ascension, has firstly fulfilled – on man's behalf – the work of 'mediation', which man must also complete in imitation of Christ. It is thus Christ the *Logos* that mediated the five fundamental divisions-opposites, while man's vocation is to eternally maintain this recapitulation through the communion of the same Logos (*Amb.* 41: 1304D–12B; see Thunberg 1995: 331ff, 373ff; Louth 1996: 72–4). The communion with the uncreated realm and the recapitulation of all levels is an inherent ability into man, because Christ, sharing these same features with man, attained it initially:

> He binds about himself each with the other, tightly and indissolubly, paradise and the inhabited world, heaven and earth, things sensible and things intelligible, since he possesses like us body and aesthesis and soul and intellect, by which, as parts, he assimilates himself by each of the extremities, to what is universally akin to each . . . Thus he divinely

recapitulates the universe in himself, showing that the whole creation
exists as one . . . [and] admits of one and the same indiscriminate *logos* . . .

(*Amb.* 41: 1312AB, trans. Louth)

Christ, the one Logos, brings about the integration of all levels in a way that the
whole universe can 'conceive' the one Logos-Creator, who consists of many *logoi.*
This is the cardinal concept of Maximus' ontology: *logoi* are the eternal God's
thoughts-as-vocations – and at the same time as the foundations – of all creatures
before creation occurred. Through these 'logoi', the one Logos is 'the whole God
in all things commonly and in each particularly' (*Amb.* 22: 1257AB). Logos, 'the
beginning and the cause of all things', is the source of all *logoi* and simultaneously the culmination, the end of them: 'the one Logos is many logoi . . . [and] the
many logoi are the one Logos to whom all things are related and who exists in
himself without confusion' (*Amb.* 7: 1077C). Distinct *logoi* in one *Logos,* united
without confusion, bearing the beginning and the telos of beings, is the essence of
Maximian 'eschatological' ontology.

The term *logos* has a long history in ancient philosophy.[16] Maximus uses *logos*
in particular contexts with different meanings: *Logos* is the Logos-Christ, Son of
God the Father, whereas *logos* is the ontological principle of each creature; yet elsewhere, it also stands for the logical psychic function, the reason (*Amb.* 10: 1112D).
However, Maximus' favourite use of *logos* is 'logos of essence' (λόγος οὐσιώσεως:
Ep. 2: 404B; *Amb.* 31: 1280A; 42: 1341CD; *Char.* IV, 45: *ACW* 199), the ontologically essential-formative principle of beings as well as their unique pattern
and potential for development that pre-exists in God's mind. According to this
logos, each created creature proceeds 'logically' towards its own 'telos' (*Amb.* 17:
1228CD). Consequently, *logos* carries the 'divine wills and intentions' according to Dionysius the Areopagite (*DN* 5, 8: 188), from whom Maximus is possibly
borrowing – also quoted by Jung when referring to the origins of the archetypes
(Jung 1954: para. 5). Despite the fact that the doctrine of the 'logoi' holds little sway
with Maximus' successors, which Louth describes as a 'lonely meteorite' (2009: 63),
modern approaches to the 'intelligence' hidden in nature (see Narby 2006) resonate
with aspects of the 'logical core' of beings that Maximus' 'logoi' denote.

The weight that Maximus applies to the doctrine of 'logoi' reveals a strong
Neoplatonic influence (i.e. a remote transformation of Platonic *forms*), which has
been investigated through different routes extensively, either through Plotinus (see
Törönen 2007: 30–1) and Dionysius the Areopagite (Louth 1993: 166–74; 2009;
Rorem 1993) or Origen and Evagrius (Balthasar 1988: 65–73; Louth 1981: 51ff;
Louth 1996: 35–8, 64–8). Despite the fact that this undisputed impact of these
'old patterns of thought', in Balthasar's formulation (1988: 82), does not concern
this study, it is noteworthy to briefly refer to significant differences between Maximus and Neoplatonics. Plotinus's triadic system *One-Good, Nous,*[17] and *Soul,*
according to which the Nous emanates from the One, whereas the Soul from the
Nous – with beings to moving towards *progress* and *return* – is partially present in Maximus. However, by his *logoi* Maximus permanently moves away from

Plotinus's idea of the 'One' as being absolutely isolated in itself (see *Enneads* VI: 8.13; VI: 9.3; V: 5.6). The Maximian *logoi* lead the beings to their eschatological purpose, to their union without confusion with their ontological source, the Logos, whereas in Plotinus the beings are finally merged with their origins:

> It is he [the Logos] who encloses in himself all beings by the unique, simple, and infinitely wise power of his goodness. As the centre of straight lines that radiate from him he does not allow . . . the principles of beings become disjoined at the periphery but rather he circumscribes their extension in a circle . . . [thus the beings do] not run the risk of having their being separated from God to dissolve into non-being.
>
> (*Myst.* 1: 668AB, trans. Berthold, cf. Plotinus, *Enneads* IV: 4.16)

Although Maximus possibly draws the concept of Logos-*logoi* from Philo and Plotinus, it is Dionysius's impact that compels Maximus to assemble his *logoi* into a hierarchy. According to Louth, Dionysius's concepts 'can perhaps be summed up under three headings: philosophy, liturgy, cosmos' (1996: 29). Maximus develops these ideas and wants his *logoi* to constitute a pyramid, whose summit is the Logos:

> The logoi of everything that is divided and particular are contained . . . by the logoi of what is universal and generic; and the most universal and generic logoi are held together by wisdom, whilst the logoi of the particulars . . . are contained by sagacity. . . . For the wisdom and sagacity of God the Father is the Lord Jesus Christ, who holds together the universals of beings by the power of wisdom, and embraces their complementary parts by the sagacity of understanding.
>
> (*Amb.* 41: 1313AB, trans. Louth)

It appears that at the bottom of this pyramid lay the 'logoi of essence' of the particular beings, whereas at the apex are the 'logoi of the universal', which constitute the modes (*tropoi*) and the qualities of virtues. Christ the Logos through the virtues of prudence and wisdom not only contains and supports ontologically all beings, universal and particular, but also permits us, through the union with the *logoi* of partial things, to experience the summit of this pyramid, the ultimate virtue that is God's divine love. Maximus defines love eschatologically, as 'the inward universal relationship to the first good connected with the universal purpose of our nature' (*Ep.* 2: 401D).

The fact that the logoi address specific qualities should be perceived within the binary concept of *logos-tropos:* while *logos* is connected with the essence of the beings, revealing at once their 'divine purpose' (*Q.Thal.* 13: 95), *tropos* is the particular mode of existence, a developmental perspective, a personal creative activation of a particular entity-as-*logos* (see *Opusc.* 10: 137A; *Amb.* 42: 1341D; or *existential tropos*: ibid.: 1344D). As Sherwood maintains, 'the *logos of nature* may be preserved with a considerable margin of variation in the *tropos of existence*' (1955: 165). The 'logoi of beings' ultimately become the 'tropoi and logoi of virtues', those spiritual qualities that the beings must incorporate (*Q.Thal.* 54: 461). Nature, as made by its *logos,* could be seen as the ground where the impact of mode or *tropos* as 'nurture' intervenes during man's development.

In addition to these ontological principles, Maximus redresses Origen's argument with regard to the initial 'satiety' and 'rest' of rational beings contemplating the Godhead, from where they, allegedly, 'fell' and were captured into the sensible cosmos – an embedded idea in Gnostic tenets upon which Jung, too, drew considerably. Maximus reverses Origen's order for beings, *becoming-rest-movement (fall),* to *becoming-movement-rest* (*perfection*; see Louth 1996: 67).[18] Maximus also adopts Evagrius's terms for psychic functions (i.e. contemplation by *nous*) and stages of development (see the next chapter). Further, he attaches equal importance to the experiential aspect of this contemplation, which was principally a Neoplatonic characteristic, namely the 'knowledge by heart'.[19] Maximus maintains a heuristic equilibrium amongst psychic functions by giving an important place to the *aesthesis* amongst the also important intellectual functions, such as the *logos* and *nous.* Psychic functions can thus develop and be transformed into spiritual virtues, reaching their ultimate purpose to experience God's love. This is attainable because the *logoi* and *tropoi* of beings carry the 'dispassionate meanings' that can be experienced by ultimately becoming the 'energies of the rational soul' (*Amb.* 10: 1108D).

Maximus clearly speaks of a transformation of the 'physical energies' of the psyche into the 'logoi and tropoi of the virtues' (*Q.Thal.* 54: 461). The relevance here is that these *logoi*-as-physical energies of the psyche are simultaneously the divine 'energies', because from 'the logoi that are in beings' one would 'contemplate the infinite energies of God' (*Amb.* 22: 1257A).[20] At this point one can trace the continuity within Christian thinkers of the idea of a divine 'portion', either as *logos* or as *energy* able to be experienced by humans – a continuity in absolute concordance with the metaphysical potential of the *spiritual continuum.* Ultimately, this developmental process leads to the status of a man being able to be deified to God through the divine love (*Amb.* 10: 1113B). It is here, however, that Maximus gives priority to the intellectual functions rather than to the senses. Such an epistemological approach is 'standing in contradiction to a modern scientific attitude, which compels us to start with facts and experiments, and thus with sensations . . .' (Thunberg 1985: 136). The experiential element through which one can incorporate qualities of a realm beyond the psychic boundaries remains nevertheless key for Maximus' vision of development.

By the *logoi* Maximus bridges the gap between his predecessors' ontology (for instance, Plotinus's 'light of the Good', *Enneads* VI: 7.22),[21] and the forthcoming supremacy of conscious experience, the 'phenomenology' of the spiritual, as discussed in the second chapter. Maximus therefore introduces an entirely different perspective on the dynamics of the psyche, the experience of a personal God, and departs from modern philosophical insights centred in man's depths (Descartes's *cogito ergo sum,* Kant's *transcendental object,* Heidegger's *dasein,* etc.; see Loudovikos 2010: 104–5). Contrary to approaches that isolate the phenomenological aspect from the ontological dimension, Maximus, by viewing the psychic functions-as-*logoi* from a teleological viewpoint, opens the path for superseding the ontological opposites and experiencing the archetypal (namely the metaphysical in Maximus' view) psychic origins – that is the *logoi* united in the person of Logos-Christ. This 'eschatological ontology' interprets human potential through its telos, namely the state of the 'likeness' with God the Logos (*deification*), the Logos who unites all the divisions of the universe. Apparently, this is a theory that differentiates crucially from Jung's archetypal system, which we are now ready to explore in detail, commencing from its philosophical context, the Kantian and the Hegelian tradition.

Jung's archetypal theory: epistemology and its philosophical background

Jung's vision of archetypes is a multifaceted notion that triggered a range of interpretations. The post–Jungians specifically signified the prevailing archetypal dimension of Jung's whole psychology (Edinger 1972; Hillman 1983), and, *inter alia*, through the 'emergence' (Hogenson 2004) the connections within neurosciences and attachment theory (Knox 2003) or links with inherited biological structures (Stevens 1982, 2006). Whatever the highlighted perspectives of archetypal theory, it must be stressed that Jung at bottom utilised Kantian concepts to frame it. Jung states that archetypal/unconscious sets of ideas could be in line with 'innate possibilities of ideas, *a priori* conditions for fantasy-production, which are somewhat similar to the Kantian categories' (1918: para. 14), which give definite form to the contents of the visible 'phenomena'.[22] Later on, Jung insinuated that the archetypes also bear the dynamics of the 'noumena' or even the absolutely unknowable *thing-in-itself*, implying 'post-experiential' dimensions of his key 'borderline concept' of the wholeness/Self:

> The concept of psychic wholeness necessarily implies an element of transcendence on account of the existence of unconscious components. Transcendence in this sense is not equivalent to a metaphysic postulate or hypostasis; it claims to be no more than a borderline concept, to quote Kant. That there is something beyond the borderline, beyond the frontiers of knowledge, is shown by the archetypes . . .
>
> (1958: para. 779–80)

However, it appears that Jung was not entirely satisfied with either Kant's *categories* or the 'borderline' concept opening up to the *thing-in-itself:* in fact 'Jung is at pains to differentiate himself, a psychologist, from these antecedents' (Samuels 1985: 24). Jung found in Kant – as Kant in Leibniz – a concept to establish the psychological foundations of the archetypes, but he implicitly extended its potential to the 'beyond the frontiers of knowledge' level. This dimension is in line with a kind of 'transcendental cognition' beyond the boundaries of the categories, inasmuch as the 'noumena' sometimes function like the 'thing-in-itself'.[23]

The question here is whether Jung is consistent with the later Kant, who endorses agnosticism and the unknowability of the 'thing-in-itself'. When Jung mentioned in his 'Face to Face' interview' that he 'was steeped in Kant' (McGuire & Hull 1977), he rather meant the early Kant and not the post-critical Kant. Paul Bishop has come to the conclusion that in dealing with Kantian concepts, Jung was taken 'not only back to pre-Kantian thought, but also beyond the critical philosophy into the post-Kantian realms of late German Idealism and Romantic philosophy' (2000: 192). Jung, in his later concepts of *psychoid* – 'neither psychological nor physical, but similar to, and transcending, both', 1947/1954: para. 368) – and *synchronicity* (a meaningful but non-causal connection between an inner and outer event separated by time and space, 1952b) implicitly incorporates a metaphysical dimension. Writing to Fordham (3.1.1957), he admits that '. . . I am equally interested, at times even more so, in the metaphysical aspects of the phenomena' (Jung 1976: 344). We nevertheless need to delineate further what was exactly meant by the term 'metaphysical aspects' and how it is related with the archetypal theory.

We can explore further the ultimate potential of the archetypes, having the intention not to provide here an extended analysis of the archetypal theory but to discuss how this potential can be investigated through the immanent dynamics of the notion of the Self/God-image – which, in Maximus' understanding, ranges up to God's likeness. Jung resorts to a kind of reduction-to-psychic level in order to address this problem, by viewing the psyche as naturally religious (1944: para. 14) in relation with God-image(s) alone – and not with the potential of God-likeness. However, despite Jung's efforts to avoid metaphysical nuances, the notion of the archetypes could meaningfully be applied to address the whole range of the ontological levels and the spiritual continuum, including metaphysics. In line with this approach, Jean Knox has explored systematically the archetypal perspectives, stating that the archetypes could range from 'biological entities in the form of information [and] organizing mental frameworks of an abstract nature, never directly experienced . . . [up to] core meanings which do contain representational content . . . [and/or] metaphysical entities which are eternal . . .' (2003: 30). Accordingly, beyond any philosophical or epistemological position by Jung, the question of the ultimate potential of the archetypes remains open.

Jung declares, 'I am an empiricist, not a philosopher' (1938/1954: para. 149): his central epistemological position is that '[p]sychic existence is the only category of existence of which we have *immediate* knowledge, since nothing can be known unless it first appears as a psychic image. Only psychic existence is immediately verifiable' (1939b: para. 769). In this respect, apart from psychic experience and image, no claim such as a religious or a metaphysical one can be valid. This epistemological statement is in line with the second pole of the bipolar epistemological frame 'Socratic ignorance – Gnostic knowledge', in Papadopoulos's formulation (2006: 43ff): although Jung is here consistent with the pole of 'knowledge', there are enough points at which he prefers agnosticism-ignorance that leave critical gaps in his theory. Indeed, as introduced above, there exist crucial differences between Kantian notions and archetypes. Whereas *a-priori* categories cannot stand as entities as such, without the things related to these categories, Jung postulated the archetypes as 'organs of the pre-rational psyche' (1935/1953: 845), as autonomous entities that yield activity and regulate behaviour. Lucy Huskinson has further analysed Jung's misconception of Kantian notions[24] and goes on, arguing that 'a more appropriate influence on Jung's archetype is Schopenhauer. . . . The Will is the Kantian thing-in-itself and grounds all life and the appearance of the reality' (2004: 78). Indeed, Jung relates Schopenhauer's 'idea' – cognised only by those who reached 'to the pure subject of cognition' – to the 'primordial image', which is not distant from the archetypal dynamics (1921/1971: para. 751–2).

In addition, the ontological potential of the 'thing-in-itself' cannot entirely exclude metaphysics, contrary to Jung's ambiguous ontology and '*anti*metaphysical methodology' (Heisig 1979: 121). For Jung, the natural religiosity of the psyche inevitably entails a fusion of certain ontological levels, namely the psychological and the spiritual-as-metaphysical: 'man can be understood as a function of God, and God as a psychological function of man' (ibid.: para. 412). Despite this critical fusion of levels, Jung, nevertheless, is aware of the multi-faceted dynamics and range of the archetypes. When he mentions Plato's *Ideas,* Dionysius Areopagite's 'immaterial Archetypes' or 'archetypal light' (1954: para. 5), Kantian 'thing-in-itself' via his 'borderline concept' (ibid.), and further refers to Schopenhauer's conception of the Idea as 'eternal forms of prototypes' (1921/1971: para. 734; Jarret 1981; Nagy 1991: 55–74), he does not entirely obliterate potentially metaphysical adumbrations. Endeavouring to incorporate all these perspectives in his concept, Jung delineates:

> Just as the 'psychic infra-red', the biological instinctual psyche, gradually passes over into the physiology of the organism . . . so the 'psychic ultra-violet', the archetype, describes a field which exhibits none of the peculiarities of the physiological and yet, in the last analysis, can no longer be regarded as psychic.
>
> (1947/1954: para. 420)

It is apparent that these features of the archetypes that 'can no longer be regarded as psychic' belong to 'the real nature of the archetype . . . [which] is transcendent, on which account I call it psychoid [quasi-psychic]' (ibid.: para. 417). Clearly enough, while attempting to leave aside 'speculative metaphysics', Jung clarifies that 'when we talk of God or gods we are speaking of debatable images from the psychoid realm. The existence of a transcendental reality is indeed evident in itself' (1955/1956: para. 787). Contemporary scholars have also emphasized the implicit metaphysical dimension of archetypal theory within its collective realm: 'Jung ultimately proffers a metaphysics of experience that is conditioned by the archetype collective' (Mills 2013: 36). This is apparently the collective unconscious and its socio-cultural dimension, insofar as patterns of behaviour have been fashioned into cultural images from time immemorial. Jung attached tremendous importance to the role of culture and the impact of the environment on individuation. Culture fashions into the psyche its tendencies and dynamics and vice versa, because 'culture expresses the depths of the self' (Bockus 1990: 43). In this fashion, Self's archetypal dynamics permeate all different levels of life (the bodily, psychic, socio-cultural, and metaphysical). Jung's statement 'no longer psychic' could therefore be considered as bearing witness to the 'beyond the psyche' dynamics.

We have seen so far how Jung misinterpreted Kantian concepts, allowing a fusion between ontological levels that appear distinct in Kantian 'realisation' – a distinction that Maximus also addressed through both the ontological divisions and the distinction between the functions of the soul. This fusion entails a clear reduction of the spiritual and/or the metaphysical dimension to the psychic level. But Jung's priority plausibly was the inner experiential/phenomenological dimension and not the ontological potential of the archetypes. In this respect, what Kant envisaged as the inner intentions of the objects was for Jung the central archetype of Self: 'there is something *inside the individual,* which knows what to do and how to act. . . . For Kant this was the experience of the categorical imperative. For Jung it was the experience of the self', notes Nagy (1991: 37). The inner meaning and potential of man for Jung is the Self, the God-image that bears one's teleological perspective. Apparently, Jung's ultimate ambition was to ground his archetypes on a variety of philosophical concepts; however, this plurality of ideas that are introduced for this purpose may have cost him the epistemological consistency and accuracy – in both phenomenological and ontological terms – such a central concept merits.

The Hegelian influence and Jung's psychological reduction of the Self

Focusing on the inner experience of the God-image as the prime epistemological criterion, Jung takes the decisive step to bridge the distance between the psychic level and the spiritual realms by identifying the 'God image' with the archetype of the Self. In a well-known statement he explains,

> It is only through the psyche that we can establish that God acts upon us, but we are unable to distinguish whether these actions emanate from God or from the unconscious . . . the God image does not coincide with the unconscious as such, but with a special content of it, namely the archetype of the Self. It is this archetype from which we can no longer distinguish the God-image empirically.
>
> (1952a: para. 757)

The psychic level, according to this excerpt, is the recipient of the 'acts of God', yet we are unable to know the exact source of these acts. In the Christian tradition, as discussed earlier, 'image' and 'likeness' are inextricably intertwined: although they indicate different ontological levels, the dynamism of the one is hidden within the other; one cannot consider the full potential of the image without acknowledging the perspective of 'the likeness'. By affirming the former and explicitly refuting the latter, Jung adopts an ambiguous position with crucial consequences with respect to his theory on the spiritual dimensions of individuation. Although the concept of Self is primarily a *teleologically* defined archetype – as the wholeness attained in mature stages of life – Jung appears not to endorse its spiritual and/or metaphysical dimension.

This approach entails serious consequences with regard to both God-image and God as such. Due to the preference of Jung's 'epistemological ignorance', he states that 'the human intellect can never answer this question [of God's existence]', because ultimately, 'the idea of God is an absolutely necessary psychological function of an irrational nature, which has nothing whatever to do with the question of God's existence' (1917/1943: para. 110). With regard to Kant's influence on Jung in the context of the 'common consent argument', it appears that the Kantian 'supreme being' and/or the 'thing-in-itself' as well as the Jungian idea of God, the archetype of 'an all-powerful Being' (ibid.), can both serve as a '*symbolical* anthropomorphism' (Nagy 1991: 153). In this respect, Jung's views match with Kant's ideas; but in the final step, Jung 'goes beyond Kant . . . namely that our thoughts about supreme reality point toward something that is really there. Jung gave even more credit to those thoughts . . . [as] facts of experience' (ibid). While Jung does not consider these 'facts of experience' separately from his own archetypal ideas of God-image(s), the spiritual potential of these experiences – emanating from God's idea/acts – appears nevertheless to require re-evaluation. Despite Jung's undeniable contribution to verify one's inner spiritual experience, as a primarily psychological experience, the spiritual dynamics of 'image-towards-likeness' are critically missing from his theory.

We discussed earlier the notion of 'supervenience' as an unexpected or inexplicable impact from a superior level to an inferior, as a *non-reductive* approach. Despite the fact that Jung implements, in Papadopoulos's definition (2006: 34), 'an epistemology' of finality and explicitly argues that 'causality' and 'finality' constitute the twofold approach necessary for the explanation of psychological facts, he is reluctant to acknowledge a certain 'inexplicable impact' of the spiritual-as-metaphysical level on the psychic level and experience. Jung thus consistently applies a reduction of the ontological depth of his archetypal theory to principally psychological dimensions.

It is now possible to understand the fact that Jung, wishing to avoid philosophical and/or metaphysical nuances in his archetypes and not being entirely satisfied with the unapproachable 'thing-in-itself', pursued additional theoretical underpinnings in Hegel's phenomenology. Hegel's fundamental position, clearly opposed to the Kantian unknowable 'thing-in-itself', is that when the 'thing-in-itself' starts to be investigated by the consciousness,

> it ceases to be the in-itself, and becomes something that is the *in-itself* only *for consciousness*. And this then is the True: the being-for-consciousness of this in-itself. Or, in other words, this is the *essence*, or the *object* of

consciousness. This new concept contains the nothingness of the first, it is what experience has made of it.

(Hegel 1807/1977: 55)

By this decisive step, Hegel departs from Kantian experience through 'reduction-realisation'. This is the *dialectic* method of the initial *thesis, antithesis,* and *synthesis* within 'what experience has made' of the first object. Such an experience is knowledge itself, because 'this *dialectical* movement which consciousness exercises on itself and affects both its knowledge and its object, is precisely what is called *experience* [*Erfahrung*]' (ibid). Theorising on the constant movements of consciousness in comprehending the *being-in-itself* as a new object of *being-for-us,* Hegel postulates that 'the way to *Science* is itself already *Science,* and hence, in virtue of its content, is the Science of the *experience of consciousness*' (ibid.: 56). Despite contemporary criticism,[25] phenomenology aspires to a constant development of consciousness up to the point at which appearance will become identical with essence – that is, the 'absolute knowledge'. By adopting the world's possibilities and perspectives through history, sciences, religion, and arts (all involved in the development of consciousness), one's experience expands and deepens towards the Absolute. This is the process in which our existence (*dasein* or the deeper 'self') is a 'gathering of the world as a human world', both collective and personal, in Brooke's concise definition (1991: 174).

The first stage of phenomenology, the 'consciousness', is in fact an actual progression of the experience from sense-certainty to perception and to understanding – terms used also by Kant in his process of reduction-realisation (see Hegel 1807/1977: 58ff).[26] It is important here to recall the distinction between experience as a 'state of mind' (*Erlebnis*), an approach of aesthetic experience that Kant narrowed down, and (the more profound) experience with the Hegelian sense (*Erfahrung*), which presents a challenge that we should 'change our minds'. Thus, the sequence-order of levels of the individual experience is closely correlated with specific features of consciousness-cognitive functions; the more aspects of the consciousness that are activated, the greater the experience is by the way of this phenomenological approach.

Jung's complex notion of an unambiguously 'dialectical process of individuation' (1958/1959: para. 1505), which in fact is 'dialectical' as both method and process, is the integration of all possible opposites: the final goal of this process, the Self, 'is a union of opposites *par excellence . . .* it represents in every respect thesis and antithesis, and at the same time synthesis, (Jung 1944: para. 22). Jung maintains that '[w]e name a thing, *from a certain point of view,* good or bad, high or low, right or left. . . . Here the antithesis is just as factual and real as the thesis' (1952c: para. 457). At these points one can recognize striking similarities between the two systems; indeed, Jung later in his life wrote that there exists 'a remarkable coincidence between certain tenets of Hegelian philosophy and my findings concerning the collective unconscious' (Jung 1976: 502). But this was not Jung's initial opinion of Hegel, whose language Jung characterises as 'arrogant' and views as a man 'caged in the edifice of his own words . . . pompously gesticulating in his prison' (*MDR*: 69).

Jung's negative attitude towards Hegel has been extensively discussed along with the argument that he never openly acknowledged the obvious loan from Hegel's dialectics (see Papadopoulos 1980; Eckman 1986; Rychlak 1991; Clarke 1992). Papadopoulos's argument is that Jung's reaction to Hegel 'might be a result of his own problematic of the Other', which 'may be understood in terms of Jung's projected fears of his unconscious' (1980: 436). Due to the fact that both the individuation process towards wholeness/Self and Hegel's progressive-consciousness towards the Absolute can be understood as a synthesis of elements from different realms and ontological levels, it appears challenging to further examine the opposing antithesis-as-other in both these processes.

Brooke remarks that for Jung, 'the Other has significance only as he/she/it facil-itates inner psychological development, *for* it is one's relationship with the Self that is the measure of individuation' (1991: 118; see also Kelly 1993: 80–1). The fact that the other is for Jung not the individual other but the Self is clear when he speaks of the achievement of wholeness, only through soul's 'other side, which is always found in a "You".' (1946: para. 454); but he rushes to add, 'I do not, of course, mean the synthesis or identification of two individuals, but the conscious union of the ego with everything that has been projected onto the "you". Hence wholeness is the result of an intra-psychic process' (1946: para. 245, note 16). Jung's tendency is to include all individual potentials into his notion of the Self, which rather absorbs any interpersonal relation (cf. Friedman 1985: 26ff, Samuels 1985: 115). Papadopoulos analysed the dynamics of the 'Other' in certain stages of Jung's life and suggests that 'once having climbed on the problematic of the Other, the centre shifts from the Ego to the Self . . . [where] no problematic any longer exists, nor any "Other"'. (1991: 88).

On the other hand, the priority that Jung's epistemology attached to experi-ence could be considered as being 'in line with Schopenhauer's sceptical episte-mology . . . insisted that we know only what is within' (Nagy 1991: 79). Jung's persistence on the experience 'within' obviously diverges from the final poten-tial of Hegel's three 'social counterparts' of consciousness: the Spirit (History and Culture), Religion (Nature, Arts, and God) and Absolute Knowledge. More-over, Jung's theory of integration of opposites does not work systematically but rather intuitively. In Brooke's further clarification, Jung 'does not question the ontological premises of terms as central as psyche' and appears to ignore that his 'continuing use of psychoanalytic terms such as psyche, and conscious and unconscious belies an *ontological difference* in his emerging conceptions' (Brooke 1991: 88, italics mine). This issue becomes crucial when Jung's concept of God-image/Self – essentially different from Christ-as-symbol – is contrasted with Hegel's interpretation of the presence of God in the subjective psyche, which stands for the actual Spirit in the world:

> The Self is a union of opposites *par excellence,* and this is where it dif-fers essentially from the Christ-symbol . . . The opposition between light and good on the one hand and darkness and evil on the other is left in a

state of open conflict, since Christ simply represents good, and his counterpart, the devil, evil. . . . The self, however, is absolutely paradoxical in that it represents . . . thesis and antithesis and at the same time synthesis.

(Jung 1944: para. 22)

But Hegel states that 'the Spirit' mediates towards human depths and that 'it is only through this mediation that it itself is subjectively present as the divestment into the objective union of love and its infinite anguish. This . . . [is] actual Spirit, God dwelling in his community' (Hegel 1985: 140). Jung's equivalent position could be that 'God wants to become *wholly* man; in other words to reproduce himself in his own dark creature' (1952a: para. 741). As we shall see, although this dark creature, for Jung, includes what has been excluded from the dominant interpretation of the Christian 'mythos', such as the body and the feminine, by indicating a 'reproduction' of God and a 'descent' to human level Jung in fact attributes to God characteristics that differentiate him from the 'Spirit of God' in a Hegelian sense – that is, 'dwelling in his community' (cf. Kelly 1993: 145ff).

Jung takes this risk to apply to God psychological features, perhaps because he might have realised that many Hegelian ideas were a projection of metaphysical truths and values. In fact, the Absolute, as containing and reconciling all opposites, 'was anathema to Jung's way of thinking', as he was fully aware 'of the inescapable presence of evil in the world . . . too massively obvious to be conjured away by clever philosophical arguments' (Clarke 1992: 66). The issue of evil is therefore a plausible *antithesis* that tremendously appeals to Jung's theoretical system to be resolved, as we shall further discuss in Chapter 8. Consequently, the Self does not appear to fully represent Hegel's *Absolute,* the *telos* of a dialectical process of stages of conscious experience (including the individual Other, History, Arts, and Religion), thereby affirming the multiplicity of levels. In the light of all these points, it is apparent that Jung is neither a consistent Kantian, as he makes a 'dubious use of Kant' in his definition of the archetypes (Bishop 2000: 192), nor a classical phenomenologist insofar as the individual Other is ultimately absorbed into the Self (Papadopoulos 1991: 88), as shown above.

Jung's epistemology ultimately permits an interpretation of the 'acts of God' through one's subjective cognitive function, insofar as by using 'our judgment . . . we are faced with the inexorable fact that . . . some acts of God are good and some bad' (Jung 1958/1959: para. 1667). Accordingly, whereas Hegel views the Absolute-Spirit as something wherein God's will participates as the culmination of conscious development, Jung treats God's acts within psychic subjective personal judgment and understanding. It is then understood that, despite striking similarities with the Hegelian dialectics, Jung deviates significantly from Hegel in his construal of wholeness/Self as full of conflicts – which appears to be defined only within a psychological antithesis-Other and not as an Other beyond psychic boundaries. Contrary to Jung, and to some extent closer to Maximus – that introduces a final union of opposites within the Logos's principles – *logoi* – Hegel follows a more consistent and progressive approach to wholeness/Absolute. It is precisely what Jung was reluctant to fully embrace, being thus trapped into the crucial limitations of his own ambiguous epistemology.

Maximian '*logoi*' vis-à-vis archetypal theory: ontological and phenomenological perspectives

Both Jung and Maximus lived in epochs in which major shifts shake the hitherto socio-cultural traditions towards unprecedented dynamics. Jung experiences the transition from the industrial revolution to the liberating post-modern societies of the 20th century, whereas Maximus witnesses the shift from the stability of the Justinian Empire to the challenges of a confrontation with religious heresies such as the *monoenergism* and eventually with the slowly emerging Islamic world. These shifts stimulated an elaboration of the rich philosophical tradition in both Maximus' and Jung's milieu, which leads to formulations of innovative concepts that shape their understanding of the psyche through, respectively, the principles-*logoi* and the archetypes.

Maximus does not address Christian faith as a mere 'religion' through a systematic analysis of doctrines, rules, and rituals but primarily within an experiential dimension that renders his system to be a 'symphony of experience' – clearly aligned with Jung's statement that 'I am an empiricist'. Yet, contrary to Jung's reduction of the spiritual dimension to the psychological, Maximus introduces an ontological system absolutely open to psychic experience, through the principles-*logoi,* that permits the spiritual continuum to range up to the metaphysical level of a personal God. A sharp distinction between the created psychosomatic world, that is the spiritual-as-psychological, and the uncreated spiritual-as-metaphysical world is thus drawn. The ontological gulf and divisions in the Maximian system are mercifully mediated by the Logos-Christ, through the integration of all 'opposites': amongst male-female, paradise-inhabited world, heaven-earth, sensory-intelligible realms, and created-uncreated nature. Man is consequently called to follow Logos's work by advancing at this hierarchy of divisions in order to acquire the spiritual knowledge through the 'logoi of beings': these are the fundamental/essential principles of creation, development, and perfection of all beings. In this way, man is gifted to ultimately bridge ontology with phenomenology by developing a spiritual knowledge-as-experience.

Almost 12 centuries later, Kant and Hegel, despite the opposition between the unknowable 'thing-in-itself' and the progressively knowable-through-consciousness 'Absolute', also established a scale of knowledge-as-experience: whilst Kant classifies the things as *phenomena, noumena,* and *in-itself,* Hegel applies six stages of consciousness: consciousness, self-consciousness, Reason, and the social-historical counterparts Spirit, Religion, Absolute. Although Hegel does not refer to God within the principles used by Maximus' ontology, the notion of God is still active (unchanged in Hegel, rather agnostically neutral in Kant), at least to the extent of acknowledgement of God's 'perfect will' for his world. Despite the different point of gravity between the ontological 'logoi of beings' in Maximus and the progressive 'consciousness' in phenomenology, the latter still 'articulates an ontology and epistemology of ambiguity by exploring the existential tensions between the revealed and the concealed . . . ' (Brooke 1991: 245). Consequently, both Kant and Hegel maintain a relative 'openness' to the ontological potential of beings, which Maximus viewed from a metaphysical angle by attributing all sources of genesis and development of beings to a personal God.

There are strong indications that Jung differentiates from Kant and Hegel, with regard to the limitations of the archetypal theory and the reduction of the spiritual to the psychological. Jung misinterprets Kant's 'thing-in-itself' as well as Hegel's 'consciousness-experience': while selectively applying aspects of both notions to his archetypes, he ultimately reduces their ontological perspectives. Perhaps not surprisingly, and despite the fact that he establishes a fascinating multi-dimensional archetypal theory that finds the highest expression into the archetype of Self/God-image, Jung ultimately fails to be fully aware of the dynamics and perspectives of his key notion: by contending to 'eschew any metaphysical or philosophical consideration' (1938/1940: para. 2), Jung renders the key concept of the Self confined to his 'psychologism'. In this respect, the Self cannot 'release' and expand its real potential to a full ontological range, in particular in metaphysics. This is a point that, as shown above, was extensively addressed and critically reconsidered by certain post–Jungians.

These challenging positions could shape an outline of juxtaposition of Maximian insights on the foundations of the psyche with Jungian archetypal theory that is constrained within psychological boundaries. Jungian archetypes find their current understanding mainly phenomenologically, via a '*functional* way as structuring our images of, or as metaphors for, typical patterns of emotional behaviour' (Samuels 1985: 44). In addition, taken into consideration is also the 'polarity – the positive and negative . . . or instinctual and spiritual' (ibid.: 53). This archetypal bipolarity (negative-positive, instinctual-spiritual) is of utmost importance in terms of both epistemological and therapeutic dimensions, as it reveals the inner dynamics and opposites that call for integration. Jung, however, does not treat this polarity systematically when referring to the spiritual dimension as such. Instead of subjecting the archetypal theory to a 'transcendental realisation-experience' – as Kant did to his 'thing-in-itself' by revolving all the psychic functions to investigate its perspectives and stages of realisation – Jung maintains that a solely psychological approach suffices for interpreting links between religious dogma and archetypal manifestations.

Despite the application of insights of modern philosophy – though subjected to his personal interpretation – and whilst he overcame Freud's reduction of the psychological to the somatic, Jung did not avoid the reduction of the spiritual phenomena to the psychological level, for the obvious fear of being criticised as a philosopher with metaphysical interests. This is apparent in the Jungian theory of opposites, according to which 'all opposites are of God' and man 'becomes a vessel filled with divine conflict' (1952a: para. 659). There is nowhere a consistent clarification as to how and under which principles psychological characteristics and ideas could be attributed to God's idea. Jung declares that the

'Summum Bonum [highest Good] is so good, so high, so perfect, but so remote that it is entirely beyond our grasp' (Jung 1976: 435), not permitting any mediation between metaphysics and the psyche – as in Maximus' systems of the mediated ontological divisions. For Jung, God, 'the ultimate reality' represents 'all the qualities of its creation, virtue, reason, intelligence, kindness, consciousness *and their opposites,* to our mind a complete paradox' (ibid.): it is an epistemology that reduces and gives little space to an independent spiritual dimension.

Jung followed both the Kantian and post–Kantian philosophical currents that ultimately, although in different ways, aspired to a conceptualization of the individual self beyond any external authorities, such as religion, political structures, or even nature as an idea of human rootedness. That the notion of the unconscious implicitly was the subject of most of the previous and contemporary to Jung philosophical strands is more evident nowadays through systematic research. For instance, Ellenberger explores the origins of the notion of the unconscious long before Freud, in Nietzsche's thought, for which human acts are manifestations of the unconscious realm: 'Even the [Freudian] term "id" (*Das Es*) originates from Nietzsche' (Ellenberger 1970: 277, citing Nietzsche's *Zarathustra* I, VII, 46–8). Ffychte, on the other hand, analyses further the dynamics of the notion of the unconscious from the Enlightenment to German idealism (Fichte, Schubart, Schelling, et al.) and develops the notion of the 'liberal unconscious' as a need for 'a new structural weight in the depiction of the individuals life' (Ffychte 2012: 22). In a more revealing way, the liberal unconscious is 'an absolutely necessary part of a theorisation of human independence' from external authorities or pre-existing determinative cause–effect constructs, internal laws, and so forth (ibid.: 32) – an independence better understood within the transitions towards liberality that the European context subjected historically in the last three centuries.

Although Jung was not fully aware of the potential perspectives of the applied philosophical ideas to his own system, he attributed to the notion of the unconscious a unique characteristic by viewing the deeper psyche, the Self, as principally related to the notion of God-image. Yet Jung ultimately restrained the fuller perspective of the Self towards the Kantian 'thing-in-itself' as well as the Hegelian Absolute that comprises forms-stages of a progressive conscious experience. In this respect, Jung appears being neither a consistent Kantian, ignoring the ontological potential of the 'thing-in-itself', nor a classical phenomenologist, challenging the reality of the real 'Other' as fundamental to psychic development. On the other hand, by synthesising inspirationally his predecessors' insights and personal intuition, Jung's archetypes exclusively explain the reason the psychic energy is formulated and conveyed through certain structured and innate archetypal ideas-images (i.e. mother, father, hero, etc.), that are at the same time collective patterns of behaviour and interaction with others. Such insights neither Maximus' thought nor phenomenology addressed and explored. Jung's insights and theory on development can now be explored in detail in the following chapter.

Notes

1. We may refer to the theology of Symeon the New Theologian, 10th century AD. This was to be continued with Gregory Palamas (14th century) until the period of *The Philokalia,* a compilation of ascetic texts in which Maximus' writings cover the second of its original five volumes (See *The Philokalia: The Complete Text.* Vol. II, pp. 48–305. Compiled by St Nikodimus of the Holy Mountain and St Makarios of Corinth. Edited and translated by G. E. H. Palmer, P. Sherrard, and K. Ware, London: Faber & Faber, 1981). Maximus' epoch can therefore be considered a productive period of genuine Christian theology, unlike the period that followed that 'became polemical and somehow lost its old fullness' (Runciman 1933: 242).

2. See Maximus' extensive biography in *PG* 90: 68A–109B, and for Syriac version, see Brock 2003.

3. The Emperor Justinian had died 15 years before and achieved re-elevating the Empire to the glory of the past: from Spain to Persia and from the North to Egypt, the citizens of the Empire could travel freely.

4. We will discuss and analyse Origen's positions in more detail in the next sections.

5. Heresies, according to which Christ had only the divine will/energy and not both the divine and human wills/energies, that means a reduction to his anthropological capacities. At this time, Maximus was living in North Africa near Carthage under the instructions of his spiritual mentor Sophronius, who later became archbishop of Jerusalem.

6. For an excellent analysis of the politicizations of theology, see Balthasar 1988: 31–3.

7. See Sherwood 1955: 24ff.

8. Pre–Socratics, in particular Democritus, considered man as microcosm (see *Diels* B34; Thunberg 1985: 133ff). Plato in the *Timaeus* postulates that cosmos came into existence as a 'living creature endowed with soul and reason' (*Timaeus* 30B, cited in Louth 1996: 64).

9. It is a holistic and synthetic view of both the visible and the invisible, by evolving further Gregory of Nazianzus's vision that man was created by God 'as second cosmos, a great universe within a little one' (*Orationes* 38, 11: *PG* 36, 321C–24B). Maximus develops it on the ground of Dionysius's idea that symbols of the intelligible realm are hidden in our body (*Coelesti Hierarchia* 15, 3: *PG* 3, 332BC).

10. Basil the Great adopted the term 'tropos of existence' to signify the hypostasis of Holy Spirit (*Contra Sabellianos et Arium et Anomaeos, PG* 31: 613A), and so did Gregory of Nyssa (*Contra Eunomium* 1, *GNO* 1: 170). For the impact of the Cappadocian fathers on Maximus, see Berthold 1982 and Blowers 1992.

11. *Genesis* 1, 26: 'God said: let us make man in our image, after our likeness'; and *Genesis* 2, 7: 'man became as a living being'. See also 1, 27: 'so God created man in His own image, male and female He created them'.

12. Gregory of Nyssa, *De Opificio Hominis* 16: *PG* 45: 185C; see also Thunberg 1995: 114–8.

13. Regarding the body–soul relationship, it is important at this point to elucidate the differences between the Hellenic and the Hebrew traditions following Ware's analysis. The biblical tradition of the composite nature is mostly based on the Hebrew holistic approach: 'The Hebrew conception of personhood is embodied and physical; I do not *have* a body, I *am* the body – I am "flesh-animated-by soul"'. (Ware 1997: 91). In fact, psyche in biblical text means precisely 'living being' (*Genesis* 2, 7), as the whole man includes the dynamic of both soma and soul. With the advent of those Church fathers well versed in Greek philosophy and the dualistic perception of man, the biblical tradition was superseded by the strong stream of the Hellenic view of soul and body as separated components.

14. See *De Opificio Hominis* 12: 177BC; 29: 236AB.

15. Jung postulated the archetypes as 'organs of the pre-rational psyche' (1935/1953: para. 845), as entities that can regulate behaviour.

16. The pre–Socratic philosopher Heraclitus postulates that *logos* pervades everything; but whereas *logos* manifests itself in the individuals, it 'is set apart from all things' (*Diels* 108), and more emphatically, 'the psyche has *logos* which increases itself' (*Diels* 115; Snell 1960: 19, 146). Maximus might have borrowed the term *logos* from Philo of Alexandria (1st century AD), who developed the Stoic idea of *logos:* for Philo, 'the *Logos* becomes a mediator between the transcendent God and the world, and has both transcendent and immanent aspects' (Louth 1981: 26; see also Thunberg 1995: 73ff; Balthasar 1988: 117ff; Staniloae 1990; Rossum 1993). Origen applies this term as a creative principle of beings and distinguishes the *logoi* from the true Logos, the God (see Origen, *On John* 2.3.22, trans. Allan Menzies and Ante-Nicene, Edinburg: T&T Clark; reprinted in 1995, by Grand Rapids, Mich.: W.B. Eerdmans).

17. *Nous* is translated as *Intellectual-Principle* by MacKenna, (in Plotinus, *The Enneads,* trans. S. MacKenna, rev. B.S. Page, Faber and Faber 1971), as *Universal Intellect* by Armstrong (1940), and as *Intelligence-nous* by Louth (1981: 36).

18. Origen's controversial influence on Maximus has been considered from different perspectives (see Sherwood 1955: 72–102; Thunberg 1995: 11, 82, 107, 134; Balthasar 1988: 81–4). In fact, rather than exercising a genuine influence, Origen seems to have provided an impetus for Maximus to correct and develop his precursor's ideas. As Blowers concludes, Maximus was 'wise enough not to make "Origenism" merely a foil for his own work' (1995: 654). Whatever the influence was, what is important is Maximus' unique craftiness in elaborating insights towards a plausible ontology with innovative characteristics.

19. The knowledge 'by heart' appears to be an influence from Macarius's *Homilies* and Diadochus of Photice, according to Louth (1981: 110–127; 1996: 25).

20. The energies of God will be the key concept of Gregory Palamas, 14th century AD, who states that 'by saying he [God] is life, goodness and so forth, and giving Him these names, [it is] because of the revelatory energies and powers of the super-essential' (*Triads* III: 2, 7–8, see Rossum 1993).

21. See also the differences between Neoplatonics and Christian thought as previously discussed in Chapter 2.

22. Kant's *transcendental realisation* starts from a 'transcendental object' prior to any experience/realisation (Kant 1781/1998: A109). This process proceeds through the functions of 'sensibility' and 'understanding' and concludes either to objects of appearance as *phenomena* or to intelligible objects as *noumena,* respectively (ibid.: A249–50, A256). The first stage of *deduction-realisation* is mediated by the 'sensible intuition' (a kind of a reception of mind by a sensory impact) and through the *a-priori forms* of sensibility (space and time); these forms are not external, but alongside the a-priori forms of thought, the *categories* (i.e. quantity, quality, modality) exist as innate 'patterns' of perception. The second stage consists of mediation through (a) 'understanding' and the *a-priori categories* and (b) 'imagination'. All modes of perception are ultimately subjected to an intellectual synthesis into a 'unity of apperception' at a third stage, which takes place in a theoretical location, our *imagination:* this is 'a blind though indispensable function of the soul, without which we would have no cognition at all' (A78/B104). Thus, our experience has both sensory and intellectual 'domains' as homocentric spheres (see Buchdahl 1992: 18, fig. 1.2). Kant emphasizes the complementary role of the psychic functions: 'with us *understanding* and *sensibility* can determine an object *only in combination.* If we separate them, then we have intuitions without concepts, or concepts without intuitions, but in either case representations that we cannot relate to any determinate object' (B314).

23. It is the case in which Kant might 'have doffed his hat, in playful gesture, to the ghost of the Leibnizian monad' as Buchdahl remarks (1992: 86). 'Monad' is non-material, an eternal-spiritual entity, which conveys to the beings divine qualities, functioning as an

entelechy – an obvious Aristotelian loan (*Monadology* § 61–9, in Leibniz, G. W., 1985, *Monadology and Other Philosophical Essays,* trans. Paul Schrecker and Anne Martin Schrecker, Indianapolis: Bobbs-Merrill Educational Publishing). By monad, a reflection of 'fulguration from the divinity' (ibid.: § 47), Leibniz devised an entity *mediating* between two realms, the *monadic* and the *phenomenal world,* respectively, which lies at the metaphysical pole of the 'spiritual'. Kant and his descendants ultimately rejected any discussion about a 'mediator' between the two realms.

24. Lucy Huskinson summarizes Jung's misunderstanding of Kant: 'The archetype is at once constitutive and beyond experience. Because it is constitutive, Jung is wrong to correlate it with Kant's "Idea", and because it is beyond experience, Jung is wrong to correlate it with Kant's "category"' (2004: 78).

25. For example, the application of the development through history of the self-consciousness to justify knowledge *prior* to such 'process' completion makes Heidemann's claim that phenomenology fails as a theory of epistemic justification (2008: 19) reasonable. However, phenomenological approaches are still applied as epistemological tools in scientific fields and sometimes serve as a new mode of ontology (see Horstmann 2008), which, without refuting the Absolute, is not at all based on metaphysical assumptions. Jung seems to have grasped this versatile reasoning, which served to verify the priority given to the psychic experience/events.

26. Phenomenology proceeds within the sequence of the progressive forms of consciousness: 'Consciousness, self-Consciousness, and Reason'. These are considered to be the basic divisions of *individual* experience, whereas the triad 'Spirit, Religion, and Absolute Knowledge' are the respective counterparts-divisions of *social* experience (see the diagram in Norman 1976: 23–4). Apparently the social counterparts serve towards the process of integration of consciousness, a position that can easily be compared to the individuation process.

5

THE DIRECTIONS AND
THE STAGES OF PSYCHIC
DEVELOPMENT

Having so far discussed the main Jungian points on religion as well the foundations of the psyche in Jung's and Maximus' understanding, we can now proceed by exploring in detail the processes of psychological and spiritual development in Jung's and Maximus' psychic models. Jung's central views on religion consider it imperative to 'understand' and 'experience' – in psychological terms – the meanings and messages of the religious doctrines, narratives, and symbols. We shall therefore explore how both Jung and Maximus describe development through processes-as-metaphors, which are grounded, respectively, in the archetypes and the essential principles/*logoi* of beings. Due to the different foundations of the psyche according to Jung and Maximus, the directions and final goals of development differ in their models, too. The Jungian process of *individuation* is primarily directed to the plurality of the archetypal dynamics following the inherent potential of psychic images, in particular of the God-image or the Self. This potential could be described as a compound 'horizontal' perspective due to the absence of a clear spiritual direction – as further analysis will show. On the other hand, Maximus' model of spiritual progress towards *deification* principally addresses the spiritual direction as 'ascension' towards God, from the God-image to God-likeness. Expanding Jung's conception of an immanent *a priori* potential, Maximus views man as being endowed with the capability of experiencing the concealed spiritual qualities of the created world, the *logoi*. This is a different conception of development that can be perceived as a 'vertical' mode of progress towards God's ultimate virtue, divine love.

Individuation as a 'natural' process: from the 'ego' to the 'Self'

As we previously discussed, Maximus reconsidered Origen's developmental scheme *becoming-rest-movement (fall)* to *becoming-movement-rest (perfection)*. This movement indicates a mono-dimensional direction from man towards the divine, which, regardless of its ontological ground, can be juxtaposed with *individuation,* a process towards the inner Self. Jung himself understands individuation as a 'biological process . . . by no means a case of mystical speculations, but of clinical observations' (Jung 1952c: para. 460), basically referring to a natural tendency or a 'democratic process', open to all potentialities (see Samuels 1985: 110). The first issue that emerges from this juxtaposition is the question of a 'monistic' or a 'pluralistic' understanding of the directions of psychic development. W. James speaks of this 'monistic form', or 'philosophy of the absolute', and the 'pluralistic form', or 'radical empiricism':

> the former conceiving that the divine exists authentically only when the world is experienced all at once in its absolute totality, whereas radical empiricism allows that the absolute sum-total of things may never be actually experienced or realised in that shape at all, and that a disseminated, distributed, or incompletely unified appearance is the only form that reality may yet have achieved.
>
> (James 1909: 43–4, *A Pluralistic Universe*)

It is apparent that the monism of James's 'philosophical absolute' is aligned with Maximus' experience of the 'authentically existing divine' and bespeaks the absolute/God's totality. On the contrary, the 'pluralistic form' or 'radical empiricism' suggests that the 'disseminated' psychic experience is found at the opposites of the conscious and unconscious territories (e.g. good and evil, instinctual and spiritual). Both the monistic and pluralistic forms carry, respectively, the dynamics of God-divine and Self-wholeness and might set the framework of psychic development. It is precisely within this framework that pluralism of directions and choices is contrasted to eclecticism/monism as well as to 'antagonism', another critical element for psychic growth towards a 'democratic process' (see Samuels 1989: 12). Despite the antithesis between the directions of psychic growth suggested by monistic and pluralistic forms, both Jung and Maximus appear affirmative of a *descriptive* mode of development, as we can follow in the next paragraphs.

Individuation is the actual process of 'the conscious-coming-to-terms with one's own inner centre (psychic nucleus) or Self' (von-Franz 1964: 169). It is a complex process of development in stages, by encountering certain archetypes (shadow, persona, anima-animus, hero, etc.), which 'begins with a wounding of the personality' and ends at 'a completely new and different orientation toward life' (ibid.: 254). Indeed, Jung initially viewed individuation as 'a process of *differentiation*' (1921/1971: para. 757) that the ego-consciousness subjects to, which 'must lead to more intense and broader collective relationships and not to isolation' (ibid.: 758). These 'collective relationships' constitute an expansion of the ego not only within the psychic but also within the interpersonal and socio-cultural levels.[1]

The process of individuation commences with the entirely undifferentiated state of psychic life and proceeds towards differentiation through the encounter with certain archetypal motives, amongst which the image-fantasy of the mother is, for Jung, the most critical. Corresponding, but rather less crucial, is the impact of the image of the father (see Jung 1909/1949; Samuels 1985: 162ff, 1989: 66ff). Jung chose the metaphor-symbol of *uroboros* (a serpent biting its tail, Jung 1944: *passim, fig.* 13), a symbolical and mythological figure of 'prima materia', to describe the primordial stage of life whereby any development occurs (1937b: para. 401–4, 460). Thus, the child's initial relation to its mother is depicted in the stage of the maternal *uroboros* from which the child's ego must gradually separate and differentiate. There have been different viewpoints between the developmental and classical schools of analytical psychology, as represented by Fordham, pointing out circles of 'integration-disintegration' (1957, 1985), and Neumann, highlighting the mother-carrier of the child's self (1954, 1955), respectively. Despite these differences, both schools develop Jung's positions in an affirmative way as regards the significance of a 'transpersonal' mother archetype. Thus, Neumann emphasizes that '[t]he dependence of the sequence "child-man-ego-consciousness" on the sequence "mother-earth-nature-unconscious" illustrates the relation of the personal to the transpersonal and the reliance of the one upon the other' (Neumann 1954: 43). These 'positive' conceptual interpretations of development also appear shaping Stein's formulation of the stages of individuation as particularly related to the mother (first containment/nurturance stage), to the father (second adapting/adjusting stage), and to the social-cultural or religious agents (third centring/ integrating stage; Stein 2006: 196ff).

The socio-cultural realm is the inexhaustible source of images from which emerge attitudes that can compensate ego-conscious norms during the ego's development. Jung views development as 'mak[ing] progress in self-culture' (1928a: para. 327), whereas Edinger (1972) links the 'religious function' of the psyche with individuation, where the images, myths, and symbols of one's particular cultural context are vital for his/her development. As shown earlier, 'cultural complexes' function as aggregates of ideas and images around an archetypal core that connects the individuation with the collective (Singer 2010: 234) and thus precipitate the 'progress' within one's cultural context.

In fact, the interpersonal and socio-cultural expansion of one's consciousness could be perceived as addressing the *spiritual continuum* should we recall the evolutionary relationship between the psychic and spiritual dimension (Chapter 2). Jung, indeed, considers the Self 'as the highest value and supreme dominant in the psychic hierarchy' identical with the God-image (1951/1959: para. 170). Moreover, he contends that 'Christ is our nearest analogy of the self' (ibid.: para. 79). However, the bipolar nature of the Self-as-archetype (good and bad poles) cannot claim a full analogy to Christ's life because 'the other half appears in the Antichrist' (ibid.). What the Self generates is thus a mutual confrontation of these opposites and splits: it is 'an integration, a bridging of the split in the personality caused by the instincts, striving apart in different and mutually contradictory directions' (1951/1959: para. 73). These 'contradictory directions' must be transcended and resolved into constructive psychic aspects. It is because individuation is 'connected with the *transcendent function* . . . since this function creates individual lines of development' (Jung 1921/1971: para. 759). It can be understood now that these 'mutually contradictory' directions, alongside the 'individual lines', as personal developmental perspectives, provide a full description of the individuation dynamics advancing in a manifold of potentialities.

Jung's understanding of the psychic growth is also affirmative to a developmental perspective that Bockus calls the 'centralising tendency' (1990: 45), through which one can establish relations to his/her lost 'nucleus' of inner lifer. Jung uses the term 'mantala symbolism', a definite category of symbols 'that refer directly and exclusively to the new centre as it comes to the consciousness' (1944: para. 45). Nevertheless, the Self is 'not only the centre, but also the whole circumference which embraces both conscious and unconscious; it is the centre of this totality . . .' (ibid.: para. 44) explains Jung. The plurality of the paths or 'individual lines of development' leading to this centre-nucleus is thus paradoxically connected with the 'circumference', which symbolizes the expansion of the ego and its integration with the unconscious elements of the Self. It is at this stage that the meanings of the symbols release the 'tension of opposite functions' and 'redeem us through their very paradox' (Jarrett 1979: 325).

The anticipating wholeness of individuation, as a 'natural' process, engages all possible aspects of life. In this respect, evil cannot be excluded but could play its vital role in an unprecedented radical manner: 'in any pluralistic metaphysics the problems that evil presents are practical, not speculative' (James 1909: 124). Jung appears at certain points to apply such a 'practical use' of God-image and evil, within the development-expansion of the idea of the Trinity to a pattern of quaternity (1942/1948: para. 258). Jung goes as far as saying that individuation could also be seen as a 'source of all evil' (1943/1948: para. 244), inasmuch as psychic wholeness 'must' incorporate the missing 'fourth element', and thus evil. Evil for Jung is one of the negative sides of personality that needs to be integrated within individuation, incorporated in the archetypes of *shadow* and *persona*. Jung states that

> If it has been believed hitherto that the human shadow was the source of all evil, it can now be ascertained on closer investigation that the unconscious man, that is, his shadow, does not consist only of morally reprehensive tendencies, but also displays a number of good qualities, such as normal instincts, appropriate reactions, realistic insights, creative impulses etc. On this level of understanding, evil appears more as a distortion, a deformation . . . and misapplication of facts that in themselves are natural.
>
> (Jung 1951/1959: para. 423)

In order to dissociate the person 'of the false wrappings of the persona' (1928a: para. 269), Jung worked out a restoration of the 'good qualities' of evil, immanent but 'distorted' in one's unconscious life. Jung claimed that one actually has to incorporate the positive aspects of his or her evil/dark side (1934/1950: para. 567; 1955/1956: para. 470–1; 1959). Debating with Jung, Father Victor White held that this was unnecessary and that the encounter and struggle with evil is sufficient to facilitate individuation (White 1952, 1960). However, what Jung means by 'incorporating' or 'integrating' evil must be considered within his theory of opposites, as an 'evil-antithesis' to the 'good-thesis' whereby a new synthesis is attained. Individuation as 'union of opposites *par excellence*' maintains such dynamics. In fact, this does not entail actual evil practices but to discovering and activating our own shadow/evil sides, which include 'good qualities' and must be integrated within the Self. Jung resorts to alchemy, where he finds metaphors of the Self in which certain opposite aspects (i.e. good-bad) are intertwined, such as the 'union between intellect and sexuality' or the 'alchemical Mercurius duplex, in the form of the lapis' (1945/1954: para. 343; 1955/1956, *passim*). Mercurius represents the supreme spirit, or the Self, imprisoned in matter-conscious, which takes the form of the philosopher's stone, the *lapis,* when freed by the alchemist.

Within the discussed individual directions of development, including the dark aspects that must be confronted within the individuation process, it is apparent that the spiritual perspective is not a priority – although this dimension, as the 'highest' achievement of the Self, has often been misconceived. Samuels remarks that 'Jung's "final" viewpoint can be misused so as to convert interpretation into sermonizing' (1989: 17). This is also obvious insofar as the withdrawal of the

Figure 5.1 Sigmund Freud, G. Stanley Hall, Carl G. Jung (front row), Abraham A. Brill, Ernest Jones, Sandor Ferenczi, in front of Clark University (1909). Printed here by permission of The Marsh Agency on behalf of Sigmund Freud Copyrights.

spiritual symbols from external objects and institutions is critical for the conscious 'to re-discover a real and "naked" self which exists beyond institutions and roles – a meta-institutional self . . .' (Homans 1990: 31). The perspective towards a meta-institutional self indicates a process clearly not having any specific spiritual/ religious orientation.

Jung ultimately understands individuation as a process 'naturally' proceeding within the psychic and the socio-cultural contexts, whereby the spiritual dimension is almost identical with the experience of the inner Self. The '*a priori* existence of potential wholeness' (Jung 1940: para. 278) indicates a strong teleological aspect; and this inner 'entelechy' in fact entails a 'synthesis' of the personal potentialities towards development.[2] Within this pluralistic and 'democratic process' naturally unfolding, Jung suggests that the immanent dynamic of ego-consciousness has to discover its unconscious possibilities and encounter the *a priori* archetypal potential, which then can reveal an evolutional character addressing all possible levels of life.

Deification in Maximus: a synergic spiritual process towards the 'deified man'

A discussion on Maximus' view of development presupposes to depart from Jung's model and to address a different ontology. It is the dynamics of the immanent potential of the 'logoi of beings' through which man can open up a dialogue with God. This perspective provides the person with an existential dimension, much discussed by existentialism in the past but also in line with contemporary insights on person-personality facing discourses of different levels of life. Wiggins's position, for example, emphasizes all kinds of evolutionary, biological, historical, and cultural facts and levels, which all form a *plateau* that constitutes the subject-person – able to experience these facts (1987: 74). Thatcher takes on a more pluralistic discussion over the term 'person' and distinguishes six uses: the ancient theological, ontological, psychological, moral, existential, and social uses (1987: 181f).

Within this plurality of levels, it is understood that a person is a 'plateau' where facts of all *levels* are gathered to constitute the 'subject of experience', since humans are both the 'subjects of consciousness and objects of reciprocity and interpretation' (Wiggins 1987: 74). Maximus does not consider such 'reciprocity' within the psychic or interpersonal levels alone but expands on ancient conceptions of the assistance stemming from the 'divine level' (e.g. see Plotinus *Enneads* VI: 7.22). Man, made in 'God-image', is able to experience the 'love . . . through which God and man are drawn together in a single embrace', experiencing thus 'the undeviating likeness of the deified to God in the good, so far as is possible to humankind' (*Ep.* 2: 401C). This spiritual state is attained only when man's will co-operates with God's will through *synergy* between the two parts – a notion that needs clarification.[3]

Maximus' analysis of 'synergy' is based on the model of the two wills in Christ: the human will and the divine will, according to his dual nature as a person

(*Opusc.* 3: 48CD). Maximus critically distinguishes between the 'natural will', which is man's ability/will to act that belongs to and is 'disposed by nature', and the 'gnomic will' (γνώμη) that belongs to the person/hypostasis as a result of the way one acts or wills: 'the way one speaks belongs to his/her hypostasis' (ibid.: 48A). This distinction cannot apply to Christ, because he is sinless and therefore cannot have a gnomic will opposing the will of his divine nature.[4] Following the prototypical pattern of the two wills in Christ, man has to abide by his inner free choice/will that follows the *logos* of his nature, or the *logoi*-as-virtues, within which divine love bears supremacy:

> Love alone . . . proves that the human person is in the image of the Creator, by making his self-determination submit to reason, not bending reason under it, and persuading the inclination [i.e. gnomic will] to fol-low nature and not in any way to be at variance with the *logos* of nature. In this way we are all, as it were, one nature, so that we are able to have one inclination and one will with God . . . through which [i.e. the law of grace] . . . the law of nature is renewed . . .
>
> (*Ep.* 2: 396CD, trans. Louth)

This passage informs us that the cooperation of self-determination and inclina-tion (natural/gnomic will) with the *logos* of nature, the metaphysical foundations of the person, may lead man to a union with Christ, reaching 'the undeviating likeness of the deified to God' (*Ep.* 2: 401C). Through this progression from 'image' to 'likeness', or deification, the psychic energies are transformed into the 'logoi and tropoi of virtues' (*Q.Thal.* 54: 461), namely the spiritual qualities that the *logoi* convey.

Maximus does not specifically use the term 'spiritual progress' but speaks of spiritual progress-development in three stages, in which he embraces both the biological and the spiritual perspective. It is 'the first birth', in which we receive the 'being itself', that is the 'bodily birth'; proceeding from this is the 'second birth' that 'comes through baptism, in which we receive well-being in abundance. The third birth comes through resurrection, in which we are translated by grace unto eternal well-being.' (*Amb.* 42: 1325BC).[5] In this concise description, the first stage apparently relates to the basic psychosomatic level, whereas the stages of well-being through the sacrament of baptism and the eternal well-being, through resurrection, belong to the 'spiritual-as-metaphysical' level, by virtue of the par-ticipation in the energies/will or grace of God. It is the spiritual dimension that consequently dominates in Maximus' vision of development. In spite of the dif-ferent priorities, as opposed to the directions in individuation towards mainly the socio-cultural realms, Maximus clearly understands the spiritual progress from one point to another descriptively – regardless of the ontological distance between the individual and the state of deification.

As shown earlier, Maximus' conceptualisation of a human being lies in a combination of such notions as in essence-hypostasis/person, logos-tropos, and image-likeness. While man obtains his own nature-essence, only by being a hypostasis-person that bears one's particular unique perspectives and spiritual potential may he reach the union of 'likeness'. In this respect, 'hypostasis' brings together the simultaneous unity and difference, the particular and universal, the distinct and unified. Törönen argues that Maximus' understanding expands beyond the dynamics of the Chalcedonian view of Christ as 'two distinct natures united without confusion' (451 AD) insofar as 'Logos draws us through the multiplicity of phenomena' and towards a 'simultaneous union and distinction' (2007: 197–8). This view is affirmative of a union which, although it is attained with all psychic parts participating in synergic cooperation with the three persons in the Trinity, simultaneously maintains the personal characteristics within a spiritual transformation:

> [The] soul can be ineffably assimilated to God . . . and wholly united to him alone inexpressibly, so that possessing the image of the archetype according to his likeness in nous [intellect], logos [reason], and spirit, they can behold the resemblance so far as is possible, and learn in a hidden manner the unity understood in the Trinity.
>
> (*Amb.* 10: 1196A)

In this process, the struggle is not towards rectification or compensation of conscious or unconscious elements opposing one another but towards the activation of the hidden *image* as a divine potential: it is exactly there that stands 'the centre of the self where our created personhood opens out upon the uncreated personhood of God' (Ware 1987: 204). The end of this process is the resemblance to the Trinity, the *deified* man: 'God and man are paradigms one of another, that as much as God is humanised to man through love for mankind, so much is man able to be deified to God through love' (*Amb.* 10: 1113B). Instead of incorporating shadowy/dark aspects, Maximus endorses a progress for 'love', which restores all the distortions of the nature caused by the 'fall'.

Maximus' spiritual path focuses on embodiment of virtues as spiritual attitudes towards objects, in order to establish a 'reasonable use of means [which] purifies the soul's condition' (*Char.* IV, 91: *ACW* 207). Opposite to this reasonable use of means stand destructive psychic attitudes, the *passions,* that entail a tug-of-war between human desires and the gnomic will. And only 'when the mind [nous] is stripped of passions and illumined by contemplation of creatures . . . can be in God and pray as it ought' (*Char.* II, 100: *ACW* 173). In this respect, it is mainly an ascetic approach that characterises Maximus' view on psychic development through the 'reasonable use of thoughts and things'. The reasonable use towards objects results in 'charity and knowledge' that supersedes egocentricity (*Char.* III, 1: *ACW* 173).

Contemporary theologians have highlighted the significance of the ascetic attitude for spiritual life. Nicholas Sakharov, for instance, explores the differences between Berdyaev's philosophy and Sophrony Sakharov's theology and points out that, whereas for the former 'creativity is the very realization of human personhood', leaving 'no theological "space" for the ascetic practice', in the latter's view the 'individualistic egocentrism can be overcome by the fulfilment of Christ's commandments about love' (N. Sakharov 2002: 92). Experiencing love of course indicates an interpersonal and social dimension in which 'the supreme factor' of love or 'charity' embraces all beings (see Thunberg 1985: 93f, 101). However, this social direction does not appear to be identical with the social adaptability and skills that individuation requires – within a context of parental complexes (e.g. the mother complex) or socio-cultural norms. Similarly, there is no specific reference to development towards socio-political perspectives, although Maximus' struggle against the heretical positions of the time was advanced within the then wider socio-political framework. These distinctions are indicative of the crucial distance between the spiritual as an individuated experience of the God-image/Self at the interpersonal and socio-cultural level and the spiritual experience of love towards God's likeness and deification.

Archetypes, creative fantasy, symbols, and the transcendent function

The encounter of certain archetypes (e.g. mother, shadow, God-image) establishes, for Jung, a psychological process that could not only shape the stages of psychic development but also construe religious beliefs by relating them to psychic elements or stages of development. The archetypes could also relate to a 'psychological myth' into depths of the collective unconscious, expanding further than the approachable personal unconscious (Jung 1934/1954; 1936 *passim*).

Jung considers the conscious and unconscious elements as subjected to a relentless reciprocal interaction, which means that changes in the conscious dimension have a serious impact on the unconscious and vice versa (1946: para. 394). According to Jung, the unconscious is a 'maternal womb of creative fantasy, in which is capable at any time to fashion symbols in the natural process of elementary psychic activity' (ibid.: para.182).[6] These fantasies and images, frequently constellated around symbolic images or symbols, maintain a decisive position in the unconscious territory as 'captivating pictorial statements' (*CDJA*: 145). Through symbols, the conscious and its functions are gradually being led to another yet unknown psychic position, to a new 'knowledge', in a process whereby the conflicts and opposites are transcended. The unconscious elements are not subject to the rules of normal logical reasoning which generates the ordinary conscious thoughts. On the contrary, the 'dreaming thinking' or 'intuitive thinking' (Jung 1921/1971: para. 830) constantly generates motives, images, and fantasies. Jung termed this function 'fantasy-thinking' (1911/1956: para. 20).

Instead of a solid, organized 'quaternary' as the pattern for the four functions of the ego-conscious,[7] unconscious elements appear chaotic: they function in a flux, conflicting with each other. Such an unceasing 'flow' of psychic activity could be understood as an endless circle around the 'maternal womb of creative fantasy': from creative fantasy to images and from images and fantasies to symbols. The symbols in turn interact with the archetypes – which once again generate images

and symbols. In this respect, images are the inner link amongst unconscious elements, insofar as '[i]mage is the world in which experience unfolds. Image constitutes experience. Image is psyche' (Kugler 2008: 77). Yet, although symbols find
their deeper expression in images and creative fantasy reveals through images, it
is the archetypes in which images-symbols integrate with the whole psychic life
and find their most vigorous manifestation. Jung uses an excellent description to
explain what archetypes are:

> Archetypes are like riverbeds, which dry up when the water deserts
> them, but which it can find again at any time. An archetype is like an old
> watercourse along which the water of life has flowed for centuries, dig-
> ging a deep channel for itself. The longer it has flowed in this channel the
> more likely it is that sooner or later the water will return to its old bed.
>
> (Jung 1936: para. 395)

Whatever the adventurous paths along which psychic energy is channelled in
the course of life, whatever the conflicts deriving from the initially inevitable
psychic one-sidedness, and regardless of the correlation between conscious and
unconscious aspects through images or symbols, there is still something under-
neath: it is the 'watercourse' of archetypal forces, which tend to direct psychic
life to flow back to these *riverbeds*-as-archetypes. Elsewhere, Jung emphatically
points out that 'the archetype as an image of instinct is a spiritual goal toward
which the whole nature of man strives' (1947/1954: para. 415). Accordingly, insofar as the symbols of totality and Self constitute the man's final goal, what under-
lies at bottom is the accomplishment of the integration of all psychic aspects and
elements within such a 'telos': and this is the symbol of wholeness, the archetype
of the 'Self', the transcendence of one's conscious experience. It is not fortuitous
that Jung terms the whole process of mediation between opposites *transcendent
function*, which is 'nothing mysterious, but merely a combined function of conscious and unconscious elements' (1921/1971: para. 184).

The paradoxical nature of the archetypes lies in the fact that although they
cannot be experienced as such, they generate the most influential images that
may function as 'symbols'. Indeed, symbols' nature 'is paradoxical and it represents the third factory or position that does not exist in logic but provides
a perspective from which a synthesis of the opposing elements can be made'
(*CDJA*: 145). Jung suggests symbols to remain in a non-logical basis, in a position in which they can function irregularly: '[t]o be effective, a symbol must be
by its very nature unassailable. It must be the best possible expression of the
prevailing world-view, an unsurpassed container of meaning' (1921/1971: para.
401). There is always a particular process-function whereby symbols convey
their important meanings to the conscious life and compensate one's opposite
aspects: it is '[t]his common function, the relation to the symbol . . . the *transcendent function*' (ibid.: para. 205). We encounter another 'circle' here: the
relationship to the symbol, namely to certain archetypal images, encompasses

the ability to generate union: this ability is precisely the transcendent function, 'the most significant factor in the psychological process' (*CDJA*: 150), and is the catalyst of this integration.

Miller explores in detail Jung's view of the reconciliation of opposites through the transcendent function in a process within different stages: it commences with the 'artificial energy needed to make symbols conscious'; as Self chooses not to supply energy to either opposites, 'energy, now "objectless", sinks into unconscious'; then, the symbol is activated and forced into consciousness, whereby the 'ego glimpses [in a] new way through union of opposites' and 'partially absorbs [the] resolution of opposites' (Miller 2004: 49). This process is repeated and the psychic opposites gradually unite. The strong relation of symbols to the resolution of opposites reveals that the inherited unconscious elements do include the innate tension towards the totality, the transcendent Self.

Archetypal patterns lie at the very bottom of any aspect of unconscious life, and development appears to a great extent to be pre-determined to pass through these archetypal 'canals'. As the individual develops, he or she first encounters those elements of the personality that are repressed and overlooked: it is the archetypal 'shadow', which could be construed as 'those qualities and impulses [one] denies . . . but can plainly see in other people – such things as egotism, mental laziness and sloppiness' (von-Franz 1964: 174). The individual must also confront the hidden aspects of the opposite sex, stimulated by the archetypal images through the 'anima/animus' bipolar dynamics by identifying elements of the opposite gender. At the final stages, psychic life is gradually led to the symbols of the 'hero' and psychic totality.

Knox describes the archetypes 'as symbolic forms which are repeated across a range of societies because the human experience of birth, life and death has so much in common, whatever the cultural context' (Knox 2003: 65). The socio-cultural parameters are therefore a constructive engagement of one's consciousness into the depths of collective experience, within which not only the elements of birth and growth are now collectively understood but also the perspectives of the spiritual and the transcendent can appear vigorously when life meets its maturity. It is the collective spiritual experience that in fact the archetype of God-image conveys, calling for a personal synthesis of conscious and unconscious psychic motives, images, and experiences. Jung is clear when distinguishing the vast distance between the conscious and unconscious dimensions of individuation:

> The difference between the 'natural' individuation process, which runs its course unconsciously, and the one which is consciously realised is tremendous. . . . In the second case so much darkness comes to light that the personality is permeated with light, and consciousness necessarily gains in scope and insight. The encounter between conscious and unconscious has to ensure that the light which shines in the darkness is not only comprehended by the darkness, but comprehends it.
>
> (Jung 1952a: para. 756)

The circular flow from the 'intuitive thinking' through images and fantasies towards symbols and archetypes is an essential function of the unconscious, whereby psychic energy can find its unique-for-every-individual way, its natural 'light', in order to integrate with conscious elements through the transcendental function. The archetypes, as 'organs of the pre-rational psyche' initially having 'no specific content' (Jung 1935/1953: para: 845), could function as the predetermined *riverbeds* in which unconscious life will ultimately find the fertile ground to provide the specific psychic content-experience for one's individuation. In other words, archetypes might represent metaphorically the coastlines that a sailor must be advised of, being the compass-light for sailing in the darkness of the unconscious. The intervention of the transcendent function, that is the 'relation to the symbols', eventually leads the dispersed psychic energy to reinvent and shed light upon its natural and simultaneously uniquely personal paths, ultimately leading to the canals of the Self-life of wholeness.

The complexes and the dynamics of logos-eros-mythos within the stages of development

Analysing the distinction between 'psyche' and 'soul', Jung considers the soul as 'personality' or a 'functional complex' (1921/1971: para. 797). Jung further explains that complexes cause a disruption of 'the unity of consciousness' and that '[e]very constellation of a complex postulates a disturbed state of consciousness' (1934b: para. 200). It was Pierre Janet before Jung that emphasized the crucial issue of 'dissociation' amongst psychic elements and realized that complexes entail 'psychic disintegration'. Jung does not see any difference between a fragmentary personality and a complex (1934b: para. 202). By viewing complexes as 'splinter psyches' (ibid.: para. 203), he also stresses disintegration as a form of a *prima materia* that obviously calls for re-integration. The constant flow between images, archetypes, and fantasies in fact constitutes the dynamics of complexes that range from collective to personal characteristics. The parental as well as the 'childhood complex' is unfolding in this wider psychic area, intertwined with the symbols of the parents:

> In the unconscious feeling-toned contents lie dormant memory-complexes from the individual's past, above all the parental complex. . . . Devotion, or the sinking of libido into the unconscious, reactivates the childhood complex. . . . The fantasies produced by this reactivation give rise to the birth of father and mother divinities, as well as awakening the childhood relations with God and the corresponding childlike feelings. Characteristically, it is *symbols* of the parents that become activated and by no means always the images of the real parents . . .
>
> (Jung 1921/1971: para. 201)

Archetypal images, addressing vital areas like parental relationship, are mingled with emotions and other conscious aspects and formulate paths of psychic growth, which unavoidably lead to conflicts-complexes and one-sidedness. Knox investigates the role of the archetypes in the formation of complexes by exploring the relationship of the 'image schemas' and the 'archetypal image' within the mental context: 'the image schema would seem to correspond to the archetype-as-such, and the archetypal image can be equated with the innumerable metaphorical extensions that derive from the image schemas' (Knox 2003: 96). These 'metaphorical extensions' deriving from archetypes shape the 'personified' images, which, through analogous complexes, can take the place of the real parents, society, or God. The complexes of a bipolar nature (positive-negative side) call for rediscovering a direction from which the dissociated elements can find new perspectives and constructive meanings.

Archetypal images are not only associated with the unconscious fantasy or the intuitive thinking but also with the four functions of ego-consciousness. J. Beebe has proposed a pattern of such correspondence: the superior function with hero/heroine, the inferior function with shadow and animus-anima, the auxiliary function with father-mother, and the tertiary one with puer-puella (2004: 103ff). An ethical aspect of individuation becomes evident when development moves towards more complex compilations of types.[8] While handling the challenges of life and paths of development, morality issues emerge and anticipate the complexes to resolve in a manner that does not seriously contradict the particular socio-cultural norms and restrictions. This is due to the fact that the individual's inherited elements and predilections directly relate to their socio-cultural background and function within the personally developed complexes. It is here that Ulanov states that

> Our complexes show the influence of our cultural milieu, the coloration of class, race, sex, religions, politics, education. At the heart of each complex an archetypal image dwells. Engaging that image takes us through the personal unconscious into a still deeper layer that Jung calls 'the objective psyche'.
>
> (Ulanov 1999: 130)

Religious beliefs and cultural symbols play a significant role in the interaction with this deeper layer, insofar as the ultimate 'image' of the collective psyche is the God-image, particular and unique in each culture. In this respect, complexes exemplify the inner connections of our unconscious to the archetypal images that are imposed in both extra- and intra-psychic dimensions, through the particular symbols and beliefs that constitute the images of the divine in each context. Whereas at the first and second stages of individuation the images-as-complexes of mother and father are the prevailing, at the final stage one has to address the 'residues' of these images-complexes: 'while the mother occupies the symbolic centre of the first stage of individuation, the father assumes this position in the second stage', whereas the third is characterised by the 'elimination of residues of childish complexes' (Stein 2006: 204), towards a balanced life, in which the spiritual perspective becomes more and more significant.

The transition from the mother-father image-as-complex towards God-image as a kind of religious complex – as discussed specifically in Jung's childhood previously – corresponds to the transition from the domination of the principle of 'logos' to the opposite principle of 'eros'. A final stage is suggested to be the union of these two through a third principle, that of 'mythos'. Jung defines the Logos as 'the paternal principle', which 'eternally struggles to extricate itself from the primal warmth and primal darkness of the maternal womb' (i.e. the unconscious; 1938/1954: para. 178). Logos can specifically facilitate understanding-knowledge, cognitive functions, and social skills, occurring in initial stages of development when one establishes his/her own identity. However, as nothing could stand alone without its opposite, 'logos' needs to be supplemented by the corresponding opposite principle 'eros', which in turn is a synonymous of '*love, intimacy,* and *relatedness*' (a tendency for constant relationships; *CDJA*: 87). Eros as love and relatedness is not far away from the *religious function:* this is 'a mythopoetic instinct of sorts and it bespeaks humankind's inherent tendency to create myth' (Stein 2004: 204) or religious symbols. Accordingly, the *mythopoetic* aspect directly addresses religion and the *mythos*-based culture of the past, contrary to the more logical modern culture, which is the *logos*-based culture (ibid.: 207–8). The further we move towards the end of psychic development, the more non-rational elements are to be integrated; and it is here that mythos can function as a mediator between the initial stages, dominated by logos, and the mature age, where the eros-relatedness prevails. The two main tendencies of approaching the 'unconscious product', the creative formulation and understanding of the meaning – linked with eros and logos respectively, subject to a similar integration: 'The two supplement each other to form the transcendent function' (Jung 1916/1957: para. 177), which also relates to the function of *mythos,* creating religious symbols for the life of wholeness.

These formulations of development as a transition from the principle of logos towards eros and mythos could be illustrated by progress in an axis, that is 'logos-eros-mythos', describing thus the stages of individuation. Neumann has envisaged the transition from the ego to the self (1954, 1955) and Edinger (1972), in more detail, advanced it to the 'ego-self axis'. In man's developmental history, 'ego' and 'self' are subject to a circle of separation and union.[9] The ego-self axis refers primarily to the second and third stages, to the progressive ego-self separation and the emergence of the deeper 'self' into the consciousness. Ego separation means that the individual begins overcoming the fragmented tensions of the sub-personalities/complexes as well as the one-sidedness, which had been inevitably developed in the initial stages. In this process, one can progressively reach the deeper meaning of the symbols and archetypal images: it is a process whereby parental complexes and images of the divine will precipitate the encounter and amalgamation between the rationality and concreteness of logos and, on the other hand, the fluidity and fantasy of mythos. The latter, as the unfathomable source of religious symbols, indispensable for resolving complexes and development, was Jung's intuitive vision of 'image' in its grander scale – from the parental to divine image. Mythos is thus a 'living force' of development. The unconscious sea of images, the collective maternal womb and *prima materia,* ultimately call for an ego-conscious emergence that leads to the rebirth of personality advancing on the ego-self axis.

The stages of spiritual life and the *logoi-as-virtues* towards 'theological philosophy'

Whereas Jung explores psychic development through the dynamics between unconscious and conscious spheres, Maximus follows a different perspective: although he acknowledges 'nature' as the *prima materia* suitable for spiritual progress, he mobilises the individual's compound function of free will in a synergic cooperation with a metaphysical agent, the intervention of the 'logoi' of God.[10] Maximus primarily explores spiritual progress within three stages, according to his favourite threefold 'triads', and relates progress to the relationship of the psychic functions with the external objects belonging to both the sensible and intelligible realms.[11]

According to this process, the function of aesthesis, being previously 'ennobled' by the logical function (the reason), undertakes the mission of the announcing of the hidden spiritual meanings (logoi) of the sensible things to the inner man, the soul (*Amb.* 10: 1116D). This is the stage of 'detachment' of the desirable object, which is related to the attitude of *renunciation,* the spirit of asceticism; it is the spiritual struggle *par excellence* toward the liberation of the senses from the impassionate approach to things – and thus the restoration of the aesthesis to its natural movement. In Maximian terminology, this stage is the *practical/moral philosophy* or *praxis.*[12] The second stage is termed *natural contemplation:* it primarily refers to the intrinsic ability of the logical function to interpret the *logoi* and *tropoi* of the intelligible realm, namely the manifold of the spiritual qualities-as-virtues. Through the latter, the logical function extends the psychic boundaries by means of spiritual knowledge and unifies all things of the visible and invisible realms.[13] At this stage, the aesthesis is free of the impassionate approach to objects and assists to the combined spiritual movement, without the conflicts that the passions cause.

The third stage is the *theological philosophy* or *mystical theology,* during which the highest of the functions, the intellect/nous, is endowed with the pure prayer and contemplation towards God, enabling thus the psyche to be initiated into the realm of the supreme knowledge of the divine wisdom of God.[14] As an inheritance of Maximus' predecessors,[15] in fact this three-fold process is more complex than merely a linear progression. The psychic elements/functions interact with the timeless principles/*logoi,* within a 'transcendent time' and from an eschatological perspective (see Plass 1980). Similarly to the view of the three stages of individuation, the three stages of spiritual development are also robustly related intrinsically to teleological approaches, which particularly in Maximus bear an eschatological character.

Maximus applies numerous threefold concepts as signifiers of the spiritual development from different angles.[16] Man initially receives the *being* of his biological birth, the second birth as a mode of *well-being* manifested through baptism, and finally the third birth through resurrection, which is ultimately transformed into the *eternal-well-being* (*Amb.* 42: 1325B).[17] The 'birth' must be followed by psychic 'motion' through virtues, to finally culminate in 'rest' (*Amb.* 7: 1073C, 1084AB, see Sherwood 1955: 172, note 63). Accordingly, it is intended that we receive the nature of 'being' as a gift from the creator but attain the mode of 'well-being' as a voluntary action in terms of communion with the qualities of God, or the *logoi*. The well-being is attained by willingly submitting our free will – that is, our 'gnomic will' – to God, as a 'wishful surrender' (ἐκχώρησις γνωμική) to the divine will (Sherwood 1955: 129).

In this process, man, as a 'portion of God' (*Amb.* 7: 1084BC), can choose through his gnomic will to develop his nature according to his own *logos* and thus attain the state of 'well-being' within God's providential love, or go against it and thus lead himself to an 'ill-being' (*Amb.* 65: 1392CD). This is another triadic description of development: *essence, choice, grace* (*Amb.* 65: 1392A). Man is also assisted by the *natural law,* given to everyone through the principles that govern the nature, the *scriptural law* (whose words and phrases comprise the embodiment of the virtues of the Logos), and the *law of grace* (*Q.Thal.* 39: 259–65), which is the final stage of spiritual progression that encounters *mystical theology.* In *Mystagogia*, Maximus intuitively bonds the three stages of progress with the three parts of the church (nave, sanctuary, altar) and at the same time with the three main parts-functions of the soul:

> [M]an [may stand for] a mystical church, because through the nave, which is his body, he brightens by virtues the ascetic psychic aspect [aesthesis], via the observance of the commandments in *moral philosophy.* Through the sanctuary . . . he conveys to God by the logical function in *natural contemplation* the logoi of the aesthesis purely and in a spirit cut off from matter. Finally, through the altar of the nous [intellect] he summons the silence abounding in hymns in the innermost recesses of the invisible and unknown utterance of divinity . . . [where] he dwells intimately in *mystical theology.*
>
> (*Myst.* 4: 672BC, italics mine)

Maximus innovatively integrates stages of development and parts of the church building along with the three psychic functions (aesthesis, reason-logos, nous). Although the symbols here function differently than in Jung's transcendent function (the *place* of integration), they cause the encounter with the spiritual perspectives of beings at the metaphysical level. This interaction is more apparent when Maximus uses the five somatic senses as 'exemplary images' of the psychic functions, because the somatic level is tightly united with the psychic one and both of them with the spiritual *logoi*:

> The senses have been called exemplary images of the psychic functions, since each sense with its organ of perception, has naturally been assigned

beforehand to each of the functions of the soul in an analogy and by a certain spiritual principle . . . the organ of sight, that is the eye, is simply the image of the nous [intellect]; the organ of hearing, that is, the ear, is an image of logos; the organ of smell, that is the nose, is an image of the anger; taste is the image of the appetite [desire]; and touch an image of life.

(*Amb.* 21: 1248AC)

Interesting as it seems with respect to the three Freudian developmental stages (oral, anal, and phallic), Maximus exemplifies further how physical senses are interwoven with psychic functions and spiritual virtues: *prudence*, by interweaving of the contemplative activity of nous and logos with the senses of seeing and hearing; *courage*, formed by anger and smell (alongside the nostril and breath), directed properly towards sensible things; *integrity*, by the synthesis of desire with taste through an appropriate use of the objects related to both desire and taste; and *righteousness*, within a similar harmonious application of the vivifying function through the sense of touch. These four virtues finally generate *wisdom* and *meekness,* which are fused into the universal 'logos and mode of love'. This is the culmination and the integration of all things, senses, functions, and spiritual *logoi* (*Amb.* 21: 1249AB; 41: 1313AB; see Balthasar 1988: 343). Accordingly, Maximus heuristically combines all levels of life, which are integrated by the highest and deeper *logos* of love, the ultimate value emanating from the Logos-Christ, both 'image' and 'likeness' of the all-embracing and loving God.

At the 'eternal well-being', the stage of *deification,* man appears to follow a 'narrower' path, the spiritual path, possibly described as a vertical ascent toward God, due to the necessary 'detachment' – renunciation – of the physical objects. It is a rather mono-dimensional course, compared to the multi-dimensional path of individuation spanning the psychosomatic and socio-cultural levels. Although this ascension includes the encounter with the 'other' and the objects through spiritual love, this relationship is ultimately accomplished through God's assistance through his grace and not in an independent and individualistic way that individuation implies. In examples of development in nature, one may find metaphors of such mono-dimensional perspective of development, for instance recalling the degrees of differentiation between the hepatic cell and the red blood cell: the former, less differentiated biologically, indicates a 'pluralistic' development in many directions without restrictions, whereas the latter, by dropping its nucleus in order to carry as much oxygen as possible, exemplifies the narrower spiritual path in Maximus' sense. This path encourages the 'impassionate' approach towards things through detachment of the objects in order to experience the 'oxygen' of God's spiritual *logoi.*

In Maximus' understanding, development is primarily a spiritual progress from the state of nature to the state of participation in God's divine life. It is a development that includes distinctive spiritual qualities-virtues, all integrated to 'love' at the divine level, the state of *deification.* Contrary to the Jungian approach, according to which during individuation 'much darkness' from the unconscious 'comes to the light' into the conscious, Maximus associates the spiritual ascension to the light and love of God by experiencing the meanings/*logoi* beyond the mere symbols, namely the concealed spiritual qualities-as-virtues of all beings.

From self-love and fragmentation to charity and integration within 'love'

For Maximus, the ultimate accomplishment of the psychic parts is spiritual love within union with God, that is a union which in turn generates further love (*Q.Thal.* 49: 353). However, this process from the state of the 'image' to the spiritual level of the 'likeness' and God's love is by no means easily attainable, due to the implications of the 'fall': the separation of mankind from God's initial plan that is the failure of human nature to follow its own 'logos' of being.[18] It is important to point out here some of the implications of the 'fall' that human nature perpetually undergoes. Maximus describes these implications in a few sentences as the longest adventure of mankind, emphasising the 'multitude of opinions and imaginations' that are generated by man's free choice:

> For since the deceitful devil at the beginning contrived by guile to attack humankind through his self-love, deceiving him through pleasure, he has separated us in our inclinations from God and from one another, and turned us away from rectitude. He has divided nature at the level of the mode of existence, fragmenting it into a multitude of opinions and imaginations. . . . Thus humankind has brought into being from itself the three greatest, primordial evils . . . the begetters of all vice: ignorance, I mean, and self-love and tyranny, which are interdependent and established one through another. For out of ignorance concerning God there arises self-love. And out of this comes tyranny towards one's kin: of this there is no doubt.
>
> (*Ep.* 2: 396D–97A, trans. Louth)

Of prime significance here is the separation of the inherent coherence of psychic elements and the 'fragmentation into a multitude of opinions and imaginations' as the main result of the fall. Individuals are now susceptible to freely generating a diverse array of images, which move them away from the natural contemplation of the spiritual meanings of creatures/objects. Contrary to this fragmentation of autonomously behaving psychic elements, all the forms of virtue 'fulfill the power of love, which gathers together what has been separated' (*Ep.* 2: 400A). What love of God unites, self-love (a mode of narcissistic love), or 'the mother of all passions . . . which is an unreasonable affection of the body' (*Char.* II, 8 & 59: *ACW* 153, 165), separates and splits into fragments. The latter disorganise seriously psychic affinity towards the realm of virtues.

Referring to self-love, Maximus, up to a point, adopts Philo's view, according to which self-love is depicted as the prevailing psychic attitude in the construction of the tower of Babel.[19] Although self-love is charged with a great degree of fragmentation and separation, as well as 'affection of the body' and the consequent vices, Maximus does not exclude a positive aspect of self-love, one that could relate to a kind of 'spiritual self-love' (*Q.Thal.* Prol. *CCSG* 7: 39ff) – through which man owes spiritual care to himself as well as worship to God. The implications of 'self-love' must be perceived from a spiritual viewpoint: although it refers to 'affection' of the body, it does not signify negligence of vital daily needs but rather a strong egocentric attitude. This attitude inflates one's narcissistic image, which implies a lack in acquisition of collective qualities. In fact, self-love is an obstacle even for encountering the Self, which openly suggests 'a better social performance than when the peculiarity is neglected or suppressed' (Jung 1928a: para. 267).

Maximus elaborates not only on the ontological feature but also on the psychological implications of the 'fall', describing precisely the disorganization and isolation of the psychic functions that fail to grasp the true knowledge of beings. The key in this process is the isolation and emancipation of the function of the aesthesis from the logical function:

> The first man was lacking in understanding the final purpose of the intrinsic motion of man's physical energies [functions] and this ignorance constituted his illness . . . and through God's ignorance he meddled his intelligible function [nous and logos] entirely to the aesthesis, experiencing the complex and disastrous knowledge by drawing the sensible things towards the passions.
>
> (*Q.Thal.* Prol. *CCSG* 7: 31)

Of prime importance for understanding spiritual progress in Maximus' thought is the role of the 'passions' complex and 'disastrous knowledge' that is caused by the entrapped intelligible function into the aesthesis and sensible things. As a consequence, the access to the whole edifice of the spiritual *logoi,* namely to the true spiritual knowledge of beings through the compound psychic function, is disrupted. The true knowledge is stemming from the divine simplicity of *logoi,* whereas the complex and disastrous knowledge that prevents spiritual progress derives from the passions complexity. As a result, a bipolar dynamics between 'pain' and 'pleasure' is developed: whilst trying to avoid the former, man is constantly rushing impulsively towards the latter (*Q.Thal.* Prol. 31.240–255). In overcoming the tensions between pain and pleasure, man has to practise spiritual love, whereby self-centeredness is superseded. We can now examine how 'pleasures and pains' of the passions must be confronted.

Passions, complexes, and 'renunciation' in psychological and spiritual development

Maximus considers psychic 'passions' as the 'complexity' of disorganization and fragmentation of the psychic functions in their attempt to assimilate the spiritual knowledge stemming from the creatures. The passions are generated by the intellect/*nous*, which 'remains behind the superficial knowledge of the sensible things within fantasies' and thus does not pass 'through contempla-tion' to the intelligible realm, according to its particular nature and function (*Q.Thal.* 49: 371.44–47). Although, for Maximus, fantasies are engaged in the improper movement of the intellect/nous, a simple image-thing cannot consti-tute a passion, but it is rather the shortage of the intellect/nous contemplation that is crucial. Accordingly, passion is defined as 'the synthesis of a sensible thing, of the aesthesis, and of another psychic aspect, namely desire, anger, or logical function, which has stepped out of its natural bounds' (*Q.Thal.* 16: 109). It is there that lies the answer to the question why evil is not in the inner nature of things; rather, it is the misuse of things which forms an 'evil' deed. However, there are also crucial questions raised from this passage, such as where precisely these 'natural bounds' stand – which will be discussed shortly. Next to the definition of passions, Maximus also provides means of healing the passions. As passions are generated, the 'nous' is trapped to the aesthesis and loses its 'investigative' aspect. This aspect is of paramount importance, insofar as it precisely has the capacity to liberate man from the 'pleasures and pains' that the passions cause:

> If the intellect/nous, as it investigates the complexity [of the three inter-related factors that comprise passions] . . . is able to view the sensible object in itself, apart from its relationship to the function of aesthesis, and the aesthesis itself apart from its association with the sensible object, and the natural desire . . . apart from its impassioned bond with the function of aesthesis and the sensible object . . . [the intellect] has then made even the slightest imagination of passions completely to vanish by restoring each of its elements to its natural state.
>
> (*Q.Thal.* 16: 109.75–90)

It is apparent that 'the God-loving mind does not war against things, or against their representations', or images or fantasies, 'but against the passions joined to these representations' (*Char.* III, 40: *ACW* 180). The object of pleasure, therefore, via its images, is not the target of spiritual struggle: the struggle is against the impassionate affinity towards it, from which one can set free 'by means of spiri-tual charity and self-mastery' (*Char.* III, 43: *ACW* 181). The mediation of the logi-cal function is once again essential to reconcile the opposites of senses-intellect, and to unite them with spiritual 'love' – while avoiding, on the other hand, the experience of 'pleasure and pain'.

From a strictly spiritual perspective, the issue of 'pleasure and pain' has fre-quently been seen as directly related to 'abstinence' or *renunciation,* the ascetic detachment from things for avoiding passionate 'complex' association. Maximus clearly connects this bipolar notion to the initial man's capacity for 'spiritual plea-sure', by which he was able to enjoy God. This capacity man later surrendered to his senses and thus experienced the pleasure-pain complex (*Q.Thal.* 61: 85f). However, one would question the exact bounds of this detachment in a contemporary socio-cultural framework, wherein numerous parameters would correlate to both pleasure and pain. This issue therefore appears to merit a closer view.

For Maximus, acquiring spiritual love is an arduous task: in fact, charity/love is the end of a long process, which starts from the detachment from objects and also incorporates additional spiritual qualities-as-virtues:

> Charity springs from the calm of detachment, detachment from hope in God, hope from patience and long-suffering; and these from all-embracing self-mastery; self-mastery from fear of God, fear of God from faith in the Lord.
>
> (*Char.* I, 2: *ACW* 137)

This progression of *logoi*-as-virtues is principally based on renunciation/ detachment, an issue of vital importance in the Maximian corpus and to other ascetic writers – which also implies a monastic context. In Maximus' definition of charity as 'the intentional doing of good to one's neighbour and long-suffering and patience; also the use of things in due measure' (*Char.* I, 40: *ACW* 141–2), he concretises the degree of detachment into the 'due measure', using the Stoic view of 'right reason/logos' as the core of virtues,[20] and particularly towards the 'other' or the neighbour.

We can explore further this 'due measure' with respect to a sequence of virtues, which compensate the opposite chain of the three main vices: *ignorance, self-love,* and *tyranny* (*Ep.* 2: 396D–97A). According to Maximus, tyranny is an arbitrary use of both psychic and physical power; ignorance stands for a deficiency of the logical function by which true knowledge is generated, whereas self-love mainly falls into the area of the senses – though all functions eventually engage a degree of self-love. In addition, tyranny can be considered a misuse of the intellect/nous, which is separated from any regulatory influence deriving from the 'lower' psychic parts (aesthesis and reason). Indeed, 'the origin of all the passions is self-love', whereas 'their end, pride' (*Char.* III, 57: *ACW* 184). Within these considerations spanning all the psychic functions, self-love results in tyranny and 'captures' the activities and spiritual orientation of the highest function, the intellect/nous.

These three vices are therefore the opposites of three spiritual qualities: instead of *ignorance, self-love,* and *tyranny*, we might have *knowledge, love of God,* and *charity.* Through the dynamics of the opposites, ignorance and narcissistic love is exactly that psychological ground which must be compensated and ultimately transformed into the experiential spiritual knowledge and love. The latter is in fact a reciprocal communion not only with God but also with others and 'our neighbour', according to Christ's prime commandment (*John* 13: 34–35).[21] We can now detect an analogy between Maximian 'passions', functioning as a second nature in individuals, and Jungian 'complexes', which 'behave like independent beings' (Jung 1937a: para: 253) and result in 'a fragmentary personality' (1934b:

para. 202). Although the two concepts are based on different ontological perspectives, both passions and complexes must somehow be resolved and overcome for the individual to develop psychologically and spiritually.

In the archetypal theory, the concept of renunciation has its own place. Jung states that '[b]ecoming conscious means continual renunciation, because it is an ever-deepening concentration' (1976: 120). Accordingly, the state of 'the inner detachment from the world' can be reached only 'when life has been lived so exhaustively and with such devotion that no obligations remain unfulfilled' (Jung 1929: para. 55); and Jung concludes: 'Whatever we are still attached [to], we are still possessed [by]' (ibid.). Jung is thus affirmative of a different mode of detachment/renunciation, attaching, like Maximus, a positive role in its engagement into psychic development. However, detachment, according to Maximus, bears a strictly spiritual character, which is applied to a specific monastic context with certain rules. Jung considers renunciation in a non-specific way and does not restrain it in a specific context; he rather indicates the tension of the consciousness to be attached to objects. The question that arises here is whether there are any 'negative' aspects of detachment/renunciation in Maximus' viewpoints.

Spiritual progress, in Maximus' view, necessarily engages in the struggle against passions, in which free will plays an important part. The role of the nous/intellect – the most important function – is crucial for both the healing of passions and the acquisition of charity: it is the nous/intellect that is able to 'restore each of the passions' elements to its natural state' (*Q.Thal*. 16: 109). Nevertheless, whatever the spiritual benefits from this process, they might encompass some remarkable 'disadvantages' from a psychological viewpoint. Being in a constant 'abstinence' from relatedness with external objects might have certain repercussions on such developmental directions as the interpersonal and the socio-cultural. We can therefore investigate certain aspects of this issue further.

Due to the fact that monasticism in Maximus' era exerted a considerable impact on social dynamics in terms of social-cultural development, societal progress was to a great extent identified with spiritual life collectively. In Brown's erudite formulation, '[s]ettled life, itself, stood under a question mark. Humanity had fallen from a state of angelic freedom into the inextricable compulsion of society' (1988: 336). On the other hand, although Jung objected to religious 'systems' that could eliminate personal experience through active imagination and free association, he acknowledges on certain occasions the importance of a 'healthy' detachment. Becker, commenting on Jung's and Ignatius Loyola's views on detachment during development, states: 'Jung, like Ignatius, sees detachments from all things as essential for the freedom to live out one's purpose and to pursue one's goal' (Becker 2001: 101). Accordingly, Maximus' considerations of renunciation – which represent at-large traditional Christian views – apart from the criticism of one-sidedness and mono-dimensional development within spiritual directions alone constitute constructive means for attaining the individual's final spiritual goal.

Maximus views psychological-spiritual development as proceeding from the state of the passions, whereby self-love dominates, towards the state of detachment of the passionate relationship with objects, a stage at which charity/love is the leading psychic quality. Despite the different ontological ground, both psychic and spiritual development demands a personal struggle to identify the complex nature of complexes and/or passions, and thus to reach one's goal: the freedom from any psychological fixation/possession – in Jung's view – or of the passionate bond with internal images and external objects – in Maximus' approach. Psychic fragmentation must progress towards integration either through the synergic co-operation between the functions and the spiritual meanings (*logoi*-as-virtues) at the spiritual level, in Maximus' case, or through the confrontation with the unconscious archetypal images via the transcendent function and symbols in Jung's understanding of wholeness.

Psychic development within the archetypal and eschatological potentialities

The stages of spiritual progress towards a personal God in Maximus become for Jung the processes narrating and stages of psychological development within archetypal images and complexes. This description-narration of psychic development is an important viewpoint that permits Jung to ground the understanding of the spiritual perspective in purely psychological terms: this is the encounter with archetypal imagery, whereas for Maximus it is the encounter with the spiritual principles, the *logoi*, of divine realm. There have been different schematic representations and conceptualisations regarding development from a point A to B – for example, the linear and the spiral models. Papadopoulos introduces a spiral model of development according to the scheme 'nature-unconscious, ego-conscious, Self-integration of both' in a recurring progression (1980: 305; 2006: 33–38). Samuels also speaks of the spiral model as 'a system with opportunity for new elements to enter, though not *ad lib*' (1985: 115). Whilst Jungian and Maximian models could stand for both the linear and the spiral models, individuation appears to spread 'horizontally' towards a wider perspective of agents within the psychic and socio-cultural levels – leaving thus the spiritual direction not sufficiently described.

More precisely, both theories consider the starting point of development being the status of an undifferentiated, in developmental terms, 'primordial' stage, a *prima materia,* of unconscious life. In Maximus' case, the starting point, slightly different than Jung's one, specifically refers to a man after the 'fall', that is the separation from his initial spiritual potential towards God. However, crucial differences and divergences emerge regarding the directions and final points towards which development unfolds in each model. Jung's insights, improved by the post–Jungians, cover a variety of directions, such as the interpersonal-parental, the social, and the cultural. Maximus views development primarily in terms of spiritual progress, which does not appear to refer to a manifold of directions but to address specifically the interpersonal level and the metaphysical realm of God's likeness-as-love. Despite its plurality of directions, the Jungian model lacks a clear spiritual dimension and thus can be described as bearing a 'horizontal' perspective. Conversely, Maximus' model addresses the spiritual direction as ascension towards God, whereby the consequences of the 'fall' are reversed; it thus acquires features of a 'vertical' mode of development. An emerging complementarity between the two models of development is obvious.

Despite the striking similarities with respect to the initial stage of development, the final goals, the 'self' and the 'deified man', are grounded on entirely different ontological grounds: the former bears the dynamics of the God-image(s), while the latter bears the features of 'God-likeness'. However, due to the 'unknown' potential of the archetypal Self, as discussed in the previous chapter, it can be argued that individuation might also advance beyond the psychic boundaries. In that respect, the dynamism of God-images could open up for man a real prospect to encounter what Maximus contemplates on the 'spiritual area', namely 'God's likeness'. Although Jung asserts that individuation is a 'biological' process, elsewhere he adopts overtly a spiritual perspective: '*individuation is the life in God* . . . The symbols of the Self coincide with those of the Deity. The self . . . symbolises the totality of man and he is obviously not whole without God' (1958/1959: para. 1624). In addition, Jung's application of religious symbols as an ordering principle with a view to precipitate the 'synthesis' of the unconscious chaos (1957: para. 541) – and by extension the mediation of opposites – might be seen as a parallel to the supreme *logos* of love in Maximus, which re-integrates all parts of personality distorted and separated by the 'fall'.

The ontological distinction between God-image, the spiritual at the psychic area, and God-likeness, the spiritual at the metaphysical/divine sphere, could represent a terminological tool for delineating the discourses referring to both the psychic and the spiritual domains. Nikolaus, for instance, exploring the differences between Jung's psychology and Berdyaev's philosophy, delineates the 'spiritual' perspective of individuation by stating that for Jung, the spiritual dimension, according to religious traditions, is 'the domain of metaphysical speculation, not of verifiable facts. . . . "God" appears within this perspective as a force of nature that drives the individuation process' (Nikolaus 2011: 79). It is apparent that this God is the immanent God-image in human nature, which can further trigger development. Considering these distinctions, one could envisage the 'ontological' hierarchy as a synthesis of both models as follows:

(a) Psychic area *before* any spiritual or mediatory process or transcendent function (*undifferentiated* state or ego-conscious)
(b) Psychic area encounters spiritual/transcendent agents at the stage of religious symbols, Self, or God-image(s)/*individuation* (union of conscious and unconscious: state of the spiritual-as-psychological area)
(c) Psychic area 'transfigured' by divine intervention/grace into God-likeness/ *deification* (state of the spiritual-as-metaphysical area)

These distinctions allow an understanding of the spiritual dimension as a *spiritual continuum* (discussed in Chapter 2) within an evolutionary perspective from psychological towards metaphysical points, through the incorporation of interpersonal, socio-cultural, and/or metaphysical elements.

The spirituality of loving God-as-Other vis-à-vis the experience of the Other-Self

The spiritual 'logoi' are for Maximus the foundations of the psyche and at once the eternal potentialities, whereby the individual is eschatologically able to encounter his/her personal God. Maximus addresses the hidden psychic elements/passions at the 'heart' of man, which must be transformed into the all-embracing virtue of 'love'. Jung, interestingly, defines the unconscious as 'something like what the Bible calls the "heart" and considers the source of evil thoughts'; it is the archetypal fantasies which must be contended with towards individuation (1954: para. 42). This deeper level of psychic dynamics is also present in Maximus, who lays emphasis on the spiritual struggle to free man from 'the hidden stains of the heart' in order to acquire spiritual love (*Char.* III, 80: *ACW* 188). There exists therefore a direct correspondence between the terms 'unconscious' and 'heart': the latter 'is the secret place of meeting between body and soul, between soul and spirit, between the unconscious and the conscious . . .' (Ware 1997: 101). However, the 'heart' in Eastern Christian tradition is also identified with the noblest part of the 'inner man', which first experiences the qualities of the spiritual love (see *Char.* IV, 72 & 78: *ACW* 203, 205). In this respect, the heart acquires a spiritual perspective with no direct equivalent within the unconscious territory.

Jung differentiates from Maximus in that he views individuation principally from a *phenomenological* viewpoint by emphasizing what the individual can consciously experience during development as 'biological' process (without intervention of external/metaphysical agents). On the contrary, spiritual progress towards deification is primarily viewed through *ontological* considerations, namely the reciprocal relationship with God and his ontological principles/*logoi* – which also determine man's foundations (see *Amb.* 17: 1228A–1229A). These principles further define the real Other as a 'person' in Maximus' model, towards which love must be directed. Jung does not particularly address a real or an eschatological Other apart from the Self or, more precisely the archetypal images and elements (the fourth element included) comprising the Self.[22] Therefore, the strong association of Jungian symbols with the cultural sources-images and their impact on the development-integration through the transcendent function, as previously mentioned, could further explain the reason individuation is inextricably linked with the social and the cultural levels. On the contrary, the engagement of these realms in Maximus' model is to a certain extent discouraged due to the attitude of detachment/renunciation: here the prime target is the real other-God.

Jung's phenomenological priority is apparent when interpreting the three stages of spiritual development, '*emundatio* (κάθαρσις, purification), *illuminatio*

($\varphi\omega\tau\iota\sigma\mu\acute{o}\varsigma$), *perfectio* ($\tau\varepsilon\lambda\varepsilon\sigma\mu\acute{o}\varsigma$)' (1955/1956: para. 644).[23] Jung attaches afresh 'psychological' perspectives to this classical scheme of spiritual progress, ignoring the implicit metaphysical dimensions – at least at the ultimate stage of perfection: 'here we have one aspect of the approximation to divinity; the other aspect is exemplified by the image of the Apocalyptic Son of Man . . .'[24] (ibid.: para. 644). It is an image that 'comes nearer to the paradoxes of the alchemists than does the Christ of the Gospels' (ibid.: para. 633). This 'deviation' from the Christian perspective is in line with the Jungian principle of applying opposites and polarities in such a way that everything, even Christ, must comply with psychological opposites. For Jung, 'wholeness' and 'perfection' are aligned with Gnostic wholeness and the alchemists' *lapis philosophorum,* in which the metaphorical opposites are mediated towards a new integrated entity that represents the Self, the union of all antithetical psychic elements.

Apparently, Jung's method of 'incorporation' of opposites into the Self can be contrasted to Maximus' emphasis on the 'transformation' of the passions into spiritual qualities/virtues. Jung departs from the 'vertical' mode of development in Maximus and follows a horizontal path, which proceeds through the 'incorporation' of hidden aspects, such as the shadow/evil, into the Self. In that respect, similarities and differences between Jung's complexes and Maximus' passions at bottom could be understood within the dynamics between 'incorporation' and 'transformation'. Maximus views 'passions' as the simplest 'complex' – in a Jungian sense – which consists of images, fantasies, objects, and an 'improper' psychic function. The passions must be rehabilitated or, more precisely, transformed into virtues – and ultimately to the love of God. Maximus clearly wants the 'eros' and 'love' of God to reintegrate the 'passible element' of the soul (*Char.* II, 48: *ACW* 162–3) and to transform desire and anger into 'divine passion/eros' (*Q.Thal.* 49: 355). Thus, Maximus ascribed an entirely new perspective to passions, having the boldness to define the end of the spiritual progress, the *deification,* as 'pleasurable suffering' (*Amb.* 7: 1088CD; Blowers 1996: 82) and a 'supernatural passion' (*Q.Thal.* 22: 141) of loving God. Insofar as passion manifests 'the primal Adamic and historic experience' within the separation of human nature from its initial spiritual orientation, 'so ultimately will passion bespeak the profound experience in which that nature regains its wholeness in Christ . . .' (Blowers 1996: 81–2).

In this way, Maximus attained through the passions a new vision of psychic functions: human desire and 'passibility', mostly condemned as negative psychic aspects in late antiquity, can now be elevated into the 'divine eros' of God, through the synergic mediation of both the logical psychic function and *logoi*-as-virtues at the depths of a loving human 'heart': it is a love of the vocations, virtues, and qualities of a personal God which the latter shares with man. On the contrary, Jung views complexes as principally functioning on an archetypal basis, and regardless of the evolution of complexes towards its positive polarity, there is no 'catalyst' to transform them into such qualities with metaphysical potential as virtues. On the other side, the archetypes as 'riverbeds' generate strong parental-interpersonal bonds (within mother or father complexes), sexual bonds (within anima-animus) – not at all present in Maximus – which all are open to be transformed into 'spiritual' figures (wise man, Great Mother, Self). As shown before, these potentialities indicate a 'pluralistic' mode of development that is absent in Maximus.

Whereas psychic wholeness addresses the collective psyche – but not specifically a real-Other – for Maximus the words/qualities of a personal God bear the dynamics of a transcendent personhood. According to Maximus, spiritual progress always faces the eschatological Other-as-love as a communion of the eternal foundations and spiritual meanings of all the 'others', the *logoi* that comprise the one Logos. By contrast, individuation precipitates the incorporation of collective norms in general and the therapeutic experience of 'transference' in particular, which both address the Other-as-Self. According to Jung, therapy is not an abstract system but a 'dialogue' between two persons: 'A person in a psychic system which, when it affects another person, enters into reciprocal reaction with another psychic system' (Jung 1935: para. 1). This reciprocal reaction and experience, however, does not necessarily engage a permanent Other beyond one's subjectivity and remains within psychic boundaries.

Current philosophical strands address similar accounts through the 'responsibility for the other' as a concern 'beyond ontology' (Levinas 1991/2006: 171). In Jung's case, the spiritual beyond any ontology and theology turns rather to a 'phenomenology of the face' in Levinas's words (ibid.), or the conscious participation in the world of the 'other', a graspable knowledge of the origins of the human being regardless of any religious context. However, Levinas's interpretation of the 'responsibility' for the Other, not distant from Maximus' real Other, is not an urgent consideration in Jung's individuation. The issue of the Other therefore highlights a weak point of the Jungian theory, regarding the non-specific interpersonal relationship of an actual loving core of one's personality – so clear in Maximus theory of love.

Ultimately, Jung responds to his 'primary concern to *understand* religious ideas' (1911/1956: para. 339) by comprehensively analysing religious doctrines, processes, and beliefs and relating them to the archetypal images and psychic processes of development. By this descriptively narrative manner, Jung bridges the gulf between the realm of the divine-God(s) and the psychological realm – a gulf that Maximus surpasses through the acquisition of the highest virtue that is 'love' for both the neighbour-other and the personal and all-embracing God. We can now proceed to explore in which ways Jung addresses his second standpoint on religion, namely the inner psychological experience as imperative for 'legitimate faith'.

Notes

1. The features acquired by this process are meant to be 'of the collective qualities' (Jung 1928a: para. 267), through the struggle of the ego to compensate for the conflicted unconscious elements which are under the impact of the interpersonal and cultural

contexts. Jung is clear that 'individuation does not shut one out of the world, but gathers the world to oneself' (1947/1954: para. 432), affirming the significance of interpersonal and socio-cultural agents.

2. Jung writes, 'The goal of the individuation process is the synthesis of the self. From another point of view the term "entelechy" might be preferable to "synthesis" . . . the symbols of wholeness . . . they can often be observed in the first dreams of early infancy. This observation says much for the *a priori* existence of potential wholeness . . .' (Jung 1940: para. 278).

3. The notion of *synergy* has been investigated from different perspectives in literature (more in Sherwood 1955: 55ff; Lossky 1957: 98–9; Farrell 1989: 139ff; Törönen 2007: 182).

4. Maximus writes, 'the Incarnate Word [Christ] possesses as a human being the natural disposition to will, and this is moved and shaped by the divine will' (*Opusc.* 3: 48), but without it being subjected to the differentiation of the *natural will* and *gnomic will* that applies to humans. This is because, Maximus explains, 'it was only this difference of our gnomic will that introduced into our lives sin and separation from our God' (ibid.: 56B).

5. See 11 such triads in Loudovikos (2010: 80); also see the subsection 'a three-fold spiritual development' in Thunberg (1995: 333ff); more in the following sections.

6. Jung developed the concept of the unconscious beyond Freud's classical position as a realm of 'repressed and forgotten contents' (1934/1954: para. 2). He also expanded Freud's idea that the unconscious is of an exclusively personal nature by introducing the distinction between *personal unconscious* as 'a more or less superficial layer of the unconscious' and a 'deeper layer' with contents of 'modes of behaviour that are more of less the same everywhere . . . identical in all men', namely the *collective unconscious* (ibid.: para. 3).

7. The Jungian four functions/typology of ego-conscious (thinking, feeling, intuition, sensation) will be explored in the next chapter.

8. J. Beebe states that when psychological processes incorporate 'both ego-syntonic functions and functions in shadow [the named ego-dystonic complexes], the ethical aspects of this development will become ever more evident' (Beebe 2004: 112).

9. Edinger (1972/1992) distinguishes among four stages of such a relationship: (a) a very early stage when ego and self are one: it means that there is no ego (this is Neumann's original uroboric state); (b) a state of an emerging ego, which is beginning to separate from the Self; (c) a more advanced stage of development in which the ego-self axis is obvious in spite of a residual ego-Self identity (this stage is considered as the more feasible); and (d) an ideal theoretical stage, non-existing in reality, in which ego is entirely separated from the Self (Edinger 1972/1992: 6). The ego-self axis therefore primarily refers to the second and third stages.

10. We will extensively explore the compound function of free will along with the main three psychic functions in Maximus' models in the next chapter.

11. Maximus refers to three functions (*nous/intellect, logos/reason, aesthesis/sensation*) that co-act with the spiritual meanings/*logoi* of beings and culminate in the divine realm: the logos is 'the interpreter of intelligible things . . . reasoning their unification's modes'; and the aesthesis, 'ennobled by the logos to imagine and make distinct the different activities of things', is the 'announcer of their spiritual meanings' to the nous (*Amb.* 10: 1116D; see Balthasar 1988: 290).

12. See: *Q.Thal.* 3: 55; 25: 159; 55: 509; *Amb.* 20: 1240B; *Char.* II, 26: *ACW* 157; *Cap.* II, 96: 1172B; and *Myst.* 4: 672BC. For *ethical philosophy*, see *Amb.* 67: 1401D.

13. See *Q.Thal.* 25: 161; *Amb.* 37: 1293B, 1296B; 50: 1369C; and *Myst.* 4: 672BC.

14. See *Q.Thal.* 25: 161; 40: 269; 55: 509; *Myst.* 4: 672BC; and *Amb.* 10: 1149B; 20: 1241C; 50: 1369C.

15. Thunberg (1995: 337–9) refers to the Origenistic-Evagrian triad, *maker, provider, discerner*, and the Dionysian one, *being, wisdom, life*, discussed by Sherwood (1955b: 40); see also Konstantinovsky (2009: 42, 89ff).

16. See 11 such compilations in Loudovikos (2010: 80); similarly in Thunberg (1995: 368f).

17. Thus, the logical beings are given the birth according to their specific 'logos of being' and they move following the 'logos of well being', whereas at the end of this movement they find rest in God according to the 'logos of eternal well being' (*Amb.* 7: 1084BC).

18. This issue covers a vast area in both Eastern and Western Christian theology, and some of its characteristic aspects come within the exposition of the features of the so-called 'garments of skin' (*Genesis* 3, 21; see Nellas 1997: 43ff).

19. See Philo, *De Confus. Ling.* 128, cited in Thunberg (1995: 234, note 22).

20. Maximus takes the Stoics' concept of 'right reason' (ὀρθὸς λόγος) – see Diogenes Laertius, *SVF* 3.473 (*Stoicorum Veterum Fragmenta*) – but his own application conveys a slightly different connotation: 'the use of things with right reason' in *Char.* I, 24–7: *ACW* 140, *PG* 90: 965AC. According to the Stoics, the 'right reason' of the psyche is the most important criterion of proper behaviour and the sensible handling of situations.

21. Maximus follows the tradition of Evagrius, Ps.-Nilus (Evagrius), and Cassian about the 'eight fatal vices'. See St John Cassian, *On Eight Vices*, in *Philokalia. The Complete Text.* Compiled by St Nikodimus of the Holy Mountain and St Makarios of Corinth, Vol. I, trans. G.E.H. Palmer, P. Sherrard and K. Ware (1973), London: Faber & Faber (pp. 73–93). Maximus, although he provides an extensive description of the passions and impassionate thoughts (*logismoi*; *Amb.* 10: 1196C–97C), does not systematically explore each passion as does John Cassian but rather considers passions as a single entity, as a 'post-lapsarian' propensity of psychic functions to generate 'complex-passionate' relationships with objects.

22. The reader here could recall the discussion on the issue of the 'Other' as unfolded in Chapter 3.

23. These stages were introduced by Dionysius the Areopagite and also used by Maximus: see *Q.Thal.* 25: 159; 55: 509; *Char.* II, 26: *ACW* 157.

24. See *Revelation* 1: 14f.

6

THE PSYCHIC FUNCTIONS AND SPIRITUAL EXPERIENCE

The dynamics between the unconscious and the conscious dimensions of development are central to understanding Jung's four functions (typology) in general and the relationship between the functions and spiritual experience in particular. Jung considers unconscious as the 'unknown' domain to our ego-conscious territory: 'unconscious phenomena are so little related to the ego that most people do not hesitate to deny their existence outright' (1939a: para. 490). There exists a dynamic relationship between these two territories, which at times becomes 'dangerous':

> Now when there is a marked change in the individual's state of consciousness, the unconscious contents which are thereby constellated will also change. And the further the conscious situation moves away from a certain point of equilibrium, the more forceful and accordingly the more dangerous become the unconscious contents that are struggling to restore the balance.
>
> (1946: para. 394)

It is apparent that Jung understands the conscious dimension as 'asymmetrical' compared with the accordingly 'more dangerous' behaviour of unconscious elements. We discussed in the previous chapter certain elements and functions of the unconscious. Jung suggests that there also exists an asymmetry between the conscious and the unconscious functions: the conscious 'directed thinking . . . operates with speech elements for the purpose of communication', whereas the unconscious, indirect 'dreaming or fantasy-thinking' is 'effortless, working as it were spontaneously . . . guided by unconscious motives' (Jung 1911/1956: para. 20). As we shall see, four functions comprise Jung's psychic model of psychological types, his 'typology', whereas Maximus names three main psychic aspects as functions or, more precisely, as 'motions of the psyche'. Regardless of how these functions are conceptualised, they play a significant role in psychic development according to both systems of thought. Moreover, the functions are decisive at the stages of development that engage in spiritual experience. Despite the fact that Jung and Maximus analyse spiritual experience differently, both maintain that at

111

advanced states of development, the spiritual dimension is experienced directly and in a 'felt' way rather than in an abstract or intellectual way. Although the boundaries between the conscious and the unconscious dimensions of the functions cannot be precisely described, it is understood that the functions primarily relate to the centre of the conscious territory, the ego (see Samuels 1985: 63, figure 3). We may now explore further these functions as well as their engagement in spiritual experience.

Individuation, typology, and spiritual experience

Jung defines consciousness as 'the function or activity, which maintains the relation of psychic contents to the ego' (1921/1971: para. 700). There is a prolific tradition in ancient and early Christian literature with regard to the conceptualisations applied to describe certain structural and functional elements of the soul/psyche. Jung appears to be well versed in classical or other sources, as he extensively refers to Origen and Tertullian, ecclesiastical writers of early Christianity, as paradigms of *introverted* and *extraverted* types (ibid.: para. 17–30). Just before the introduction to *Psychological Types* (Jung 1921/1971), the Platonic and Aristotelian impact on the Jungian typology is directly acknowledged:

> Plato and Aristotle! These are not merely two systems, they are types of two distinct human natures, which from time immemorial, under every sort of disguise, stand more or less inimically opposed. The whole medieval world in particular was riven by this conflict. . . . Although under other names, it is always of Plato and Aristotle that we speak.
>
> (Heine, *Deutschland,* p. 81, cited in Jung 1921/1971: 2)

By contrasting the 'visionary, mystical, Platonic' with the 'practical, orderly, Aristotelian' natures (ibid.), Jung not only presents them as examples of introverted and extroverted types – as he did with Tertullian and Origen – but he also draws on their thought to formulate the terms for the four functions of his own system, the 'typology'. Although there is no specific reference to Plato's relevant terminology in *Psychological Types,* a closer look reveals striking similarities between Jung's typology and Platonic/Aristotelian terms. However, as further analysis will show, Jung's typology has rather little to do with spiritual/religious experience, which was an important aspect of psychic functions in Greek philosophers, and in Maximus, too.

Despite different approaches and interpretations from the Homeric epoch to the Aristotelian school, psychic activity and functions were always related to the knowledge of the moral and spiritual attitudes of the psyche, the virtues (ἀρεταί). Referring to this rich inheritance on morality, Snell points out that 'the knowledge of one particular right is true knowledge only if it is founded upon the knowledge of the good as such' (1960: 187). For instance, Socrates argues that the craft of know-how (ἐπίσταμαι, ἐπιστήμη) is determined by the fact that one should investigate the depths of his/her actions according to the ability of distinguishing between good and evil: he 'reduced all the virtues to one and described that one as wisdom or knowledge – the knowledge of good and evil', as stated by Guthrie (1967: 104–5). The development from psychic experience to knowledge and further to a mode of spiritual 'knowledge-as-experience' of superior qualities-as-virtues is one of the distinctive aspects of the understanding of the psyche in antiquity.

By introducing new terms describing the psychic elements and functions, the pre–Socratics laid the foundations of conceptualising the human thought as functions. Snell states that 'in Greece, and only in Greece, did theoretic thought emerge without outside influence, and nowhere else was there an autochthonous formation of scientific terms. All other languages are derivative' (1960: 227). For instance, Anaximander's attempt was one of the first 'to explain the origin of man, as well as the world rationally' (Kirk & Raven 1960: 142). Parmenides radically established a phenomenological method when he effected the transition 'from truth to seeming' (ibid.: 278, n.353). Anaxagoras introduced the *Nous* (mind/intellect) as the principle of all beings; and though this Nous is corporeal, it addresses a dualism of mind and matter. More intriguing is Heraclitus's principle of *logos,* which governs both world and human behaviour (ibid.: 215) through the axiom that 'the psyche has logos which increases itself'.[1] Thus, the pre–Socratics did not only define the world governing principles but also laid the foundations of the psychic functions as 'organs of knowledge'.

A crucial moment for the future of both philosophy and psychology was Plato's classification of these functions into *superior/intelligible* and *inferior/aesthetic* realms: in the former, it is the reliable functions of the *nous* (mind/intellect) that contemplates alongside the *logos* (thinking) that interprets the experiences of the nous; in the latter, we refer to the *senses* such as the *aesthesis* and *doxa*.[2] A further distinction Plato makes is amongst the three parts of the soul: (a) the *rational* part of nous/intellect and logos/reason, symbolised allegorically by the driver of a chariot, and the *irrational* part of (b) the *thymikon* (anger) and (c) the *epithymitikon* (desire), which both are represented as the two horses pulling the chariot (*Phaedrus* 246f, 253c). The nous/intellect, a mode of psychic vision as introduced by Homer,[3] in fact stands for the function of the 'contemplation of the beautiful', which leads to the true beauty, the *bios biotos* (a life worth living; see Plato *Symposium* 211D). It is apparent that the Platonic view of the psyche did establish a *dualism* present in both Freudian and Jungian psychology, disguised under various forms (i.e. id vs. superego, ego-conscious vs. unconscious, rational vs. irrational). Whilst Plato gives priority to the nous/intellect, in Aristotle the logical/aesthetic approach to knowledge and truth appears to be the principal.[4] The distinction between superior and inferior functions is apparently present in both traditions and goes on within the following centuries. Even during early modernity, it is understood that the psyche bears some functions that are dedicated to grasping the supreme knowledge which might be located beyond the soul as such (see Michael 2000: 150, figure 7.1).

Contrary to this classical inheritance, Jung's approach is aligned with modern trends that depart from traditions affirmative to a locus of the divine and/or supreme knowledge beyond the psyche. Psychic experience is understood to be the only valid means through which one could approach the spiritual perspective. As a result, Jung does not structure his psychic model directly open to spiritual experience. Despite the fact that Jung is aware of the intractability and polarity of human psyche present in Plato's trinitarian system (*Phaedrus* 246, 253–4), he opts to adopt 'the idea that the soul was a square' from the Pythagorean school. Jung thus appears to be content with a fourfold model comprising the 'four aspects of psychological orientation, beyond which nothing fundamental remains to be said' (1942/1948: para. 246).

Jung's 'typology' is based on two broad types, the *extraverted* and *introverted,* and comprises a two-dimensional model with four functions in opposite pairs: the superior (dominant function) – inferior (less differentiated) functions, and the auxiliary – tertiary functions. In this scheme, four functions can be consecutively adapted: *thinking* and *feeling* (rational, evaluative functions) and *sensation* and *intuition* (irrational, perceptive functions). The four functions of the ego-consciousness are meant to orient human activity in daily life and, as Jung points out, are engaged in the individuation process: '[l]iving consciously is our form of individuation. A plant that is meant to produce a flower is not individuated if it does not produce it – and the man who does not develop consciousness is not individuated . . .' (Jung 1934/1976: 296–7, cited in Beebe 2004: 88). Echoing the significance and centrality of consciousness for individuation, Beebe comments that 'the various functions of consciousness . . . will be the petals of his or her flower' (ibid.). These functions may constantly develop throughout one's lifetime. Thus, the less differentiated, namely the inferior function, is subjected to the potentially greatest growth.

Jung eschewed delineating the role of functions with regard to specific types of experience, in particular of spiritual experience. His treatment of typology primarily aimed at establishing paths of development of consciousness, according to which one might relate to and adopt specific attitudes towards objects. However, Jung's aim was to address psychic experience, too. But here one needs to overcome certain contradictory points in Jung's understanding beyond the distinction between rational and irrational. For instance, whereas Jung defines the (irrational) *intuition* as a mediating 'perception in an *unconscious way*' (1921/1971: para. 770), he describes irrational types as '*empirical* . . . [because they] base themselves exclusively on [conscious] experience' (ibid.: para. 616) – though in such an experience, rational functions such as thinking are also main contributors. There is also a question of how emotions are engaged in experience and through which functions, since *feeling* does not signify any emotional state but mainly the sense of objects' value, something of 'like-dislike' (see 1921/1971: para. 724).

Consequently, it appears that a distance emerges between 'inner experience' and the four functions. This gap increases when taking Hillman's view that inferior functions (i.e. inferior feeling) could signify repressed material: 'inferior feeling is loaded with anger and rage and ambition and aggression as well as with greed and desire' (von-Franz & Hillman 1971: 111). Hillman's interpretation in fact allows a direct comparison of the inferior function, with the unconscious material it conveys, to Plato's irrational/passionate psychic part where desire and anger dominate – contrary to the rational part in which the nous contemplates the *forms* by the impulse of eros (*Symposium* 210ff). However, although Jung follows a similar dualistic model, he does not describe the processes in which the functions co-operate with each other to forge an area that may lead to spiritual experience. Thus, the phenomenological considerations of the four functions outclass their spiritual and/or ontological perspectives.

This is because Jung gives priority to psychological experience as such, before any other mode of experience. Discussing in *Psychological Types* the problem of the particulars and universals (i.e. eternal patterns of beings), Jung argues that for resolving the antithesis between *nominalistic* and *realistic* arguments, neither mind/ intellect nor senses are sufficient: '*esse in intellectu* lacks tangible reality, *esse in re* lacks mind' (1921/1971: para. 77). Consequently, a third mediating stand point is needed: '[l]iving reality is the product neither of the actual, objective behaviour of things nor of the formulated idea exclusively, but rather of the combination of both in the living psychological process, through *esse in anima*' (ibid.).

Apparently, *esse in anima* is for Jung the psychic 'essence' or 'area', which can stand for the whole psychic experience, far away from the polarity intellect-senses, in deeper (unconscious) layers of the psyche. However, Jung avoids naming the specific functions that operate within this crucial area, in which both 'ideas of things' (nominalism) and 'things as such' (reality) are experienced together. More precisely, he prefers to assign such a role to the complex function of 'active imagination':

> The psyche creates reality every day. The only expression I can use for this activity is *fantasy*. Fantasy is just as much feeling as thinking; as much intuition as sensation. There is no psychic function that, through fantasy, is not inextricably bound up with the other psychic functions. . . . Fantasy . . . fashions the bridge between the irreconcilable claims of subject and object, introversion and extraversion.
>
> (Jung 1921/1971: para. 78)

Psychic reality is for Jung what is created by the function of fantasy, 'the autonomous activity of the psyche' (ibid.: para. 78), which integrates all other functions, and through which psychic images emerge as experience. No longer is the real experience dependent on eternal forms or matter or any kind of spiritual counterparts, but it is now grounded in the depths of the psyche. Images for Jung are constituent elements of psychic reality; they generate fantasies, which are linked to the objects. Jung's notion of 'fantasy' in fact relates closely to Klein's 'phantasies' and to deeper-unconscious psychic contents.[5] Nonetheless, it is questionable if any kind of psychic experience based on the reality of images, as created by these phantasies, could substitute psychic experience-as-knowledge – particularly the mature conscious knowledge concerning spiritual experience. Is therefore Jung's argument that beyond the four functions 'nothing fundamental remains to be said' (1942/1948: para. 246) entirely convincing?

For Jung, the value of image is principal: one could only recall the key role of God-image(s)/Self in his developmental model and the importance of linking the symbols with psychic reality: 'the psyche consists essentially of images' (1926: para. 618). Yet could fantasy, image, or active imagination bear and express the totality of the psychic spectrum in terms of an experiential wholeness? It seems that desire and anger, as well as the 'type of seeing' in the Homeric view (nous), are not contained by what 'fantasy' implies. In post–Jungians' understanding, however, attainment of consciousness 'would appear to be the result of recognition, reflection upon and retention of psychic experience, enabling the individual to combine it with what he has learned, to feel its relevance emotionally, and to sense its meaning for his life' (*CDJA*: 36). Here there is exactly a description of almost the whole spectrum of functions: senses, emotion, thinking, and understanding/ contemplation of life meaning. Does Jung's typology and active imagination specifically address the totality of psychic/conscious functions that can constitute psychic or spiritual experience? This critical question must be investigated further.

In religious contexts, spiritual experience is a result of activation and engagement of functions within the whole psychic spectrum – a process which engages all levels of the *spiritual continuum*.[6] W. James describes certain features of religious experience: *inexpressibility*, namely the 'state of consciousness . . . insusceptible of any verbal description' (1902/2002: 407); *cognitive aspects*, that is an impression of 'revelations of new depths of truth' (ibid.: 408); and *ecstatic or 'mystical' conditions* and *passivity* (individual's will held by an external power; ibid.: 411ff). Although spiritual experience, according to Jung, is to address *sine qua non* the psychic wholeness, Jung is extremely unclear about what illustrates such an experience. In one of his rare references to 'religious experience', he writes: '*in religious experience man comes face to face with a psychically overwhelming Other. . . .* Only something overwhelming, no matter what form of expression it uses, can challenge the whole man and force him to react as a whole' (1958: para. 655). Despite the fact that at this point Jung addresses both psychic 'wholeness' (echoing an integration of psychic functions) and the 'Other' (standing for an external factor), there still appears a gulf between *esse in anima,* or the active imagination/fantasy that conveys psychic reality, and the specific functions that might engage in attaining this experience (such as James' *cognitive aspects*). It is subsequently understood from all these discussed points that Jung's functions are not specifically engaged in spiritual experience.

The post–Jungians on typology and inner experience

The post–Jungians developed the perspectives of typology primarily towards the basic principle of the variety of psychological types. By focusing on the phenomenological aspects of the functions, the one's distinctiveness was addressed further through a pioneering pattern describing the features of the eight basic types. The Myers-Briggs Type Indicator (MBTI) explores types in a pluralistic basis by focusing principally on the extraverted function, either superior or auxiliary, which indicates the most easily identifiable behaviour in the outer world.[7] On the other hand, the participation of functions in the process of spiritual experiences has also been addressed.[8] For instance, Repicky lays emphasis on the significance of the existence of a minority within a group so as to function similarly to the *inferior* function; he also highlights the ability to share the diversity of giftedness 'in order for each person to relate more fully to God' (1988: 204). In this respect, the ability to discover the less developed psychic aspect and to share talents and weaknesses within a group does improve personality's undeveloped areas; yet the 'locus' of spiritual experience still remains within Jung's typical psychological boundaries.

In addition, there has been criticism on the simplicity of typology. Storr argues that 'the opposition of the four functions it too neat a pattern, which is actually of little help in grasping how different personalities perceive the world' (1973: 78). However, at a closer look, it appears that typology bears a potential towards an archetypal dimension with ontological characteristics. Meier develops this idea within the pattern of a 'compass' and states that 'it is possible to deduce laws or even predict them from the quaternity schema' (1977: 57). Beebe openly relates the four functions with the archetypes of hero/heroine, father/mother, anima/animus, and puer/puella, respectively, in one 'basic orientation' and its 'shadow counterpart' (2004: 110). Archetypal complexes and unconscious material are directed towards the conscious primarily through the inferior function, which thus plays a crucial role insofar as it bears greater potential for development than other functions. During psychic development, at least one of the functions might not be able to follow the others, 'in a way that is not in tune with the person's constitutional personality' (Samuels 1985: 64). Von-Franz (1971) investigates further how typology works when the inferior function begins to grow; she presupposes a layer of 'the preconscious structure' below the fourfold structure that typology normally signifies. At the moment in which the conflict between superior and inferior function turns out, it might emerge as an outlet the *sacrificium intellectus*, that is,

> the humility to go down with one's other functions onto that lower level. This, then, produces a stage between the two layers at about the level where everything is neither thinking nor feeling nor sensation nor intuition. Something new comes up, namely a completely different and new attitude towards life in which one uses all and none of the functions all the time.
>
> (von-Franz 1971: 17)

The emergence of 'a new attitude' opens up a new dimension for psychic experience, located in *esse in anima.* In this case, the conscious is no longer constrained by the ego, but its point of gravity is to be found 'in another dimension, a dimension that can only be created by the world of imagination . . . the transcendent function . . . [that] creates the uniting symbols' (ibid.: 63). This 'fifth function', or the *transcendent function,* generates a new phenomenological prospect and simultaneously an ontological potential of deeper experience towards a realm in which the symbols can acquire new 'meaning'. The new perspective is something entirely novel: it is a fruit of the differentiation of the inferior function to the maximum possible degree, which now 'can successfully emerge as a *competitive* function' (Meier 1977: 56).

It is then understood that the archetypal dimension of typology could lead to a development that 'is not simply a linear model . . . rather, it is ultimately a way to establish the ego and prepare the individual to enter into the inner world of psyche itself' (Spoto 1995: 156). What Jung ultimately stresses is the struggle to avoiding one-sided and imbalanced development. It is within this one-sided development that impulses and conflicts are suppressed into the unconscious, 'unless an understanding of the indirect route taken by the unconscious impulses brings with it an understanding of the one-sidedness of the conscious attitude' (1921/1971: para. 910, 346–7). These constant ramifications through the activation of the opposite contents/functions generate a 'process of development that proves on closer inspection to be cyclic or spiral' (Jung 1944: para. 28), which ultimately leads to *esse in anima.* Thus, the emphasis is laid on those developmental features that lead to the emergence of one's 'uniqueness' (Jung 1921/1971: para. 895). This is a point which was underestimated by psychic models in antiquity, as they describe humans collectively rather than individualistically. Contrary to the ultimate goal of the Platonic model, aiming at the contemplation of the 'forms' on a level beyond the psyche, Jung's phenomenological approach opens up a new perspective to increase substantially the insights of man's uniqueness towards an understanding of one's 'psychological type'.

Maximian psychic model-functions and spiritual experience

The Jungian model, based on a fourfold pattern of psychic functions, as shown above, has been considered and developed through a primarily phenomenological approach, shedding light on the individual's uniqueness. Maximus' psychic model is rooted in a different ground with a prevailing ontological dimension; it also bears an essential eschatological perspective. Contrary to the poor engagement of the Jungian model in attaining spiritual experience, Maximus' psychic model does yield priority to the spiritual experience and 'authentic knowledge'.

Maximus' psychic model is an evolution of the previously outlined Platonic one, through certain decisive improvements: (a) Maximus withdraws the sharp line between the superior and the inferior levels and introduces a holistic co-operation between the functions; (b) introduces a dynamic connection between the three main functions (*aesthesis, reason, nous*) and the *volition-will*, and (c) applies a hierarchical relationship between the functions and the essential principles/*logoi* of beings. Although Maximus applies in some cases the dualistic model, too, with rational logos and irrational desire/anger,[9] he basically introduces the trinitarian model comprising the 'nous/intellect, logos/reason, and spirit [aesthesis]' (*Amb.* 7: 1088A, 1196A).[10] It is of importance here to mention Nemesius (c. 390 AD), who attributed rational aspects to irrational-instinctual parts (see Nemesius: 75) and whom Maximus almost copies in his *Ambigua*.[11] This is an important advance, in which Maximus innovatively introduces the view of the irrational/passible aspects (anger and desire) as parts of the internal 'aesthesis'. Aesthesis now constitutes an activity of the 'sensible aesthesis' that integrates rational elements (*Amb.* 10: 1116A). More crucially, psychic potential expands now far beyond psychic boundaries and touches the divine level, the *logoi* or the spiritual meanings of beings. Maximus writes that the sages,

> illuminated by grace [teach that] the soul/psyche has three modes of motion that converge into one: that of the nous [mind/intellect], that of the logos [rational function/reason] and that of the aesthesis [sense/perception]. By the first [motion], which is inconceivable, the soul ineffably approaching God, knows him in a transcendent way . . . by the second, which distinguishes according to the causes of the unknown, the soul physically applies its knowledge to all the natural principles of those things, which are known with regard to causality . . . [whilst the motion] of the aesthesis is a synthetic one and, through symbols of the sensible things, gains some impression of their innate logoi. . . . Within these motions . . . the aesthesis, by perceiving the logoi of the creatures in the visible world, is ascended up to the nous through the logos; the logos conceiving the logoi of the intelligible creatures unify them with the nous in a simple inseparable prudence; in this way the nous, freed and pure of any motion around any creature . . . is raised up to God.
>
> (*Ambigua* 10: 1112D–13A)

Maximus refers elsewhere to different versions of these three functions-as-motions,[12] occasionally replacing 'aesthesis' with the 'practical part' or 'desire and anger' (see *Myst.* 4, 5: 672B–73A; *Q.Thal.* 22: 145–6).[13] But these differences in names and terms are of secondary importance. Maximus proceeds with the evolution of a 'static' psychic part to the dynamism of a 'motion': these are the Aristotelian *dynameis* (faculties), which replace the static parts of Plato's model (see Guthrie 1967: 143). In Maximus' view, *nous, logos,* and *aesthesis* are not motionless at all, but through their relationship with the essential principles/*logoi* of beings they are able to extend their activity from the psychic level to the spiritual/divine level. The aesthesis does not include only the physical senses but ranges from the bodily to the inner feeling/emotional state and furthermore to the intelligible level (the *intelligible aesthesis,* see *Amb.* 10: 1116A). The aesthesis is thus able to perceive the sensible things through 'symbols' in its attempt to investigate and understand their essential principles/*logoi* along with their spiritual meanings. The logical function, which also encompasses many partial faculties and 'enlarges upon nous, intellect, conception and pensiveness . . .' (*Amb.* 17: 1228B) interprets the *logoi*-as-spiritual meanings of the intelligible world and unifies the aesthesis with the nous. The nous, in turn, eventually acquires a spiritual perspective and wholeness by absorbing and integrating all the other functions: it becomes the most contemplative function, identified with 'wisdom, knowledge, contemplation, and irremovable knowledge' (*Myst.* 5: 673C).

Due to their relationship with the spiritual *logoi,* Maximus' functions-as-motions acquire a spiritual potential as a whole and not as separate aspects. In fact, the three functions are subject to a constant evolution through the *logoi* respectively to their perceptiveness: it is a state not far from prayer whereby mind and heart are directed towards the divine. More specifically, the compound logical function is the location of comprehension of the spiritual meanings that creatures are endowed with, whereas the aesthesis interprets the symbols stemming from the sensible things. The nous, in turn, has received the knowledge from the logical functions (the logos) and the aesthesis becomes the noblest psychic part, the 'inner man' (*Char.* IV, 80: *ACW* 205; see Thunberg 1995: 112). Indeed, Maximus ultimately views the three functions as having their particular but simultaneously common task, which is very similar to prayer: the nous to be occupied 'by the excellences of God', the logos to be 'the interpreter of intelligible things . . . reasoning their modes of unification', and the aesthesis, 'ennobled by the logos to imagine and distinguish the different activities of the things', to become the 'announcer of their spiritual meanings' to the soul (*Amb.* 10: 1116D; see Balthasar 1988: 290). It is thus this high degree of interdependence and co-operation amongst the functions that ultimately leads to the union with the 'excellences of God'.

P. Sherwood recognises a strong twofold influence when commenting on the features of Maximus' functions, considering that his model 'is alien neither to Evagrius[14] nor to Denis'[15] (Sherwood 1955: 143). The strong impact of Evagrius is displayed in the supremacy that is attributed to the nous; however, the nous accomplishes the 'union' with God not as 'pure-mind' and by excluding any 'above nature', as states Evagrius, but, as Maximus points out, by a certain process and synergy with God (see Sherwood 1955: 137–149; Thunberg 1995: 355–368).[16] However, features such as 'pure-mind' or 'the naked intellects' in Evagrius eventually 'retain some somatic characteristics' and are 'not entirely hostile to the fundamental concerns of orthodoxy' (body-soul bond), as Konstantinovsky explains (2009: 170).[17]

The psychic functions in Maximus in fact resonate his apophatic anthropology, which introduces elements from different ontological levels. Thus, while Maximus draws a sharp distinction between the psychological (the functions-as-motions) and the metaphysical/divine level (the *logoi* of beings), at the same time he affirms both these levels without confusion: the end of the integrated process through the compound psychic motion of the aesthesis-logos-nous is located beyond the boundaries of the psyche, which is the union with God and his eternal words or *logoi.* Aligned with the idea of a man as *microcosm,* Maximus innovatively envisages the intelligible world of the spiritual *logoi* and simultaneously the meanings of all beings to exist within the sensible one – that is, within the microcosm-man – through the symbolic forms (*Myst.* 2: 669C). In this respect, man has to develop a dialogue, a constant communication with the symbols and meanings connected to the beings, in order to enrich his knowledge about the cosmos and its creator – a knowledge primarily conveyed by the meanings that the *logoi* bespeak. But before we further investigate this mode of 'spiritual knowledge', it is necessary to introduce another significant function, that of the will.

The compound function of 'will' and psychic-spiritual experience

So far, we have seen man's psyche as an aggregation of partial functions-as-motions. This is only the one side of the coin; the human 'will' is the other. Maximus can be considered 'as the first in the Christian East to have understood it [the will] as a fully-fledged faculty', as Bathrellos terms it (2004: 189). In order to conceptualize and elevate the 'will' as a distinct but at once compound function, Maximus had to take some crucial steps, that is, *inter alia,* to emphasize the rational aspect of the 'will' more than the irrational one. Plato, for instance, in his classical 'trichotomy', attributed both volitional and intellectual features to each psychic part: the rational element contains rational apprehension and rational aspiration, the irascible element conviction and arduous striving, and the concupiscible one conjecture and appetite (see Thunberg 1995: 177). Aristotle follows a different approach with respect to these features, as he never fully elaborates on the function of will.[18] In a different vein, Nemesius, whom Maximus occasionally uses as his paradigm,[19] considers that 'desire' does not relate to the mind or choice (Morani 1988: 101–3). But it was Maximus who eventually established an ontological link of the 'will' with the sensible desire and the intellect and dissociated it from the instinctive (irrational) desire.

Maximus discusses the distinction between 'natural will' and 'gnomic will' by distinguishing elements that emanate either from nature (e.g. determination) or from hypostasis and the person's uniqueness (e.g. choice and *gnome*; *Opusc.* 1: 12D–13A, 153AB). The natural will, through man's actual capacity to choose, can develop towards a gnomic will, which leads to choice (ibid.: 17C). In this way, Maximus introduces the distinction between the will as 'related only to what is natural' and the *proairesis* (that may lead to gnomic will) that is 'a deliberate desire for things that are up to us' and 'capable of being brought about through us' (*Opusc.* 1: 12C–13A). Consequently, proairesis/gnomic will is directly related to choice, being innate in rational beings, according to Maximus.[20]

It can therefore be understood that the constituent elements of the compound function of Maximus' 'will' are linked with most of the psychic aspects and functions (mind, intentions, desire). Maximus attaches particular significance to the relationship between will and the nous/mind, insofar as the latter is considered a leading function in spiritual life. Both the will and the nous can operate either 'according to the 'logos of nature' or against it; this is because, '[t]he "gnomic will" is closely related to the activities of the mind', as states Thunberg (1995: 213), and thus can operate towards the acquisition of a superior knowledge (*Char.* II, 26: *ACW* 157).[21] At this point, however, it must be said that there exists a partial independence of the constituent elements of the will that are integrated in the same compound function. As Bathrellos points out, '[t]he function of the will to hold together all the attributes of man's being is something that happens more or less independently of man's reason and any rational decision on his part' (2004: 123). It is therefore important to follow exactly which way the will advances through certain stages, by specifically relating to other psychic aspects:

> Every logical being has a rational desire as a natural function, which is called will of the intellectual soul, in accordance with which we willingly think and . . . wish, and . . . investigate, and . . . consider, and . . . deliberate, and . . . judge . . . and are inclined towards, and choose [decide] and rush [decisive impulse] and use.
>
> (*Pyrr.* 293BC; *Opusc.* 1: 21D–24A)

Thunberg (1995: 211–3, 218–26) and Bathrellos (2004: 127ff) explore this passage from certain viewpoints; yet, beyond the deep analysis of both, the important question that emerges from our scope is the particular way in which the will is linked with the three main functions-as-motions. Thunberg clearly sheds light on the relationship of the will with such aspects as desire and choice and suggests that '*all* the major acts of human willing are seen by Maximus as a kind of *desire* . . . Maximus may therefore be said to follow Aristotle more closely than Nemesius' (1995: 224). However, regardless of the degree of interrelation amongst the functions, what must be stressed via the analysis of the 'will-in-process' is the fact that the will basically permeates all the functions: 'willingly wish' falls within 'rational desire', and alongside the 'decisive impulse', it could stand for the integrated psychosomatic aesthesis; 'consider' and 'judge' fall within the logical function/reason, whereas 'choose' falls within the mind/nous, as discussed earlier.

Consequently, on the one hand the will is realistically a 'fully-fledged faculty', whilst, on the other, it could be seen as a particular volition with which each of the three functions (nous, reason, aesthesis) is charged. The vast area that 'will' covers in Maximus' view, and the priority it takes in the account of the ultimate integration of human will with Christ's will, directs the whole discourse of 'will' towards the person of Christ, the perfect archetype-person of man. Due to Christ's dual nature, the dipole 'natural will – gnomic will' of humans turns out to be the co-operation between human will and divine will – where the former is now consciously and intentionally subordinated to the latter (see *Opusc.* 3: 48AD; *Ep.* 2: 396CD; *Amb.* 10: 1113B).[22]

The multifaceted function of the will therefore exceeds desire or self-determinacy. It can cover the depths and the heights of the entire spectrum of psychic functionality. Due to this innate relationship of the will with almost all functions, at the points where Maximus speaks of psychic functions-as-motions he might also mean 'willing functions'. In addition, insofar as the will is a determinative part of the conscious, all activities of the will may also refer to psychic experience. We can now explore how Maximus clearly suggests two different kinds of psychic experience that generate knowledge:

> there is relative knowledge, rooted only in reason and ideas, and lacking in the kind of experiential perception of what one knows through active engagement. . . . On the other hand, there is that truly authentic knowledge, gained only by actual experience, apart from reason and ideas, which provides a total perception of the known object through a participation [μέθεξις] by grace. By this latter knowledge we attain, in the future state, the supernatural deification [θέωσις] that remains unceasingly in effect.
>
> (Q. Thal. 60: 77, trans. Blowers & Wilken)

It is apparent that 'actual experience' is essential for spiritually 'authentic' knowledge. Such an experience is attained through genuine engagement of all functions and especially through synergy amongst human will and God's 'grace'. This grace is a metaphysical agency conveyed by the *logoi* of beings. Consequently, psychic experience-as-authentic knowledge surpasses the level of any psychic function and reaches 'the spiritual' at an ontological level beyond merely psychic boundaries, that is to say at higher areas of the *spiritual continuum.*

It has been shown how the Maximian three functions-as-motions co-act with the spiritual meanings-as-*logoi,* culminating in the divine realm: logos is 'the interpreter of intelligible things . . . reasoning their unification's modes', whereas the aesthesis, 'ennobled by the logos to imagine and make distinct the different activities of things', is the 'announcer of their spiritual meanings' to the nous (*Amb.* 10: 1116D; see Balthasar 1988: 290). After all these, it is understood that Maximus not only integrates the main strands of his predecessors (Plato, Aristotle, Evagrius) into his model but also innovatively expands their insights towards a new, versatile shape.

As discussed previously, Maximian functions are primarily directed to a spiritual dimension, in a state of 'prayer' and 'union' with the essential *logoi* and spiritual meanings of all entities – and not towards development of particular functions and attitudes for relating to objects, similarly to Jung's psychological types. In Maximus' corpus, we will never encounter a development of functions in a phenomenological sense, which is towards an external context (such as parental, social, or cultural setting) – unless this context is the divine – but always with respect to spiritual progress towards deification. On the other hand, Maximus elaborates the interdependence and co-operation of all functions towards a constant flux of knowledge-as-experience, from the complex function of the aesthesis (that includes desire) to the all-embracing nous/intellect, always through the reason/ logos – which is the mediatory function between the physical and the divine. This co-operation in fact is an integrated 'development' of all functions, including the will, in all levels, which leads to the experience of the spiritual *logoi*-meanings beyond psychic boundaries.

Active imagination, prayer, and
spiritual experience-as-knowledge

It has hitherto been shown that Maximian and Jungian models engage their functions in spiritual experience differently. According to Jung, *esse in anima* is the psychic area in which mind and senses can be integrated and generate the psychological fact-experience. It is this psychological experience that is the proper ground for authentic or valid faith: '"Legitimate" faith must always rest on experience' (Jung 1911/1956: para. 345). Jung, nevertheless, does not indicate which precise function corresponds to *esse in anima*. Post–Jungians have attributed to the 'active imagination/fantasy' the integration of all functions, which can now be either the 'transcendent function' or 'the fifth new out of the four' (see von-Franz 1971). Active imagination in fact 'is a channel for "messages" from the unconscious by any means' (Samuels 1985: 12), or the mechanism through which one can 'translate the emotions into images', as Jung explains (*MDR*: 177). Aligned with Jung's second standpoint of a 'legitimate' spiritual experience or faith, Maximus does not consider merely 'faith' that is based on an intellectual belief alone as an essential part of spiritual experience, insofar as the latter comprises a synthesis of all functions with the spiritual *logoi*. For Maximus, as for Jung, psychic experience is indispensable for authentic spiritual experience. The critical difference lies in the fact that, whilst in Maximus all functions, emotions, and images are 'translated' through prayer into spiritual experience and ultimately into union with God, in Jung the functions principally operate to analyse psychological types.

Jung seeks the source of spiritual/religious experience principally within the unconscious area, which is 'the only available source of the religious experience . . . simply the medium from which religious experience seems to flow' (1957: para. 565). However, he also acknowledges that 'knowledge of God is a transcendental problem' (ibid.) – without nevertheless discussing any process of the ego-conscious aiming the approach to this 'transcendence'. Maximus, instead, provides a clear path to the transcendent knowledge of God. More precisely, he considers such knowledge possible only through the synergic cooperation of God's qualities (the *logoi*-as-virtues) with all the psychic functions, through prayer and contemplation of the 'excellences of God'.

At a closer look, Jung does not adopt in his typology what Greek philosophers applied to the functions, that is the capability of the innate 'seeing-vision' (a function of the nous/intellect), which, in Maximus, can further be educated by God's intervention to experience true knowledge. More precisely, the Jungian model of typology does not clearly engage (a) an emotional state (*feeling* refers just to the *evaluation* of objects), as well as the desire and anger in a Platonic sense, and (b) the 'inner vision' or 'nous', which Festugière interprets as the 'intuitive aspect' of the rational function (1967: 247–9). Indeed, Jung's equivalent function of the nous appears to be the *intuition*, which overlaps but does not coincide with *nous*, having the potential for creative and authentic thinking.

Maximus, on the other side, considers the integrated logical function (reason-understanding-intellect-nous) as a locum where all conceptions are gathered and synthesised: it is the state of spiritual contemplation-as-prayer as a synergy between man and God. Maximus also incorporates both corporeal and sentimental elements into the *aesthesis*, including the dipole of anger and desire. It is then understood that *active imagination* that conveys unconscious material – as the hallmark of psychic activity in Jung's model – critically differs from the compound function of *nous-reason-aesthesis* in Maximus, which attains spiritual knowledge by mobilising the entire psychic energy (conscious and unconscious) in prayer. The former is the source of intuitive and creative fantasy that generates psychic equilibrium or even artistic creativity, whereas the latter is the state of ultimate concentration of nous and thus a co-operation among all the functions and the spiritual *logoi.* Prayer bears both a 'therapeutic' and a divinising power, whereas active imagination appears to principally convey artistic and creative features, although it includes a therapeutic aspect, too: 'the imagination creates symbolic images and stories that express the mood or emotion in a way that may be more bearable', explains Chodorow (2006: 223). Instead, Maximus lays emphasis on the eternal spiritual meanings and qualities of psychic images and thoughts – that is, the encounter with their *logoi* – during the endless movement of the psyche towards God.

Ultimately, Maximus considers the all-embracing compound function of will the key function for attaining spiritual experience at the depths of the heart/unconscious. Jung, on the contrary, takes Driesch's view that 'volition' is always conscious: 'there is no willing without knowing' (Jung 1947/1954: para. 380). Jung acknowledges that 'the motivation of the will must in the first place be regarded as essentially biological' (ibid.: para. 379). This approach differentiates from Schopenhauer's view of will, as the latter treats it as an 'absolute' – which, however, might generate 'the emergence of higher manifestations of mind as the source of human suffering' (Clarke 1992: 68). According to Schopenhauer, '[t]he will, as the thing in itself, constitutes the inner, true, and indestructible nature of man; yet in itself it is unconscious. For consciousness is conditioned by the intellect . . . that the will is warmth, the intellect is light' (1819/1995: 87). It is the unconscious dimension, therefore, that plays the significant role here, in line with Jung's understanding of the unconscious as the only source of spiritual experience. On the contrary, Maximus does lay emphasis on conscious processes in which we are in principle voluntarily participants. Teleologically, however, the will finds its archetypal fulfilment in the harmonically synergic co-operation of Christ's two wills (human and divine). Expanding Jung's approach, Rychlak takes a view analogous to the Maximian one, that 'freedom of the will and psychic determinism are . . . simply different perspectives on the same telosponsive process' (1991: 52). After all these, the two models' correspondent functions could be tabulated as in Table 6.1.

It is worth exploring further the differences between Jung and Maximus on spiritual experience/knowledge. As previously shown, for Maximus the point of gravity is not the psychic functions as such but the experience of the spiritual

Table 6.1 A Comparison of Jung's and Maximus' psychic models and functions

Concepts/functions	Jung's model	Maximus' model
Higher/deeper area 'inner vision'	*Esse in anima* intuition (?? not clear)	nous/intellect (as 'inner vision') and *heart*
Area of thinking-understanding	thinking, feeling?? = judgment	logos/reason as thinking and judgment
Area of emotion, desire and anger	?? (not specified) irrational function? or active imagination??	aesthesis: integrated with desire and anger
Senses	sensation	corporeal aesthesis/senses
Free will	'a matter of sciences of mind'; not specific action in Jung's model	'a compound function' integrates aspects of other functions, plays a principal role
Locus of synthesis Mode of interdependence	'active imagination'? union of opposites	the logos must dominate to the aesthesis and the nous upon the logos; union via *logoi of beings*
Locus of spiritual experience	*Esse in anima*?? not specified: 'unconscious is the only source of spiritual experience'	co-operation of functions/will with God's will and *logoi* by means of prayer
Developmental directions Psychological types	a pluralistic model, through the *inferior* function (see MBTI)	?? a rather monistic model (not specified)
Archetypal/collective dimension	Archetypal typological scheme; connections with archetypes	Christ is the archetypal man and the ultimate paradigm of development

meanings/*logoi* of beings through these functions. This process engages all the functions consciously and encompasses the whole psychic spectrum, from the (unconscious) desire to the nous/intellect. By contrast, Jung's functions and active imagination do not address the entire psychic spectrum, which entails some crucial consequences on spiritual experience. Jung states that modern man holds faith valid 'only so far as their knowledge-content seems to accord with his own experience of the psychic background. He wants to *know* – to experience for himself' (1928/1931a: para. 171). However, there is no further elucidation of how such an experience could become conscious, insofar as the spiritual experience stems from the unconscious (see Jung 1957: para. 565). Thus, Jung rather views spiritual experience as an 'instinctive' process, driven by unconscious archetypal images, in which the functions are not specifically engaged. On the contrary, in Maximus' model, the individual is fully aware of the engagement, consciously and willingly, of his/her functions in the process towards spiritual knowledge-experience.

Indeed, Maximus draws a sharp distinction between 'relative knowledge', within the boundaries of psychic functions, and the 'authentic knowledge' based on active engagement, which surpasses the functions and extends to the metaphysical level 'through participation by grace' (*Q.Thal.* 60: 77). In Maximus, spiritual experience is the outcome of a process in which the functions are hierarchically (and consciously) united with the *logoi* to generate authentic knowledge. This process, in which the aesthesis is subjected to the reason/logos and then both aesthesis and reason to the nous that ultimately offers the *logoi* to God (*Amb.* 10: 1112A), could be understood as a parallel to the Hegelian *synthesis.* The latter indeed unfolds as 'a sequence of different forms of consciousness, each of which is subjected to criticism and thereby gives rise to its successor' (Norman 1976: 24). However, unlike the Maximian processes of integration of the *logoi,* the Hegelian synthesis does not explicitly engage the metaphysical level but addresses the historical progression of the cosmos in which the ideas of God and religion are embedded.

On the other hand, Maximus does not at all address the development of one's unique psychological 'character' or 'type' in terms of identifying the prevailing function. In addition, the archetypal dynamics of Jungian psychic functions towards an encounter with archetypal images is not present in Maximus, unless one assumes that the Logos-Christ is such an archetype. The fact that Maximus' model remains the same for all individuals raises the question of where exactly the psychological uniqueness of a person is grounded. Despite one's potential to become a 'deified' person according to his/her particular spiritual *logos-tropos,* there is apparently a psychological 'monism' in man's development towards deification.

By contrast, Jung's typology provides a pluralism of perspectives towards one's *individuation.* The anthropological 'dangers' of the vertical 'Christomonism' versus the pluralistic although horizontal 'resemblance' of types, as Hillman interprets typology (1980), has been discussed further by Melissaris (2002: 116ff). The 'monism' of development in Christian contexts, the latter suggests, can be resolved by introducing the charismata-as-virtues – in other words, the psychological manifestations of the *logoi* – endowed by the Holy Spirit during the personal process of deification. This issue, although going beyond the scope of this study, is indicative of the controversies raised by Jung's typology, a typology that provides a pluralistic view on the individual and claims 'uniqueness' within the archetypal perspectives of the personal Self.

Notes

1. See *Diels, fragm.* 22B115.
2. Plato's *Republic* IV: 412b, 428b–432b, 435e–436b, 440b, 441b–412b, VI: 511a–e, 533d–534a. See also Thunberg 1995: 177ff.
3. The Homeric legacy terms two psychic functions, the 'noos', related to thinking, a 'type of seeing . . . the mental act which goes with the vision', and the 'thymos', generating motion and agitation (Snell 1960: 8–10, 13).
4. Aristotle also follows a dualistic pattern: *aesthesis* (sense) and *doxa* (opinion) on the one hand and *episteme* (knowledge) and *nous* (intellect) on the other. The term

episteme could be correlated with the true knowledge, attained by the rational part. With regards to Aristotle, the knowledge based on the *aesthesis* is always real, while *nous* and *episteme* are true, but they can falsify the truth during the synthesis of their contents (*De anima* III, 3: 421b, 428A, 430a, 431a).

5. M. Klein states that 'phantasies' emanate from the unconscious and link psychic functions, such as feeling, to various objects, generating a world of imagination that is crucial for the infant's psychic growth. On the contrary, fantasy is an imagined unreality, like a daydream, that can be consciously generated (e.g. fantasies about our future): 'Phantasies – becoming more elaborate and referring to a wider range of objects and situations – continue throughout development and accompany all activities' (Klein 1997: 251).

6. The reader might recall here the discussion on the fuller potential of the *spiritual continuum* in Chapter 2.

7. The result is a list of 16 possible configurations/types, which, in fact, could be 32 should the introverted main function also be considered. MBTI is a competent tool for clinicians and demonstrates the potential of the 'typology' to address the distinctiveness of one's development (Myers & Myers 1980; Beebe 2006).

8. For example, T. E. Clarke (1988) discusses connections of typology with the spiritual perspective by providing descriptive modes of prayer in which one of the functions dominates.

9. See *Q.Thal.* 16: 107–9; *Char.* I: 78, *ACW* 148.

10. Thunberg has extensively discussed the rich inheritance on dichotomy-trichotomy (1995: 169–95) in Maximus' predecessors, pointing out significant evolutions of the basic Platonic model in earlier Christian times.

11. See, for example, *Amb.* 7: 1196C. More in Nemesius (Nemesii Emeseni) in Morani (1988: 141).

12. *Amb.* 10: 1153C, 1193D–96B, *Amb.* 15: 1216A–21B, *Amb.* 21: 1249BC.

13. Louth contrasts these functions-as-motions (1996: 205 n.7) with those of Dionysius Areopagite, who is referring to the circular, spiral, and straight motions. Thunberg also discusses this passage in the wider framework of the trichotomy of soul without laying any specific emphasis (1995: 172). When Balthasar translates it, he names the three motions of psyche as 'intelligence, discursive reason, and sense perception', which could remind one of Kant's notions of perception and reason (Balthasar 1988: 289–90, n.44). Nevertheless, none of these scholars has extensively analysed this extract, which appears to merit closer attention.

14. Evagrius of Pontus (345–399 AD).

15. (Pseudo)-Dionysius the Areopagite (fifth century AD).

16. The citation of 'in a transcendent way' and 'to the exceeding excellence' (*Amb.* 10: 1112D–13A) is certainly a Dionysian apophatic element of 'monism' within the psyche, a divergence from Maximian 'pluralism' and holism based on the three functions' cooperation. In this respect, Maximus' aim was rather to refrain from a pure intellectualism and a mere use of a 'naked mind', a kind of 'pure prayer' well known as Evagrius's teaching (see Evagrius, *Tr. Pratique* 66, *SC* 171: 650).

17. Despite the fact that these issues find an extensive analysis in the literature, they do not concern this research (more in Thunberg 1995: 366ff; Sherwood 1955: 88f, 95f; Konstantinovsky 2009: 78ff, 168ff). Thunberg concludes that Evagrius considers a 'pure mind' to be the mind purified but staying within itself, whereas Maximus' view of psychic activity, especially within pure-ecstatic prayer, is 'a formless contemplation of God' by the mind/nous wholly participating 'in the qualities which He shows by grace' (1995: 367).

18. This is because Aristotle describes *appetite* (a precursor of will) as inclined to obey mostly irrational instincts: it is 'closed to the voice of reason', as states Gauthier (1954: 58 *cited in* Bathrellos 2004: 125); see also Thunberg (1995: 221–4).

19. Maximus copies Nemesius in many cases, e.g. see *Amb.* 1196–7. For a fuller account of this issue, see the index in Nemesii Emeseni (Morani 1988: 141).
20. However, Maximus does not consistently apply these distinctions throughout his corpus (see *Opusc.* 1: 28A; further details in Bathrellos 2004: 149).
21. This knowledge is accomplished by leading 'the participant to the essences of the incorporeal and corporeal creation' (*Char.* II, 26: *ACW* 157).
22. The reader may wish to recall here the relevant discussion on gnomic will in Chapter 5.

7

THE ULTIMATE GOAL

A question of wholeness or holiness?

Commenting on the possibility of a constructive combination of Jung's and Freud's psychological theories, G. Adler emphasizes the limitations of such an attempt and suggests that this might be 'a task transcending the possibilities of psychology' (Adler 1979: 114). Analogous attempts of juxtaposing the Jungian model with the Maximian model as well as their final goals appear to face similar limitations. Jung's understanding of wholeness appeals to God(s)-images and culminates in the concept of a multifaceted polycentric Self. The Self incorporates aspects of human life ranging from the psychosomatic (i.e. bodily and gender issues) to the socio-cultural levels (archetypes of shadow, evil, hero, or great mother, etc.). On the other hand, Maximus' model, although it does not address the socio-cultural realm as extensively as Jung's, provides a clear view of the spiritual-as-metaphysical perspective that is 'christologically' determined. It is therefore a significant divergence that characterises the final goals of the two models. In this consideration, Jung's third major standpoint on religion, namely the incorporation of the missing 'fourth element' – that is, aspects of the dark side, feminine, and body – towards psychic wholeness calls for further investigation.

God-image and the fourth element in Jung's
understanding of the Self-wholeness

In previous chapters we discussed the notion of the Self in certain contexts, for instance, by exploring its relationship with philosophical concepts such as the Kantian 'thing-in-itself' and Hegel's 'self-consciousness' or by viewing its proximity to the God-image. The aim here is to explore further the implicit aspects of the Self, such as the dark side, the feminine, and the body, as essential ingredients of a multifaceted 'wholeness'. At certain points, Jung directly relates the Self to both the God-image and the wholeness of personality, as an advanced stage of integration of all possible psychic potentialities. However, the wholeness indicated by the Self is not fully aligned with the wholeness typically implied by a God-image/symbol. Indeed, an ambiguity emerges when, for instance, Jung defines the Self as 'God within us' (1928a: para. 399), but immediately he hastily adds that this does not imply 'a deification of man or a dethronement of God'

130

(ibid.: para. 400). This is a position that leads to an unclear relationship between the psychological and the spiritual. Jung maintains an uncertain distance from both the human and the divine: for him the Self is a term on the one hand 'definite enough to convey the essence of human wholeness' and on the other 'indefinite enough to express the indescribable and indeterminable nature of his wholeness' (1944: para. 20). According to Jung, to address 'the essence of human wholeness', one needs to incorporate neglected aspects of modern culture such as the dark side and the feminine.

The dark side and the multiple 'luminosities' of the Self

Jung writes: 'The self, as a symbol of wholeness, is a *coincidentia oppositorum,* and therefore contains light and darkness simultaneously' (1911/1956: para. 576, cf. ibid.: para. 460; 1958: para. 779). Hence, he draws a sharp distinction between the Christ-symbol and the Self, accepting the latter as the broader term: 'The self is a union of opposites *par excellence,* and this is where it differs essentially from the Christ-symbol' (1944: para. 22); for, whereas 'Christ simply represents good', the Self 'is absolutely paradoxical in that it represents in every aspect thesis and antithesis, and at the same time synthesis' (ibid.). In this respect, one of the most important God-images/symbols does not include the totality of wholeness that the Self paradoxically incorporates, because the dark side is absent. It now becomes clear why in his mature work *Answer to Job* Jung takes one more crucial step, challenging the meaning of Christ's incarnation and giving a much clearer idea of what a 'wholly man' must include:

> At first, God incarnated his good side in order, as we may suppose, to create the most durable basis for a later assimilation of the other side. From the promise of the Paraclete we may conclude that God wants to become *wholly* man; in other words, to re-produce himself in his own dark creature (man not redeemed from original sin).
>
> (1952a: para. 741)

Leaving aside Jung's 'provoking' approach, from a theological viewpoint, to Christ's incarnation, it appears that Jung's most vigorous representation of the Self is that of a God becoming *wholly man.* This representation, however, appears to lie exactly at the opposite side of the *wholly deified* man, which is Maximus' counterpart of psychic progress and perfection. Jung claims that a 'wholly man' incorporates the dark, evil, and feminine aspects without these elements being subjected to the process of spiritual struggle and to the transformation that the process of *deification* describes. Jung then takes a further step by characterising the symbol of the Trinity as 'of exclusively masculine character' (1938/1940: para. 107); he thus attributes to the divine nature human traits to create space for the accommodation of the feminine. Indeed, the unconscious transforms the Trinity symbolism 'into a quaternity, which is at the same time a unity, just as the three persons of the Trinity are one and the same God. The fourth constituent . . . was τὸ σώματον the earth or the body' (ibid.). But the unconscious is also personified by the archetype of anima, the feminine part of God, which, in Jung's view, 'would be the matrix of the qua-ternity, a Θεοτόκος or Mater Dei, just as the earth was understood to be the Mother of God' (ibid., para. 107). In this consideration, along with the essential parts of evil/dark in certain quaternary patterns (i.e. father-spirit and son-devil; see 1942/1948: para. 256–9), the body and the feminine are also essential parts of the 'wholly man'.

It is apparent that Jung opts for a 'personal' reading of traditional symbols, defying theological principles – attribution of masculinity to the Trinity and God's incarnation into a 'dark creature'. What matters most, in his view, is the psycho-logical impact of these symbols on 'real time' and in a contemporaneous context as a means of integration of the human and the divine. Jung's vision of wholeness is a *man* carrying his God-image in its earthly dimensions of time and space. The implementation of the God-image is therefore cut off from the dynamics of an image towards its prototype, that is, the eschatological God-likeness. Jung clearly acknowledges that 'in its scientific usage of the term, "Self" refers neither to Christ nor to Buddha but to the totality of the figures that are its equivalent' (1944: para. 20). In this respect, the plurality of images of God(s) constitutes the inner pluralism of the Self.

It can now be understood why 'the Christ-symbol lacks wholeness in the mod-ern psychological sense' (1951/1959: para. 74) and why 'wholeness', as an integra-tion of light and dark, masculine and feminine, has little to do with 'perfection'. As Jung highlights, there may occur 'an integration or *completeness* of the indi-vidual, who in this way approaches *wholeness* but not *perfection,* which is the ideal of certain world philosophies' (1955/1956: para. 616). The feasible goal is therefore aligned with the psychological reading of God-images and not with the dynamics of perfection in the metaphysical sense; and the 'more accessible goal of approximate completeness' is encouraged instead of pursuing the 'ideal of per-fection', Jung adds (ibid.).

As a result, the Jungian approach to wholeness departs from traditional/linear developmental models that advance from one point to another. Jung applies per-plexing processes of development from alchemical equivalents or Hebrew-Gnostic traditions that open paths to 'transformation' while deviating from classical Chris-tian narratives. The feminine personification of *prima materia* now becomes the 'dark figure' of the unconscious anima at a primordial stage:

> The darkness comes from Eve's sin. Sulamith (the Shulamite) and Eve (Havva, earth) are contaminated into a single figure, who contains in herself the first Adam, like the mother her child, and at the same time awaits the second Adam, i.e., Adam before the Fall, the perfect Original Man . . . to be freed by him from her blackness.
>
> (Jung 1955/1956: para. 592)

At this point, the 'original hylic-psychic man' is contrasted with the later 'pneumatic man' (ibid.) in a reversion of the Christian position according to which the latter is the prototype of the former (*A Corinthians* 15: 45, 47): the first hylic-somatic man, bearing the wholeness, is able to set free and integrate the 'blackness' of the unconscious-nature. The dark side of the psyche, nevertheless, is also a rich source of creativity and productivity; it is also closer to its feminine aspect, related to the archetypal great mother (*maternal uroborus*; see Neumann 1954: 39ff, 1955: 18). Accordingly, whereas the pneumatic man is supposed to be illumined and transformed by the Spirit alone, the dark Lucifer, the ἀντίτιμον πνεῦμα, 'spirit of imitation', now can play its significant part in the process of transformation: it is 'both the Above and Below undergoing a process of mutual transformation (1955/1956: para. 644). The dark spirit/side becomes an essential part of the multifaceted wholly/original man.

The multifaceted man becomes a 'multiple consciousness', or an ego-consciousness that is 'being surrounded by a multitude of little luminosities' (1947/1954: para. 387). These luminosities, the archetypal living psychic forces, are the numerous sources of the psychic transformation that culminates in the multifaceted Self.[1] Post–Jungian literature has signified the pluralism of the Self in diverse standpoints: as the 'primary union' (Neumann 1954), the primary Self/archetype of order (Fordham 1985; Urban 2005), a Self as a constant process (Colman 2000), or an 'ethical Self', struggling to be in terms with its shadow that 'brings pain and requires sacrifice' (Solomon 2000: 212). The Self can also be an agent taking the place of 'Freud's superego' (see Jung 1942/1954: para. 396), or, on the other hand, even 'a dethroned self', within a 'democratic' individuation (Samuels 1990: 295). The *coniunctio oppositorum* of the Above (spirit) and the Below (matter) is a coagulation of dark/shadow and light, feminine and masculine, inner and outer, within *unus mundus* – the wholeness of matter and spirit – following circles of integration and disintegration (see Fordham 1957). This process proceeds toward the anticipated equilibrium of all the 'luminosities' of a constantly changing subject by incorporating all the potentialities of the psychic life through paradoxical mediums and symbols so that the tension of the opposites may be accommodated in the 'more accessible goal' of the Self.

Culture, body, and the dynamics of the fourth element

In Jung's understanding, cultural development is aligned with psychological development. This is due to the fact that culture, through ideas, images, and artistic symbols, shapes the directions towards development: it is the 'progressive subjugation of the animal in man' (Jung 1917/1943: para. 17). Jung meticulously considered the links between culture and psychic development: '[t]he secret of cultural development is the *mobility and disposability of psychic energy*' (1911/1956: para. 17).[2] However, Jung also criticised the limited perspective of the Western civilisation: '[w]estern mind, lacking all culture . . . has never yet devised a concept, not even a name, for the *union of opposites through the middle path,* that most fundamental item of inward experience . . .' – such as the Chinese Tao (1928a: para. 327). Finding this middle path is for Jung already an achievement of wholeness, which surpasses the polarisation of the opposites that the Western civilisation imposes.[3]

The post–Jungians have explored further the dynamics of culture as a decisive factor whereby individuation advances within the concept of 'cultural unconscious'. This is a concept conveying historical memory, as states Henderson, 'that lies between the collective unconscious and the manifest pattern of the culture . . . and also promotes the process of the development of individuals' (Henderson 1990, cited in Singer & Kimbles 2004: 182). The cultural-historical memory is the locus where the archetypes of dark side and shadow as well as the anima/animus potentially find their personification to generate the cultural identities-as-complexes. As Singer and Kimbles suggest, these cultural complexes 'are expressions of the need to belong and having a valued identity within a context of a specific reference group' (2004: 201), despite the consequences that this may cause. It is on these complexes that the 'organising' Self crafts one's particular identity, which now comprises personal preferences for overcoming what the archetypes/complexes impose and opting for personal choices. This apparently is a developmental process from the collective to the personal, 'from an idealized and collectively determined ego, to an individuating Self-oriented ego' (Salman 2008: 73).

In this fashion, the cultural context might be the primary source or even the *prima materia* of the 'here and now' upon which the psyche potentially draws for images and experiences. Upon this culture, the spark of the Self could 'spark off' the suitable preconditions for the individual 'to make progress in his self-culture' (Jung 1928a: para. 327); and this means that the interaction between the 'outer culture' and the inner 'self-culture' of the psychic world may generate development. Although individuation is a 'natural process', it is also considered as challenging the natural/archetypal forces. In fact, it is an *'opus contra naturam'* (Jung 1945/1954: para. 414) towards our inner self-culture. In this respect, culture constitutes a complexity of challenges that one must confront in order to resolve the tensions leading away from the experience of the totality of one's inner and outer worlds.

In this process towards self-culture and wholeness, the body becomes a decisive factor. The Self embraces both the psychological world and 'the bodily sphere' (Jung 1955/1956: para. 717). Accordingly, just as society and culture may function as the locus where the Self is crafted in its spatial and temporal dimensions, so the body can be the locus of the specific imprints that culture and society generate on the dark or the feminine/masculine aspect of individuals. It is well known that Jung has been critiqued for not providing an adequate theory on the body's role in development, equivalent to Freud's libido. Samuels, for instance, stresses Jung's one-sidedness as theorising of 'no sex infancy', in contrast to the Freudian stance of 'nothing but sex in infancy' (1985: 150). Despite the criticism, Jung genuinely contributed on early development and promoted a better understanding of the transformation and canalization of the libido (1911/1956: para. 204–250);[4]

134

he also attributes equal significance to the body–spirit bond, since 'the spirit is the life of the body seen from within, and the body the outward manifestation of the life of the spirit – the two be really one . . .' (1928/1931a: para. 195). Although Jung's approach to gender initially appears limited to sexes, there is further scope for a 'feminine' perspective. Indeed, as Rowland delineates, 'despite Jung's habitual collapse of gender into bodily sex . . . it is as a critic of culture that Jung tends to detach "feminine nature" from biological women' (2002: 43). The reason, then, why Jung introduced the feminine symbolism into the divine becomes clear.

Jung views the body as having a higher role to play at the final stage of *coniunctio* within the Self. A closer association between the sexual instinct and the pursuit of wholeness is then considered. Indeed, spiritual experience is compared to sexual experience: 'only something [so] overwhelming . . . can challenge the whole man and force him to react as a whole' (Jung 1958: para. 655). Nonetheless, maintaining a safe distance from equivalent Freudian positions, Jung views sexuality to eventually develop 'into an intellectual or spiritual system' (1928b: para. 43), due to the fact that his ultimate vision is the *unus mundus* – in which the mind and body become one world and sexuality merges with the intellect.[5]

To address this integrating perspective, Jung introduces a more challenging vision of the body, namely the 'subtle body'. This is a notion inspired by the concept of resurrection and the union of body and soul: it is 'the "subtle body" in the state of incorruptibility' (Jung 1940/1950: para. 202; 1938/1940: para. 160; Romanyshyn 2000). As Schwartz-Salant observes, the subtle body 'can be experienced imaginally as a kind of energy field that extends from our physical being': it is a 'field' within which the subtle bodies of the therapist and the patient 'can interact and manifest in a state of fusion' (1989: 132). This fusion, as a key issue in Jung's theory of wholeness, echoes to a great extent the archetypal *coniunctio* and the *hierosgamos* in which both soma and psyche find their most rigorous and profound manifestation. This is a union among multiple levels, the bodily, the psychic, the social, and the cultural: 'the final synthesis of male and female is an achievement of the art . . .' that results in 'self-knowledge, which, like the knowledge of God, is needed for the preparation of the Philosopher's Stone', Jung states innovatively (1955/1956: para. 657).

Jung's application of Christian, Gnostic, and alchemical ideas results in numerous metaphors and representations of the subtle body in connection with the *lapis philosophorum*. Commenting on the interpretation of the holy liturgy by Nikolaus Kabasilas,[6] – a respected work in Eastern theology – Jung equates the transubstantiation of bread and wine into Christ's body and blood with the transformation of a 'natural, soiled, imperfect material state into a subtle body' (1937b: para. 417). However, Jung ultimately resorts to alchemy for exemplifying this vision of union: '[t]he coniunctio does not always take the form of a direct union, since it needs – or occurs in – a medium . . . Mercurius is the soul (anima), which is the "mediator between body and spirit"'. (1955/1956: para. 658). Despite a degree of misunderstanding of Gnostic tenets (see Segal 1992: 31–3), Jung reflects further on the dialectic between Christ (male-spirit) and Sophia (feminine), whose true Spirit can free man from the bodily entrapment.

135

By misinterpreting and reversing historical elements of Christian theology, Jung explores the worship of Mary as a heritage of Isis and other mother goddesses via the principle of opposites.[7] According to this scope, God, surrounded by the 'four wheels of four Seraphim', is married to its own Sophia – where the four wheels represent 'a fourfold synthesis of unconscious luminosities, corresponding to the tetrameria of the *lapis philosophorum* . . . a single hermaphroditic being, an arche- type of the greatest universality' (Jung 1952a: para. 727). This 'hermaphroditic being', the archetypal manifestation of 'greatest universality', which encapsu- lates ingredients of the fourth element embodied in the Self, appears altogether to comprise the ultimate stage of development. This is Jung's supreme vision of the body in a union with the psyche and particularly with the neglected – by both contemporary culture and the Christian church – feminine aspect.

It can now be understood that it is no accident that the Self, 'in accordance with its paradoxical nature, it can only be expressed by means of symbols' (Jung 1946: para. 474), challenging therefore its own manifestation in a realistic context. In this respect, the alchemical and Gnostic representations (*Mercurius, hierosgamos,* etc.), and the non-personified illustrations of the Self (*mandala, lapis*), apparently manifest once again the lack of the real Other in Jung's vision of wholeness/Self. As discussed previously, Jung appears to maintain an ambiguous approach to the Other, insofar as the Self absorbs any interpersonal dimension: '[n]obody can know himself and differentiate himself from his neighbour if he has a distorted picture of him, just as no one can understand his neighbour if he had no relationship to him- self' (1955/1956: para. 739). The supremacy of the knowledge of the true 'inner picture' is accordingly the dominant factor for comprehending the external object, which must first be internalised for the maturation process to proceed. Beyond the inevitable vital engagement of the real other-therapist, and due to the fact that in the final phases of development the subject must eliminate the dialectic of the other in favour of the Other-Self (Papadopoulos 1991: 88), the inner Self ulti- mately becomes the sole 'Other' for the psyche at higher stages of development.

According to Jung's dialectics, the feminine and the body within its cultural embodiments are essential agents of his conception of the 'fourth element', which appears to have been seriously neglected by modern culture and religion(s) and which is now an essential part of the *lapis philosophorum* – the ultimate expres- sion of the polycentric Self. We can now proceed to look at what Maximus estab- lished as the ultimate accomplishment at the end of man's development within his vision of spiritual perfection and to which extent the body and the feminine participate in this process.

Theosis (deification) in Maximus and the membership of Christ's body

To explore Maximus' conceptualisation of the ultimate goal of development, we must depart from the psychoanalytic theory and Jung's understanding of psychic wholeness. Maximus grounds his vision of development on a different ontological basis, which, nevertheless, includes a dynamic experiential aspect. According to Maximus, the ultimate purpose (σκοπός) of spiritual development is conceptualised through *theosis* (θέωσις, *deification*), a notion that, despite its 'divine' connotation towards 'holiness', embraces the totality of the human person comprising body and soul. Philosophers have investigated the encounter of human nature with the divine since early antiquity. Plato applies the terms *homoiosis* and *methexis* to signify a relation in which an entity shares the qualities of another without losing its identity (see Russell 2004: 2). Early Christian writers, such as Clement of Alexandria, Origen, and the Cappadocians, utilise and explore *deification*, too. Dionysius the Areopagite defines it as 'the attaining of likeness to God and union with him as far as possible' (*EH* 1.3: *PG* 3, 376A). However, it was Maximus that introduced deification 'as the goal of the spiritual life' (Russell 2004: 296).

The ontological dimension of deification

As shown in Chapter 4, Maximus' view on ontology is a combination of cosmology and eschatology, which considers the creatures teleologically within their ends, that is, their ontological *logoi*. In addition, this ontology incorporates a strong experiential dimension through the sacraments (i.e. Baptism and Eucharist) as well as the union of the psychic functions with the *logoi*. Academic research has emphasized the fact that, in Maximus, like in Aristotle, 'the cosmos is viewed not as a static, metaphysical unit, but in terms of its goal (*telos*) or purpose (*skopos*), which for the Confessor is christologically determined' (Cooper 2005: 84; see Plass 1980: 277). The teleological perspective is a direct consequence of the fact that Logos's descent to earth opened the way for man to ascend to heaven. It is a principle that is encountered in numerous expressions, from Athanasius of Alexandria – 'God became human that we might become divine' (*De Incarn. 54*) – to contemporary scholars (e.g. Mantzaridis 1984; Nellas 1997). Deification is a dynamic incorporation of eschatology into our cosmos; and '[w]hen cosmology is reconciled with eschatology, we get the eschatological community in the divine Eucharist and the body of the Church', states Zizioulas (2008: 131).

Maximus refers to Christ, the incarnate Logos, as the perfect model and goal of the deified man, a person whose 'flesh and blood' bears the whole potential of deification: 'the flesh of the Logos is the return and restoration of human nature to itself through virtues, while his blood is the anticipated deification, which will sustain human nature by grace unto eternal well being' (*Q.Thal.* 35: 241). In parallel to the ontological aspect, Maximus robustly embeds an experiential dimension, through the all-embracing virtue of spiritual love: 'nothing is more truly Godlike than divine love . . . nothing more apt to raise up human beings to deification' (*Ep.* 2: 393B). In this way, Maximus' understanding of deification is that this concept is not at all an unattainable theoretical accomplishment but a spiritual experience as a result of the attuned psychic functions with the *logoi* of the Christ-Logos, of which the ultimate is love.

We mentioned above how the incarnate Logos integrates in himself all the divisions of the creation. The whole cosmos is ontologically and physically present in Christ's flesh and blood, because his flesh stands for the *logoi* of the sensible things, whereas his blood stands for the *logoi* of the intelligible things (*Q.Thal.* 35: 239). As previously discussed, these *logoi* are explicitly connected with the psychic functions of the aesthesis/senses, reason/logos, and intellect/nous, all of which are 'willingly' offered to God.[8] It is a 'wilful surrender', following the dynamic relationship 'between an image and its archetype: a seal conforms to the stamp against which it was pressed' (*Amb.* 1076BC). It can then be understood that deification is not attained by man alone: it is not an accomplishment that belongs to our personal abilities, nor a reward given 'in requital for righteous works, but is proof of the liberality of the Creator, making the lovers of the beautiful by adoption . . . indicate[d] the supernatural power that brings about deification . . .' (*Opusc.* 1: 33C–36A, trans. Russell 2004: 276–7).

Deification is the pivotal point of Maximus' vision for man and cosmos. In focusing thus, Maximus attains to synthesise all aspects of human nature with the divine by avoiding heretical connotations of his predecessors – that is, managing to exclude both the fusion of the divine and the human as well as the ascent of only the pure intellect to God.[9] Human functions, bodily and psychic, become 'as an image' the vehicles of the Logos-Christ's *logoi*-as-virtues and share their supreme qualities in God's likeness, the stage of deification, without incurring any loss of one's own identity.

The experiential dimension of deification: symbols and reality within the 'twofold world'

The ontological aspect of deification, which is 'christologically determined', is only one side of the coin. Deification also holds a robust experiential dimension through both the sacramental communion and the participation of the psyche in Christ's *logoi* – identical with the *logoi* of beings. Maximus adopts the symbolic and allegoric language of the Alexandrian hermeneutic school[10] to describe the participation of the humans to the divine. It is therefore necessary to initially discuss the role of symbols in Christianity, insofar as they were popular means of expressing doctrines of faith. In fact, in early Christianity, 'everything could be or become a symbol, a sign, an image of God . . .' (Ladner 1995: 7). Symbols could thus bridge the natural and the transcendent by highlighting essential aspects of the metaphysical realm.

Although in Christian tradition symbols are treated mostly spiritually, it is important to emphasize that the locus of the interaction with symbols is the bodily senses. The icons and the paintings therefore are not only means of spiritual progress but first and foremost of sanctification perceived by the senses – that now become 'spiritual senses'. Symbols and reality are intertwined as the artist contributes to the unity of the visible and invisible worlds by integrating the symbols and entities of the invisible reality with the colours and means of the tangible world in an icon. In this respect, the transcendent object can become known through the spiritual senses: and now man is capable 'of consuming the substance of the knowing object' (Balthasar 1988: 168). Maximus combines the symbols with the individual's participation in the symbolic order, which becomes a source of spiritual experience. Consequently, one can speak of 'symbolic identification' of Christ's symbolism – through his flesh or the *logoi* – 'with their intelligible contents or meaning' (Cooper 2005: 41). This becomes important for understanding Maximus' use of symbols.

Maximus interprets numerous historical events, resorting to insightful analogies to describe man's adventurous journey towards salvation and, eventually, deification. For instance, referring to the Israelites' exodus from Egypt, he compares the 'desert' to human nature, whereas the intellect, which has attained the spiritual knowledge by contemplation, is compared to Moses. The latter is summoned by God to lead the Israelites away from Egypt – that is, far from the 'passions' of the senses (*Q.Thal.* 17: 111.24). In this way, imagery and reality, past and future, external historical events and internal personal experiences are all ontologically linked, because 'the sensible world is understood within the intelligible one through the *logoi*' (*Myst.* 2: 669C). On this ground, Maximus is able to envisage the church building as

> an image of God, in that it accomplishes the same unity among the believers as God. However different they are by their characteristics and their differences of place and ways of life, nevertheless they find themselves unified in it through faith.
>
> (*Myst.* 1. *PG* 91: 668BC)

The church is also an image of the twofold world, visible and invisible (ibid.: 668D), as well as of man, who is 'a mystical church': through the body, representing the nave, man illumines the practical aspect of the soul, whilst through the sanctuary, that is the intellect/nous, he conveys to God the sensible things by the natural contemplation in spirit as purely detached from matter (ibid.: 672BC). The fact that the grace of deification is bestowed upon the people through the sacraments is an essential element throughout Maximus' *Mystagogia:* 'the reception of the holy and life-giving mysteries signifies the adoption, the union and intimacy, and the divine likeness and deification' (*Myst.* 24: 709C). Yet, whilst the church unites believers who partake of the sacraments, this union and deification is not at all an individualistic process but a result of openness to the others' needs: 'nothing brings us more easily to justification or deification . . . than mercy towards the needy offered from the soul with pleasure and joy' (ibid.: 713A).

Deification is ultimately attained through loving God and the neighbour, a love 'that imitates and reciprocates the divine philanthropy' (Russell 2004: 273). Man, borne in God's image, is simultaneously bestowed with the all-embracing psychic potentiality of 'love', whereby he is able to ultimately act as a deified man in 'God's likeness'. In fact, man shares God's energies within the 'hypostatic union' of the double nature, human and divine, of Christ (*Amb.* 4: 1044D; *Opusc.* 1: 36BC). A portion of this union belongs to all those that attain deification through their own specific *logos* of nature, inasmuch as Christ-Logos 'came to deify wholly that nature which . . . he willed to unite to himself in one and the same hypostasis, with everything that naturally belongs to it, apart from sin' (*Opusc.* 7: 77C).[11] In this hypostasis-person of Christ, cosmos and nature, body and soul, along with their symbols and senses, find the ultimate spiritual manifestation. It is because both the physical and the spiritual/intelligible world, the 'twofold world' that challenges the limitations of the human mind, are intertwined through the *logoi* – the virtues – of which the highest is divine love.

The experiential dimension: the union of the body and soul with Christ's body-limbs

Maximus considers deification to apply to the whole human nature, of body and soul, in a 'mutual relationship'. Cooper (2005) has extensively explored the participation of the body in the state of deification in a study characteristically subtitled 'holy flesh, wholly deified' (see *Opusc.* 7: 77C). But despite the fact that Maximus' corpus provides numerous references for the body at the stage of deification, it must be stressed that the precise context of these references is the ascetic: it is there that God calls us 'to subject the flesh to the spirit, mortifying and enslaving it by every sort of ill-treatment' (*L.Asc.* 41: *CCSG* 40: 109; CWA 132). Whilst the eschatological perspective for the body is to be 'wholly deified', in fact, in real time, and during the spiritual struggle, this body – in the ascetic tradition – was particularly under 'vigilant attention':

> In the desert tradition, vigilant attention to the body enjoyed an almost oppressive prominence. Yet to describe ascetic thought as 'dualistic' and as motivated by hatred of the body, is to miss its most novel and its most poignant aspect. Seldom, in ancient thought, had the body been seen as more deeply implicated in the transformation of the soul; and never was it made to bear so heavy a burden.
>
> (Brown 1988: 235)

The narrow circles of social life in the medieval context as well as the prevailing attitude of renunciation/detachment from objects – and by extension from bodies and sexuality in both monastic and secular life – indicate the limits of the then bodily activities compared with a modern man's diversity of bodily expressions in personal or artistic life. Even within marital life, the body was not the protagonist. The dualistic Hellenic conceptualisation of body and soul,[12] exerting an influence on patristic writers such as Athanasius and Gregory of Nyssa, is present in Maximus, too. Maximus thus 'even takes the view that marital union has been approved by God only because of the fall' (Ware 1997: 97). It is nonetheless important to highlight that Maximus' strong Hellenic and Neoplatonic inheritance, as well as his profound knowledge of Gregory of Nyssa's positions, resulted in a more personal point of gravity for theorising the body (see Cooper 2005: 208–11). Maximus speaks of 'limits' regarding the role of the body, restricted into a sexual union for reproduction – thus also deprived of certain activities at multiple levels (i.e. social or cultural). In Maximus' ultimate vision, still, 'the unity of man and woman retains . . . that reflective glimmer of God's own unity' (Balthasar 1988: 204). In this respect, these limits did not finally prevent Maximus from his vision of a 'deified' body – that is Christ's 'holy flesh' – which is able to embrace the whole cosmos:

> Man . . . is just as much included in a larger whole through his natu-
> ral mutual relationship to the two realms of creation . . . he is included
> through his essential way of being, and he includes through his intellec-
> tual function. By being extended, then, into these two realms through his
> double nature, he is able to draw both of them together to himself in a
> synthesis. . . . He is included among both intellectual and material things
> because he is himself a soul and a body; but he can include them in
> himself through the functions of his intellect, because he also possesses
> reason-logos and senses.
>
> (*Amb.* 10: 1153AB, trans. Balthasar)

The body therefore undertakes an action of 'recapitulation' of all sensible things, whilst the soul takes that of the integration of all the intelligible things. This outstanding potential is described precisely by Maximus in the case of the archetypal man, the Christ, whose body and soul are the 'reservoirs' of the total-ity of *logoi*: '*logoi* of sensible things are to be comprehended the flesh of Christ, *logoi* of intelligible [things] his blood . . . while the bones [are] the logoi of deity above any comprehension' (*Q.Thal.* 35: 239, cf.; *Th.Oec.* II.10: 1129A). In this respect, Christ's flesh-limbs 'functions as the 'bridge' between the intelligible and the sensible spheres' (Cooper 2005: 38) and signify man's ultimately metaphysi-cal potential.

However, the path to this union is not always clear in terms of the participa-tion of the body, because Maximus' application of the symbols leads directly to the Archetypal-Logos. What is for man a potentiality, for the archetypal man, the incarnate Logos-Christ, is a reality. Logos embraces the whole world within his body and soul, being the 'definition' of the spiritual and ontological recapitulation into the 'hypostasis' of Christ. As a result, the very limbs/body of Christ acquire an extraordinary value, being the very means of man's perfection. Maximus views these limbs as the recapitulation of the *logoi*-as-virtues; and when a man attains a virtue, at the same time he partakes of the correspondent to this virtue of Christ's limb, according to Maximus' innovative passage:[13]

> [One will partake Christ's] *legs and feet,* if he keeps unwavering and
> steadfast the soul's underpinnings on the ground of faith, virtue and

knowledge . . . and overcomes with exaltation the mountains of ignorance and the hills of evil . . . [65ab]; *hands* if he . . . maintains the
practical psychic aspect alert and robust for the fulfilment of the divine
commandments [64d]; *knees,* if he is disposed with compassion and
providence to those that are poorly and overwhelmed in faith, imitating
Lord's mercy to us . . . *lower parts,* if he reasonably stands with prudence in front of the things and . . . preserve undefiled his flesh alongside
his soul, shaping in it the Logos through the virtues . . . [65ab]; *head,*
if he has attained faith . . . whereby the entire edifice of virtues and of
knowledge is attached together and grows within spiritual progress . . . ;
eyes, if he appreciates the creation in a spiritual manner and smoothly
brings together all the spiritual logoi of sensible and intelligible beings
into a pure fulfilment of God's glory . . . ; *breast,* if he fills his heart with
notions of theological contemplation . . . ; *abdomen,* when he . . . keeps
on being enriched in spiritual contemplation and maintains unquenched
the dispassionate desirous eros [love] for the celestial intercourse . . .

(Amb. 48: 1364C–65C, 64cd, italics mine)

Maximus interprets with boldness the spiritual communion of Christ's limbs
not only as an ontologically determined perfection but also as a recapitulation of
the whole spiritual struggle towards spiritual development: this is due to the fact
that the communion of Christ's feet, hands, and lower parts stands for the *practical philosophy* (first stage); knees, head, eyes, for the *natural contemplation,* that
is the interpretation of the spiritual meanings; whereas breast (heart) and abdomen
stand for the highest stage of *mystical theology* and profound experience of the
divine union.[14] Aside from Loudovikos, who attributes to this passage the foundation of Maximus' 'Eucharistic ontology' (2010: 33ff), this extremely interesting
description of Christ's body has evaded scholars' attention.[15]

Maximus' approach opens new avenues in terms of philosophical understanding of objects as symbols, as a further result of the discussed earlier 'twofold
world'; and he does so by interpreting Christ's limbs/body not only as virtues
but also as supreme symbols or means of knowledge. This is an intriguing case
where spiritual symbols, divine qualities, psychic experiences, and bodily senses/
parts are deeply interwoven without confusion: a synthesis of all of them leads
par excellence to experiencing the deified man-Logos. Discussing the verse from
Matthew 17, 7, in which Jesus approached his disciples and touched them, after
his transfiguration in the mountain,[16] Cooper wittily remarks: 'The sensible symbol by which the Word draws near is not other than himself . . . in becoming flesh,
he has become his own symbol' (1995: 33). The spiritual path in Maximus obviously offers this kind of ontological 'intimacy' with the symbolic, because man
becomes, in 'God's likeness', the source of all spiritual symbols/meanings, the
Logos in many logoi. Instead, Jung's usage of the symbols is different, insofar as
symbols convey meanings or images of the Self but can never be identified with
these very meanings or the Self *per se.*

Both the ontological and the experiential aspect of deification illustrates the particular paths that the body and soul follow towards 'likeness', which integrates and ultimately deifies the whole man via Christ's limbs-as-virtues. In Christ's body, all levels of the creation are united, such as the divisions between male and female or earth and heaven, as well as between created and uncreated (*Amb.* 41: 1304D–12A; *Q.Thal.* 48: 335.71–80). This union becomes possible only through the 'dispassionate desirous eros for the celestial intercourse', which is the divine love (*Amb.* 48: 1364CD). Although this ontological union towards deification is rarely attainable in the present time, it comes with the eschatological vision of man's ultimate development, as a prospect of an 'inaugurated eschatology', in Ware's words (1967: 30). We must not forget that the Neoplatonic dualistic tradition and the monastic context, both prevailing in the early Christian and Maximus' era, determined the range of perspectives that he could attribute to the body. The body in Maximus is an essential part of wholeness/perfection, as in Jung's fourth element, but first needs a transformation towards Christ's body and its limbs-as-virtues. Yet, despite these challenging visions of the body, we also must address the question whether and how the body, in Maximus' vision, may interact with the socio-cultural summons that modern life openly proposes. To answer this question, we must further consider synthetically all the perspectives opened by Jung and Maximus' final goals.

Wholeness or holiness?

Maximus and Jung envisage the final stage of development by engaging multiple levels of life in that both refer to the union between matter and spirit, earth and heaven, man and God(s). Individuation culminates in the polycentric Self, integrating the potentialities and perspectives of a life as 'wholeness', whereas deification is directed to the incarnate Logos-Christ, who endows people with the communion of his *logoi*-as-virtues through his body/limbs. Accordingly, the final point is a contrast between a Self-determined individuation process and the 'christologically determined' spiritual life towards deification. We can now discuss the differences between *wholeness* within a polycentric Self, namely a 'wholly man', and *holiness,* that is a 'wholly deified man'.

Although Jung explores the crucial role of God-image for attainment of the Self, the Self/God-image is deprived of 'divine' qualities, because the God-image bears psychological characteristics alone. By failing to attribute metaphysical perspectives to the Self, Jung rather drains the God-image of any ontological potential and relationship to God as such. Consequently, when Jung speaks of the spiritual level, he views it in psychological/phenomenological terms, not valuing the ontological underpinnings of the applied concepts. Furthermore, Jung introduces the missing elements (dark, feminine, body) for the God-image to constitute wholeness. However, he does not provide convincing examples for lively representations of this wholeness/Self but gives alchemical and Gnostic equivalents, which rather signify symbolic *metaphors* of the Self rather than paradigms of the missing elements in real time and space. By departing from classical theological interpretations of God (image), for the fear of charges of mysticism, Jung unintentionally resorts to tenets that are not at all distant from mysticism. The amalgam of elements from different and often contradictory traditions ultimately endangers the clarity of the real potential of the Self.

Maximus, on the contrary, proposes the concept of *deification,* a process bearing both ontological and experiential aspects. Despite the pre-condition of a metaphysical God as such, this God is not inaccessible: he manifests himself through the incarnate Logos-Christ, who can be experienced by means of the sacramental path and the transformation of psychic functions to his *logoi*-as-virtues. Maximian theology therefore leaves sufficient space for the ontology to become, in the end, 'wholly experienced', precisely because the dynamics of the 'many *logoi* in one Logos' can embrace all levels of life.

Deification is equally dependent on the synergy between the psychic functions/will and God's will as well the communion of Christ-Logos through the sacraments. These two ways comprise a concrete path leading to the attainment of this goal through spiritual struggle. Moreover, the Christ's bodily limbs function as both symbols and sources of experience of the divine due to the fact that they ultimately identify with virtues. Spiritual wholeness includes the union of male-female and of all the divisions of universe in the person of Christ-Logos, as well as the transfiguration of the body. However, such a transformation of the body is eschatologically determined and presupposes a certain degree of renunciation and ascetic context. The paradox of a body at once 'dangerous' and 'sacred' (Turner 2008: 75) provides the ground to Maximus' discourse on the body, potentially both 'fallible' and 'deified'. Despite the fact that Maximus includes aspects of Jung's 'fourth element' in the final stage of development, he also challenges Jung's equivalent view on the condition of a necessary spiritual transformation of these elements – within the communion of Christ's body/limbs.

On the other hand, the possible 'weakness' from a theological perspective on the Jungian points might provide the grounding for fostering a pluralistic vision of wholeness within the polycentric Self. Whereas Maximus speaks of the union of ontological divisions from an eschatological perspective, Jung's interest is in the emergence of the feminine aspect in current culture and society (mother/nature/feminine *as equal* to masculine/church/God) or in the confrontation and realisation of the evil/shadow as both reality and potentiality. This view works towards new insights into the dynamics between individual and external reality by enacting the hidden-shadowy aspects of personality within the socio-cultural dynamics. This integration becomes crucial when considering the ways in which both theories handle the body and its feminine and masculine aspects. Maximus indeed views the psyche as a virgin/feminine, capable of 'conceiving and giving the birth to Logos' and its virtues, taking thus the place of Holy Mother (*Ep.* 4: 592A; see Squire 1966). This is, however, a 'christologically' determined view and does not refer to contemporary cultural attitudes. The body in Maximus' and the Christian context is allowed to undertake only spiritual activities, which renders sexuality and eros – especially in their creative aspects – rather repressed in the interpersonal and cultural dimensions (see Schubart 1994: 209f, 226–8). By contrast, Jung's views differ: 'gender', although initially limited to bodily sexes, can be amplified and 'conceived as a plural within any one being' (Rowland 2002: 69) interacting with the socio-cultural context. Moreover, the post–Jungians clearly value the body 'on its own matrix level', a value that 'does not require its transformation into spirit, meaning, communication, dream body . . . or metaphor' (Samuels 1990: 305).

Despite these divergences, Jung's notion of the 'subtle body' can be juxtaposed to Maximus' 'deified body' and both can constrictively contribute to the contemporary post-modern debates on the body. Both notions illustrate 'wholeness' that appears to overcome the Cartesian body–mind split, based on the ancient disgrace of body (but not its *beauty*) in Plato's dualistic view – a tradition which was passed on to Descartes through Augustine (see Matthews 2000). However, the subtle/alchemical body cannot simultaneously function as a 'recapitulation of all sensible things' and, like the deified body, as an object of experience/communion of virtues such as divine love: the former is the symbol of the matter–spirit union, whereas the latter is both the symbol and object of wholeness/deification.

Contemporary understanding of the human 'body' addresses a multifaceted object-body from a sociological viewpoint, such as of 'sporting bodies' or 'technological bodies', that leads to a '*multi-dimensional medium for the constitution of society*' (Shilling 2005: 1). The body can also be understood as a cultural product: for instance, 'music provides an excellent example of how the body is a source of a cultural product . . . ' (ibid.: 145). In this respect, the body is an object that conveys specific cultural meanings. Post-modern views on the body, expanding Marx's analysis of a body as locus for capitalism and discussing how political/social forces formulate bodily behaviour-sexuality,[17] also address the body through cultural discourses but do not attribute to it any independent meaning. Instead, in Maximus' view, Christ's body/limbs not only convey symbolic or spiritual meanings but also principally are a medium of development through their spiritual communion.

Jung's subtle body is, to a considerable extent, aligned with the post-modern body, on which the impact of society and culture is unquestionable. As Rowland notes, Jung, like the post-moderns, 'did not regard the body as a self-explanatory source of meaning' (2002: 134) but rather as a source of constant psychic development through certain canalisations of the libido. What Maximus' vision of Christ's limbs can contribute at this point is that the encounter with the body of the 'Other' – despite the initial disengagement from socio-cultural dynamics – recapitulates the wholeness of human expectations, being thus the locus of all discourses and experiences. The parts of the Logos-Other's body epitomize the profoundest meanings and values. It is therefore essential to understand that the two models may supplement each other in an emerging complementarity. Jung's failure to accurately address the potential of the Self can be substituted by Maximus' robust ontology. The lack of socio-cultural engagement of the body and the feminine in deification could be enriched by the Jungian concepts of 'cultural unconscious' and 'the fourth element' within an individuated polycentric Self. Through this mutual understanding, Jung's multifaceted individuation may complement the renunciation/detachment from objects in deification. It is not accidental that a post-modern philosophical mind gives an insightful vision for such integration:

> Renunciation of love and fulfilment of love: they are *both* wonderful and without equal only where the entire experience of love may assume a central position along with *all* of its nearly indistinguishable thrills . . . that is then also the place (in the ecstasy of a few lovers and saints of *all* times and *all* religions) where renunciation and fulfilment become identical. Where infinity occurs *entirely* (whether as a negative or positive), the prefix drops away, that which had been the, ah, all too humanly achieved way, which now has been followed – and what remains is the state of having arrived, *being itself!*
>
> (Rilke 2005: 195–6)

   Although wholeness and holiness ultimately appeal to different levels of life (socio-cultural vs. spiritual/metaphysical), both aim at the elevation of psychic and bodily aspects towards a spiritual level, 'where infinity occurs *entirely*'. The body, along with other 'neglected' aspects of human life – which Jung incorporated in the fourth element – becomes a means of higher 'meanings', cultural or spiritual, necessary for the union of all developmental potentialities. Although the two models anchor the acquisition of their final goals on different grounds (unconscious, cultural symbols vs. Christ's *logoi*-as-limbs), a synthesis of their complementary aspects might generate a new constructive viewpoint for rethinking modes of union between 'wholeness' and 'holiness'.

Notes

1. These luminosities, the archetypal 'living psychic forces', bear both an elementary and a transformative character according to Neumann (1955: 24ff). The transformative aspect indicates the developmental potential of the psychic archetypal forces towards individuation.
2. Jung introduces a striking metaphor of the psyche like a 'night sky', that is, of a 'darksome psyche as a star-strewn night sky, whose planets and fixed constellations represent the archetypes, in all their luminosity and numinosity' (1947/1954: para. 392). All these luminosities are subject to further growth within the individual's life, through the decisive impact of the cultural symbols and the interaction between the external and internal worlds.
3. This middle path is for Jung significant, as it is 'the most legitimate fulfilment of the meaning of the individual' (1928a: para. 327).
4. Jung specifically explored the mother–infant relationship, considering it 'the deepest and most poignant one we know' (1928/1931b: para. 723) – before the Oedipal complex emerges.

5. Jung resorts to alchemic metaphors to integrate certain opposite aspects such as the 'union between intellect and sexuality' (see 1945/1954: para. 343; 1955/1956).

6. A Christian writer and mystic who lived in Thessalonica in the 14th century AD.

7. Jung writes: 'When one considers how strongly the Church Fathers were influenced by Gnostic ideas in spite of their resistance to these heresies, it is not inconceivable that we have in the symbolism of the vessel a pagan relic that proved adaptable to Christianity, and this is all the more likely as the worship of Mary was itself a vestige of paganism which secured for the Christian Church the heritage of the Magna Mater, Isis, and other goddesses. The image of the *vas Sapientiae,* vessel of wisdom, likewise recalls its Gnostic prototype, Sophia' (1921/1971: para. 398).

8. See *Amb.* 10: 1112A–16D; these functions are offered through the surrender of our 'gnomic will' (ἐκχώρησις γνωμική) to God; see *Amb.* 7: 1076B.

9. Russell explains that Maximus surpassed the risks of 'both an Eutychian fusion of the divine and the human and an Origenistic ascent of the pure intellect [alone] to an undifferentiated assimilation to Christ' (2004: 293–4).

10. Mainly represented by Clement of Alexandria, Origen, and Cyril of Alexandria. More in Blowers (1991, 1995).

11. For an analysis of this issue, see Balthasar (1988: 237ff) and Garrigues (1976).

12. For the distinction between the Hellenic (dualistic) view and the Hebrew (holistic) view of the body, see Ware (1997: 91–3), also discussed in Chapter 4.

13. We have slightly changed the order of Christ's 'limbs', from the external to the internal and from the lower to the higher, to emphasize the three stages of spiritual development: the practical philosophy (*foot, hands, lower parts*), natural contemplation (*knees, head, eyes*), and mystical theology (*breast, abdomen*).

14. About these three stages, see Chapter 5, at the section: *The stages of spiritual life and the logoi-as-virtues towards theological philosophy.*

15. Maximus follows the earlier usage of Christ's flesh as a source of virtues by Evagrius; see more in Thunberg (1995: 352), who makes only passing references to several of the limbs (ibid.: 381, 391, 398) without attaching to them any particular significance.

16. See *Matthew* 17, 7: 'Then Jesus came over and touched them. "Get up" he said. "Don't be afraid"'.

17. For example, we may refer here to the theories by Foucault (1981) and Turner (2008: 49).

8

'ANSWER TO JOB'

A *dark side* or an *eschatological light*?

Aside from the body and the feminine as aspects of the fourth element, the most challenging and perhaps the most ambiguous aspect of Jung's *tetrameria* is God's *dark side* as it is understood within the notion of evil. This exceptionally vital issue for Jung's 'wholeness' will be explored in juxtaposition with Maximus' theory of 'final restoration' (*apokatastasis*). The discussion lays emphasis on the fact that Jung's understanding of 'the fourth' or God's dark/evil side could be construed as a result of the polarities and dualities, and thus limitations, of the archetypal theory within the space-time continuum. As a result of these limitations, Jung follows a chronological understanding of time, an important parameter to understand the implications of evil. On the other hand, Maximus unfolds an eschatological view of time as he articulates his theory of final restoration beyond the space-time limitations. The comparison is thus an issue of *perspectivism* and in particular of time perspectivism. Accordingly, the two thinkers attribute different qualities to the dark/evil side.

In Jung's understanding, God's dark side is the problematic core concerning divine 'wholeness', as it is dealt with in his innovative work *Answer to Job* (1952a). Jung addresses so extensively the dark side of God's image – and goes so far with this 'darkness' – as to describe the Son of God as 'a conflict situation *par excellence*' (1942/1948: para. 272). This statement thoroughly describes Jung's vision of wholeness that must incorporate – and not transform in Maximus' understanding – the primordial conflict of good-evil opposites. The challenge now is not the perfection, the 'likeness' and the divine, but God's 'dark side' in a new perspective: 'The dark side of God is a merciful one, effacing useless images, stretching, pushing us beyond even the best of what we have found in our traditions and created in our prayers' (Ulanov 1999: 71). This deviation from classical Christian interpretation is possible for Jung as he follows Keopgen's view that considers man as 'the bearer of the mystery': and this means that 'the *opus Christi* is transferred to the individual' (Jung 1955/1956: para. 531). In fact, this 'mystery' constitutes the new avenues of development that human consciousness is gifted within human history as well as is 'ordered' to 'further' God's work. We must discuss now this challenging view extensively.

Evil and time in Jung's progression of the Self

Although irrelevant at first sight, *perspectivism,* and particularly perspectivism of time, may demonstrate the core of the different conceptual schemes between Jungian and Maximian approaches to evil. Despite the fact that modern *perspectivism* rejects any metaphysical dimension, any *thing-in-itself,* it provides an effective interpretative tool for many applications in science. In particular, in modern physics it is understood that the parameter of time-velocity changes dramatically the ordinary way we perceive daily formations. In this fashion, just as Einstein had intuitions beyond the graspable reality in order to understand the perceptible in more than one dimension (that is, the space-time continuum), one has to draw upon that which is beyond the conscious/psychological realm in order to fully understand the 'spiritual' perspectives of evil and time – in line with the ultimate metaphysical potential of the spiritual continuum (Chapter 2). Einstein's *relativity theory* perceives the notion of time in relation to both the dynamics of the matter-field and the issue of observation-participation. In such a reality in which '[t]here is no place . . . both for the field and matter, *for the field is the only reality*' (Einstein, cited from Capek 1961: 319), we are not distant observers but participators.[1] The universe, therefore, is 'a participatory universe' (see Capra 1975: 153), which means that the way we participate in a phenomenon may change dramatically the outcome of our understanding of this phenomenon.[2] Despite the oppositions to this approach by such scientists as Popper,[3] it is understood that similarly to the importance of conscious experience in psychic facts, for a profound understanding of a phenomenon, one needs the highest possible degree of observation/ participation therein.

Perspectivism within time and space may provide an understanding of different approaches to 'evil' according to the limitations that we set over the 'field' of time and personal choice. Both Jung and Maximus appear to maintain a partial knowledge of evil, a knowledge that is limited by their specific viewpoint. This limitation occurs due to the particular 'glimpse' or 'slice of time' that is taken when viewing evil. This conceptualisation of time has been addressed both by physics and philosophical insights that explore the ontological validity of things by focusing either on the present or on the absence of a space-time 'slice' (Craig 2008: 597, fig. 35.1). Jung adopted reductionism as his principal observational method and made little use of personal participation beyond the purely psychological implications of the shadowy or dark/evil aspects (transcendentally). Furthermore, Jung does not seem to make a distinction between the collective evil and one's free choice or evil side. As a result, he ultimately fuses human activities and evil choices, such as wars, with God's dark side/evil. We can now explore how Jung reached this synthesis and its impact on his theory on evil.

At many points thus far, we have discussed Jung's methodological premises grounded on the archetypal dualities (personal-collective, good-evil, etc.) through the antithesis and synthesis of opposites. In his *A Psychological Approach to the Dogma of the Trinity* (1942/1948), Jung brings forward Plato's trinitarian approach (quoting *Timaeus*, ibid.: para. 243), the quaternitarian *tetraktys* in the Pythagorean school, Goethe's *Faust,* and Schopenhauer's fourfold root of his 'Principle of Sufficient Reason' (ibid.: para. 246). It is at this point, along with his *Aion* (1951/1959), that Jung lays the foundation for the burning questions of his later *Answer to Job* (1952a). One could start with realising that Jung's vision of the fourth element has decisively been influenced by Hegelian antithesis:

> Good and Evil were the specific differences yielded by the thought of Spirit as immediately existent. Since their antithesis has not yet been resolved . . . each of them having an independent existence of its own, man is a self lacking any essential being and is the synthetic ground of the existence and conflict.
>
> (Hegel 1807/1977: 469)

Jung, however, furthers the Hegelian antithesis acting on a historical space by applying it into the psychic life. As Dourley remarks, Jung 'departs from Hegel when he removes the conflict of absolutes from projection into historical events understood as outside the psyche and relocates the process within the psyche' (2008: 124). It nevertheless appears that historical events played a crucial role in Jung's formulation of the dynamics of evil. In this respect, amongst the equivalents of the fourth element – matter/body, the feminine, dark/evil – the latter seems to predominantly occupying Jung's thought, especially in his *Answer to Job*.

It is commonly known that Jung's 'Christian' epoch, with the world suffering from the worst manifestations of the human dark side and evil through two world wars, was Jung's hidden impetus for challenging the 'good' aspect of man and, by extension, of God (Jung 1945, 1952a, 1959). Jung went as far as saying that '"God-Almightiness" does not make man divine, it merely fills him with arrogance and arouses everything evil in him' (1945: para. 439). Nevertheless, this 'God-Almightiness' was rather a manifestation of how humanity perceived God (as an archetypal image with polarities, good and evil), especially at a 'certain' time, when man had declared God 'dead': it is rather one's, and also Jung's, unconscious and subjective projection-as-understanding of the idea of the death of God, namely the total absence of God's 'good side' as well as of any of God's 'divine' interventions in wartime. It is when the God-image, previously 'projected' into a superpower outside the psyche, 'returns to its origin', following a 'way back into the subject' and potentially leading 'to catastrophe' (Jung 1945: para. 437). But the crucial question that arises here is whether such a catastrophe could convincingly prove the existence of God's dark side.

Jung introduced the idea of the 'development of Trinity into a quaternity', precisely because this development addresses the perspective of psychic wholeness comprising opposites. What is principally important for Jung is once more the reduction of any religious perspective or 'metaphysical figure' to the psychological, 'to man and his psychology': 'any statements of this kind . . . must be reduced to man and his psychology, since they are mental products which cannot be presumed to have any metaphysical validity' (Jung 1942/1948: para. 268). We followed in detail in Chapter 3 Jung's reductive treatment of metaphysical figures as 'projections', that is, unconscious identification with objects subjectively. These projections must be traced back to the discussions with his father, a Protestant pastor, who was irritated when the child Jung questioned him on faith and who would answer, 'You always want to think. One ought not to think but to believe' (*MDR*: 43). In his reply 'No, one must experience and know' (ibid.), Jung frames his future 'reductions and projections' in a creeping uncertainty between experience/knowledge and religious belief. After many years, Jung progressively reaches the compound conclusion that the symbol of Trinity is

(a) 'to be thought of as a process of unconscious maturation taking place within the individual' (1942/1948: para. 287), namely it is understood in three phases: the unconscious as father, the conscious as son, maturation/individuation as spirit;

(b) 'a process of conscious realisation continuing over the centuries' (ibid.: para. 288); and

(c) 'the Trinity lays claim not only to *represent* a personification of psychic processes in three roles, but to *be* the one God in three Persons, who all share the same divine nature' (ibid.).

It is apparent that Jung speaks of (the symbols of) the Son-Logos as processing from the Father, just as consciousness proceeds from the unconscious, whereas the Spirit/Self is introduced in order to unite the opposites of Father and Son (ibid.: para. 270–2). However, to complete Jung's understanding of the Trinity, the Logos-Christ is not the only Son of the Father, it is also the Satan that emanates from him:

> If God reveals his nature and takes on definite form as a man, then the opposites in him must fly apart: here good, there evil. So it was that the opposites latent in the Deity flew apart when the Son was begotten and manifested themselves in the struggle between Christ and the devil . . .
>
> (Jung 1942/1948: para. 259)

Is it not obvious here the Hegelian vision of good and evil as 'the specific differences yielded by the thought of Spirit', as shown above, that Jung incorporates in his essential reasoning? This reasoning together with the fact that God is viewed through his archetypal dimensions (according to statements a and b) explains the reason Jung's insights cannot go beyond the dualities that determine the archetypes. Despite Jung's third reference point (the Trinity 'to *be* the one God in three Persons'), it appears that he does not take this point into serious consideration. Instead, Jung primarily refers to such dualities as good-evil and collective-personal to construe this doctrine (see 1911/1956: para. 351–2).[4] As a result, what Jung attained as knowledge and 'answers' to the questions posed by his *Answer to Job,* appears to be predetermined by the dimensions and boundaries that he applied to the archetypal God.

The discrepancies between a 'good' God and a 'bad' God and between personal and collective manifestations of evil are richly depicted in Job's life: this is, for Jung, part of a 'divine drama' (1952a: para. 560) focusing on the problem of 'suffering'. Challenging the classical Christian interpretation of evil via the dogma of *privatio boni* (evil is an absence of God's presence, introduced by Augustine), Jung principally states that the '[p]sychological experience shows that whatever we call "good" is balanced by an equally substantial "bad" or "evil"' (1952a: prefatory note). In this fashion, Jung views Job's history as a collective process of consciousness advancing within time and space from an unconscious state of an undifferentiated God-image, as of the Father, to the consciousness of the incarnate God-image in Christ – an image that, however, was not completed by the revelation of the Holy Spirit but has to be further incarnated by the Antichrist. This is a central symbol in the book of *Apocalypses,* standing for God's not-yet-revealed dark and/or evil side (ibid.: para. 688–95).

In fact, Christ 'remains outside and above mankind': due to 'his virgin birth and his sinlessness, [he] was not an empirical human being at all' (ibid.: para. 657). For this reason Jung re-interprets Christ's incarnation in purely psychological terms: '*Incarnatio* means first and foremost God's birth in Christ, hence psychologically the realisation of the self as something new, not present before' (letter to Erich Neumann 10.3.1959, Jung 1976: 494). Man needs this Self's incarnation-realisation as an essential part of development. This process further implies that man's individuation, a 'heroic and often tragic task' (Jung 1942/1948: para. 233), is analogous to 'God's suffering on account of the injustice of the world and the darkness of man' (ibid.). Both God's pain and human darkness account for the Self's realisation of the 'drama' of Christ's archetypal life as well as of a man 'who has been transformed by his higher destiny' (ibid.). Consequently, God's passion is projected into the Self's realisation, its dark side included.

It is not difficult now to realise in which precise way Jung's reduction and projection works: it is in line with the strong links-as-projections between the archetypal (God-image) and the personal God-Yahweh (Job's God), resulting in the reduction of the latter to the former within Jung's subjectivity. According to this reduction, the most important problem is the 'chronological' implications of the dark side as it is experienced in one's psychological life. In this respect, when Job endures with perseverance inflictions by God, he 'stands morally higher than Yahweh'; and as a result, Jung deduces, 'Yahweh must become man precisely because he has done man a wrong' (1952a: para. 640). This is the reason the Self, for Jung, is 'bigger' than the incarnate Christ.

The acting person is now the Antichrist, a key figure in *Apocalypses*: Jung's basic question and at the same time answer to the man privileged now with the *opus Christi* is, 'In spite of his misdeeds and in spite of God's work of redemption for mankind [through Christ and Spirit], the devil still maintains a position of considerable power and holds all sublunary creatures under his sway' (ibid.: para.

697). It is exactly the point at which the archetypal polarities of good and evil find their most dreadful manifestation. Because *nothing exists outside the archetypes*, there is no redeeming power from outside to cast out the devil and man's evil side. At the final analysis, *Answer to Job* stands as 'a self-portrait of Jung in his inner struggles with God' (Heisig 1979: 88), and 'despite the exegetical distortion' (ibid.), it manifests the writer's struggles projected towards God's actions, which, as being limited within the archetypal dualities, are also doomed to confine man's *opus Christi* within his dark/evil side.

The post–Jungian insights into the Answer to Job

Certain psychoanalytic interpretations construe the relationship between Job and God as the ego's 'emancipation from the super-ego' (see Britton 2006). Expanding classical psychoanalytic approaches on primary processes, Hoffman, amongst others, provides a constructive developmental perspective of man's capability for good and evil, following Ricoeur's view on evil (Ricoeur 1967). It is a view within man's inherent potential, 'capable of relationship with the transcendent and one another, capable of creativity and choices for good' (Hoffman 2012: 165).

In the same vein, post–Jungian insights on Job's paradigm fruitfully contribute to our understanding further the development of one's consciousness through the impact of God's 'suffering'. Corbett, for instance, comments that Christ's incarnation 'humanises the archetype [Self] by Jesus' ability to integrate aspects of the Self that were previously unconscious'; and '[b]y emphasizing qualities such as love rather than only law or justice, Jesus began a radically new consciousness of the Self' (Corbett 1996: 133). The new Self-as-Jesus consequently has to expand by incorporating aspects that appear to be negative or 'evil'. This is applicable in cases of 'a developmental deficit', when the individual particularly seeks 'a powerful need for soothing' (ibid. 191) – in which case good and evil become relevant. In this respect, when a 'good' like love becomes destructive, one must 'neither love or be loved' (ibid. 192). What appears crucial here is that the characterisations of good and bad are considered closely within the developmental, namely the chronological, perspective.

In a similar line, Bishop takes the view that the wrestling of Job with Yahweh accounts for 'the conscious life of humanity . . . our "destiny"' (2002: 85), so that the conscious to elevate is nothing less than 'the second cosmology' (ibid.: 175; also *MDR*: 337ff). According to Jung, the opposites of love and fear play a significant part in that as being inflicted by God's archetypal dualities: 'the pair of opposites united in the image of God, i.e. Yahweh, [are] Love and Fear . . . [and] such an opposition must be expected wherever we are confronted with an immense energy' (Jung 1976: 623). This is also evident in Jung's understanding of God, as 'love and fear were acquired by a single means: the personal experience of the God-archetype, of which the story of Job became, for him, the supreme expression' (Bishop 2002: 176). This is another account of Jung's statement of God's 'injustice, and cruelty' with regard to the original dimensions of God's archetype.

According to this rationale, a consciousness that advances in maturity must 'find it difficult to love, as a kind father, a God whom on account of his unpredictable fits of wrath, his unreliability, injustice, and cruelty, it has every reason to fear' (Jung 1952a: para. 665). As a consequence, 'love and fear' seem to ultimately mark the Jungian version of Heracletian *enantiodromia* in the case of the God's archetypal idea as it is understood by consciousness within time and space.

On the other side, discussing *Answer to Job*, Dourley highlights the fact that the *Sophia* (God's wisdom) reappears as the feminine element that Yahweh is missing: 'her gentle urging pushes Yahweh further toward becoming an embodied human' (2008: 115), which whilst 'in its deepest meaning is really his own suffering, now becoming fully conscious in humanity' (ibid. 116). By highlighting the fact that God shares his 'suffering', the religious implications become crucial: the focus moves from the archetypal God to the personal God, who desires to share his 'suffering' and 'dark' aspect with humans. The action of this sharing results in broadening the boundaries of human consciousness, also 'urged' by God's feminine side, the Sophia, towards an understanding of personal pain.

However the post–Jungians look at and reflect on the aforementioned dualities of both God's and man's consciousness, their considerations remain principally within the archetypal boundaries (good, evil, fear, love, personal, collective, masculine, feminine, etc.), and their contribution is limited to the way they appear to question the extent to which the human 'consciousness' might develop towards a new understanding of God as an 'active' image. In effect, they remain essentially still Jungian, insofar as they retain Jung's basic 'chronological' framework that is located within his previously discussed stated limits: that metaphysical figures 'cannot be presumed to have any metaphysical validity' and must be treated as 'projections'.

Maximus' theory of 'final restoration' and the eschatological light

Maximus takes an entirely different stance from Jung's 'chronological' viewpoint on dark/evil. By applying an *eschatological* approach through Christ's 'economy' (providence), namely God's work for man's salvation, Maximus considers good and evil through eschatological principles. The reference to 'the last things' (*ta eschata*) is the creed in which 'the whole of Christian doctrine – creation, incarnation, redemption and deification – finds its fulfilment' (Louth 2008: 233). Whereas for Jung little distance seems to separate the archetypal God from the personal (subjective) experience of God-image (through his reductions/projections), Maximus draws a sharp distinction between God as such in eternity and God as perceived by man within time-space continuum – that is to say, within Christ's 'economy'. Whilst for Jung good and evil, Christ and Antichrist are entities within the Hegelian 'antithesis', Maximus views the dynamics of good and evil within a process of transformation of the latter to the former. This is because Maximus is an heir of a robust tradition addressing the question of the final outcome of the cosmos, especially through Origen's 'final restoration', which Gregory of Nyssa appears, to some extent, to endorse, too (see Balthasar 1988: 356).

In fact, whereas Maximus addresses the antithesis between good and evil – that is, the struggle to freely choose good instead of evil actions (see *L.Asc., passim*) – he does not apply this antithesis to the ultimate God's will for mankind: 'The purpose of divine providence is to unify by right faith and spiritual charity those whom vice has sundered in various ways. Indeed for this the Savior suffered – *to gather together in one the children of God that were dispersed*' (*Char.* IV, 17: *ACW* 194, *John* 11, 52). Although Maximus lays much emphasis on wrestling against the 'devil' and 'desires of the flesh' (*L.Asc.* 41: *ACW* 131–3), he also strongly suggests Paul's paradigm, according to which he 'blessed the revilers and suffered the prosecutors' (*A Corinthians* 4, 12ff, ibid.). In addition, through this wrestling, Paul 'defended himself against these machinations of the demons, ever conquering evil with good in imitation of the Savior' (*L.Asc.* 15: *ACW* 112).[5] It is clear that Maximus does not recognise collective evil as something absolutely evil; he does so only when he refers to the evil that is espoused by individuals' will with the intention to sin. We now can follow Maximus' main positions describing the theory of the final restoration (*apokatastasis*):

> The church acknowledges three restorations. The first is that of each one according to the *logos* of virtue, in which one is restored having fulfilled his/her intrinsic *logos* of virtue. The second is that of the restoration of the whole creation into incorruptibility and immortality through the resurrection. The third, which actually Gregory of Nyssa misused in his own works, is that of the restoration of the psychic functions fallen in transgressions into their natural condition before the fall. Just as the whole nature will receive in resurrection the incorruptibility of flesh in hope through ages, so the diverged functions of the psyche throughout the ages must expel the memories of evil imposed to them . . . and culminate in God. And thus they will receive back the [God's] strengths in a certain understanding, though not the communion of his excellences, being restored in their initial stage. And thus God will be proved as causeless of sin [and of evil, too].
>
> (*Q.Dub.* 19: 18, 796ABC)

In this excerpt, Maximus raises the issue of the participation in 'God's excellences' according to the degree of the consent of one's freedom/will to God's will and life of virtues. Even those who have not followed him will regain their original 'nature', latterly distorted by evil, but not on the level of a spiritual communication with God's virtues. Florovsky elucidates this point, speaking of an *apokatastasis of nature* and not of restoration of the freedom/will:

> 'Nature' will be restored in its entirety. This does not mean, however, that freedom, too, will be redefined as good. . . . To recognize good does

not mean to love or choose it. Man is also capable of not falling in love with the recognized good.

(Florovsky 1931: 244)

In this consideration, by choosing the beyond-space-time eschatological view, Maximus appears to take the position of an absolutely 'external observer' of dark/ evil actions, outside of the space-time boundaries – contrary to Jung's subjectivity and confinement by the space-time continuum; and from a beyond-psychic boundaries viewpoint, what is evil in the present will cease to be evil in the end, in eternity: 'the works of sins will disappear into nothingness', because of God's mercy (*Q.Dub.* 157: 111, 848A). What will matter in the end is the degree of one's free participation in God's excellences. However, even those who will not 'receive' God will not be punished in a state of eternal 'evil', but they will just be deprived of God's 'strengths'.

There is a long debate on the theoretical and practical implications of the *final apokatastasis* (see Louth 2008: 244–7). It appears that there is no conclusive point that could summarise this debate. According to Balthasar's astute conclusion, '[t]o want to overcome this final antinomy through a premature "synthesis" is not appropriate for theology in this present age' (1988: 358). Nonetheless, it is undeniable in Maximus' view that 'those whose piety Divine Providence exercised in life' are subject to 'the infliction of grievous things' (*Char.* II, 91: *ACW* 171) and should recall Christ's words: 'in your patience possess your souls' (*Luke* 14, 33). Accordingly, the personal 'possession' and 'transcendence' of the external/collective evil lies in 'patience', which once again echoes a remote impact of Maximus' dominant eschatological viewpoint.

A long tradition has preceded these Maximian viewpoints. According to Clement of Alexandria, Christ is the *Philanthropic Paedogogus* who 'ministers all good and all help, both as man and as God: as God forgiving our sins, and as man training us not to sin' (Clement, *Paedagogus* 7, 1: *SC* 70, 122).[6] As a result of this pedagogy, what man can experience as 'dark side of God' is not God's dark side as such but is the whole difficulty and 'suffering' of his training as well as the 'patience' needed to 'possess his soul'. There are still diverse approaches amongst Christian writers in their interpretation of God's 'dark side'. Dionysius Areopagite's 'gnofos' and 'skotos' (cloud and dark), Gregory of Nyssa's 'divine darkness', or John of the Cross's 'dark night' are expressions that do not stand for symbols of spiritual experience, but 'they are, rather, external and occasional motifs, used by doctrinal speculations anxious to mark the limits, or to fix certain necessary modalities, of the mystical vision of God' (Louth 1981: 176–7). It is therefore within the dynamics between cataphatic and apophatic approach that spiritual experience and struggle are described. The 'apophatic attitude' provided the 'freedom and liberality' through which Church fathers 'employed philosophical terms without running the risk of being misunderstood or of falling into a "theology of concepts"' (Lossky 1957: 42). It is thus not the terms as such but what precisely these terms bespeak beyond their intrinsic antinomy. In Sophrony

156

Sakharov's experience, the dark side is conceptualised in the term 'godforsaken-ness', which recapitulates the whole man's sufferings in his struggle to encounter God. It is clear in which ways these sufferings 'in darkness' are transformed in the spiritual light of eternal God's mercy through man's struggle:

> [W]e find ourselves in a paradoxical situation: we suffer but in a hitherto-unknown way. This suffering inspires us. It does not destroy. There is an uncreated strength in it. . . . Our initial suffering of repentance is transformed into the joy and sweetness of love which now takes a new form – compassion for every creature deprived of divine Light.
>
> (S. Sakharov 1988: 46–7)

As Nicholas Sakharov comments on this approach, 'for Fr Sophrony the divine "darkness" as "godforsakenness" is only a stage on the way to the fulfilment of communion with God in divine light, and not the fulfilment itself' (2002: 186). By overcoming the boundaries and dualities of an archetypal God (as an image) and by distinguishing between evil-as-choice and evil-as-afflictions – that is, experienced through spiritual wrestling within God's providence – man is finally gifted with the knowledge of the true dimensions of God's 'dark side'. Advancing towards deifica-tion, the dark side of the spiritual struggle eventually becomes light and life in God.

'Darkness' as a stage of spirituality within time and eternity

Jung's and Maximus' analyses of God's dark/evil side, radically different yet cog-nate in terms of *perspectivism,* reveal the different weight both thinkers attribute to the function of space-time as a four-dimensional continuum wherein develop-ment advances. Taking the position of an 'internal' observer/participator in this continuum, Jung's subjectivity perceives the impact of the two opposites, good and evil, as non-resolved within the space-time continuum. Thus, Jung's analysis of good and evil, reduced from the Hegelian historical realm to the psyche as such, precludes a transcendental understanding of development and its pertinent dark side. On the contrary, Maximus endorses a holistic-eschatological viewpoint by taking the position of an external observer outside subjectivity and beyond the boundaries of physical (and psychic) space-time. As a result, he understands the dark/evil as being a certain stage of conscious development, which will ultimately be transformed into eternal light in the transcendental time or eternity. On the other side, Jung attaches prime significance to an eschatological-as-permanent perspective of 'evil' – which however, is, for Maximus, only temporal and even-tually 'providential'. Furthermore, Jung, within the space-time continuum, raises concerns on the fourth element as necessary for individuation, which Maximus, in turn, by taking a different viewpoint and living in a different time, does not consider essential – while proposing transformation of the body and the feminine in the final stages of spiritual progress.

More specifically, when Jung asks, '[w]hat kind of father is it who would rather his son were slaughtered than forgive his ill-advised creatures who have been corrupted by his precious Satan?' (1952a: para. 661), he does not seem to understand the 'eschatological economy' of a God acting – beyond psychic boundaries – out of his own providential love for the world. Regarding this question, Maximus responds that Christ's purpose was to 'obey the Father until death, for our sake, keeping the commandment of love. . . . Christ was crucified in weakness;[7] through this weakness, Christ killed death and destroyed him who had the empire of death'[8] (*L.Asc.* 13: *ACW* 111). The dark and the weak in God-Christ are treated through an *economical* perspective within the hypostatic union between God and man in the person of Christ – who suffers temporarily in order to transform both death and human darkness/sin into eternal light. Due to the exclusion of metaphysical perspectives in his epistemology, Jung fails to consider the outcome of Job's afflictions as a 'teleology' of God's love, according to the narrative: 'and the Lord gave Job twice as much as he had before' (*Job* 42, 10). Apparently there exists a perspective in which evil afflictions could be superseded by the opposite of God's 'love' after some indeterminate time, through the development of Job's spiritual experience and trust to God. Time and evil are thus placed in a transitory perspective that is exactly echoed in Ezra Pound's candos, 'time is the evil' (Pound 1948: 458). Time will reveal how 'evil' is a permanent, or not, 'evil'.

Treating the concept of evil as confined in history, Jung appears to also limit God's manifestation within space-time. Yet, as Abraham remarks, '[t]he future planned by God is not fully realised in history, but it has been inaugurated' (2008: 585). Maximus treats eschatological matters by introducing some crucial distinctions: (a) between God as such, beyond space-time, and God as 'economy', namely the ways whereby the Trinity enacts God's love on mankind within space-time; (b) between evil as a personal choice and evil as externally afflicted by God as 'pedagogues'; and (c) between temporal power of evil and eschatological God-Christ's dominion over death and evil. Collective and personal evil are not, as in Jung's thought, in fusion or confusion. In Maximus, every logical being takes personal responsibility on the basis of his/her own free will. The external occurrences and afflictions, not being caused by one's own will, can therefore be understood and experienced only as a temporal *stage*, as an inevitable source of grief necessary for spiritual growth. In no way they are permanent opposites of the 'good' side with which one's dark-evil side is in tension.

These distinctions would have helped Jung, should he have not applied the limits and dualities of the personal – and at once archetypal – experience of 'dark/evil'. Jung projects his own unconscious 'fear and love' on a super-personal 'God' bearing his 'dark side' only because dark/evil is so powerful in human consciousness; or he tries 'to exorcise some inner demons to do with his upbringing as the child of a dysfunctional Protestant pastor's family' (Bishop 2002: 164). By contrast, in Maximus, weakness, fear, and evil are the psychic grounds absolutely capable of transformation by God's love – on the condition of human consent and co-operation with God – into virtues, good, and light. We could thus summarise, in light of the earlier discussion, that if Maximus were to comment the book of *Job*, he would have emphasized the following:

Firstly, although Job profoundly experiences the (archetypal) polarities of good and evil, these polarities cannot be projected from the human to the divine level. In other words, God does not contain 'good' and 'evil' in human terms. However, man experiences a God as *Pedagogues,* within his Providence-economy for his creation, who is critically different from God as such. Yet those who progress spiritually towards deification will ultimately experience God as an all-loving Creator.

Secondly, the archetypal dualities of dark and light, good and evil are in fact certain stages that man must experience and pass through, from a state of struggle against vices to a state of God's love, where no evil can exist. Evil is to 'vanish' when time reaches the *telos-eschata*, which is the eternal dominion of God's love for the whole mankind beyond space-time – harmoniously to the *telos* narrated in the book of *Job*. It is important to re-emphasize that within the actual biblical text of this book, God in fact rewards Job for his unwavering faith, regardless of all 'provocation' and 'temptations' (*Job* 42, 10). It is also important to mention that Jung's 'exegetical distortion' chooses to ignore this outcome, full of God's light and love.

Finally, the consequences of the collective evil (e.g. wars) afflicted on man at the individual level, against one's own will, are crucially different from the evil that man himself experiences as a result of the voluntary separation of his own will from God's will and virtues. Thus, whereas God ultimately fully restores these consequences on the nature of man, he 'respects' man's personal will. Hence, according to Maximus' view of final restoration, the human will is not fully restored. As a process of spiritual development, deification addresses the encounter with the evil/dark side of man's free will, but this evil side must be transformed in the opposite good-as-virtues psychic attitudes through God's providential love.

On the other hand, Maximus, not being a psychologist in a modern sense, is not concerned about the collective dimensions of evil and its tremendous psychological impact on the masses, also present in institutions such as the church. Jung challenges the good aspect of God who is confronted with and often invalidated by such contemporary occurrences as wars and also by the inappropriate behaviour of spiritual leaders in 'Christian' societies. In this respect, evil becomes a 'missing element' the unconscious produces as a negative response to one-sidedness of the conscious 'good', compensating the tension of opposites. According to Jung, 'the expectation of the Antichrist is a far-reaching revelation or discovery, like the remarkable statement that despite his fall and exile the devil is still "the prince of this world"' (1952a: para. 697). Maximian and, by extension, Orthodox Christian theology now is challenged to decipher and explain to contemporary man the consequences of the collective evil: how the power of evil, from a status of personal choice, can take incalculable forms at the collective level holding a dreadful sway over mankind's destiny and why a loving God may allow human beings suffering when they have not chosen evil themselves.

To ultimately achieve, either through psychological development or spiritual struggle, a consciousness that encompasses the implications of the collective evil, however Jung interprets it, is of immense importance for both psychology and religion. Jung ultimately views the discourse of evil not as an 'opposite' of Christian virtues but as a psychic potential, something that Christian theology appears not to discuss. In Jung's insightfulness, 'the evil spirit must be a factor of quite incalculable potency' (1942/1948: para. 249). It is because the symbol of Cross and Crucifixion bears the psycho-spiritual dynamics of a union and redemption within human consciousness (see 1942/1954: para. 406–8, 431; 1951/59: para. 79). Human consciousness is thus the unique locus of such an indispensable quest as redemption between the opposites of good and evil; and it is individuation of that process through which one can experience and integrate these opposites. Maximus, on the other hand, looking towards the *eschata*, provides the paradigm of Christ-Logos as the redeemer and simultaneously the reminder of the fact that deification is offered as a possibility and gift to all humans. The good and evil deeds will be under God's loving justice in an eschatological perspective. By remaining faithful to God's loving providence, the temporal inflictions by evil will be restored within the eternal light of God's love and justice.

Jung takes a further step by elevating the feminine aspect, along with the dark-evil, as crucial for maturation and the individuation process.[9] Jung's preference reflects on Mary's assumption as an important complement to the doctrine of the Trinity (1942/1948: para. 252ff). In spite of these references to an epoch vastly different from that of Maximus, the feminine aspect, neglected critically by the contemporary church, also functions as an additional challenge that the Christian theology has to confront, insofar as this aspect is more or less restricted by the prevailing attitude of the *renunciation* in a 'masculine church' – one that cannot be fully applicable in contemporary life (as discussed in Chapter 5). We can follow Jung's and Maximus' main positions on God's dark side and evil as being summarized in Table 8.1.

In modernity, the body and the feminine function as essential and valuable expressions of psychic life towards union of the sexes: both serve as means of sexual pleasure, fulfilment of personal goals, and expression of both personal maturation and social status in a Foucauldian sense. Maximian analogous insights are rather problematic when applied beyond monastic contexts, at least to the degree to which they do not determine where the exact limits are of using our psychic energy/functions 'according to nature' or, conversely, in a passionate way 'contrary to nature' (*Char.* II, 16: *ACW* 155). Only in Christ's resurrected body do the feminine and the body as 'flesh' find their definitive place. It is God the Logos-Christ that sets an example for individuals to progress spiritually and attain union with him. Yet not all individuals will reach this final perfection. Deification is an open challenge beyond individuated life and psychic wholeness (feminine, dark/evil side included) in a Jungian sense. But it is Jung who openly challenges the Christian church(es) to secure a realistic 'place' for these elements, essential for wholeness, within human consciousness and experience and the space-time continuum.

Table 8.1 Jung and Maximus on evil and God's 'dark side'

Book of Job's themes	Jung's approach	Maximus' positions
Origins of good and dark/evil	In both God and man, within the bipolarity of archetypes.	God does not include evil; exists beyond archetypal dualities.
Manifestations of dark/evil	Evil is manifested in nature, man, and God. As human conscious develops, evil emerges as an unconscious counterpart of good.	Evil is a result of humans' free will, not of God prompted by Satan. Dark/evil only as a stage of spiritual development.
Collective evil and its consequences	Evil 'permanently' present, decisive for mankind's destiny.	Inflictions of the collective evil temporarily only, ultimately restored.
Personal evil as a result of choice	Not distinct from the collective, treated under the same discourse with the collective.	It is the only 'true' evil and will not be abolished. God respects one's choices.
Redemption of evil	Within human consciousness only, by experiencing and integrating good and dark/evil side within *individuation* process.	The personal dark side/evil is transformed into light and God's love at the state of deification. Implications of the collective evil are fully restored in the eschata.
Feminine aspect, Sophia	Essential element of individuation process and of Self/God-image.	A division (male–female) integrated in God (the Logos-Christ). In *deification*, man exists beyond sexes and divisions.
God's incarnation	God's incarnation is a realisation of one's Self, an essential stage of psychological development and *individuation*.	*God becomes man in order for man to become God.* Christ is the paradigm-model for humans towards spiritual development and *deification*.

Insofar as God's loving providence for mankind works towards the restoration and transformation of human suffering and its eternal implications beyond space-time, as Maximus states, Jung's theory on God's dark/evil side can be reconsidered and redressed. Although individuation confronts one's dark side through the inevitable encounter within the archetypal polarities and certain unconscious elements (the shadow, instincts, etc.), it does not offer a transformation of good and evil within God's providential charity in the *eschata* – through one's spiritual struggle according to Maximus. By acknowledging the free will as the crucial factor in choosing evil, Maximus' *final apokatastasis* restores the implications of the collective manifestations of evil, in which evil is no longer permanent. On the other hand, although deification as a spiritual process ultimately restores the consequences of one's evil actions (but not of one's freedom), it does not convincingly address within the contemporary space-time either the occurring 'chronological' implications or the 'immense potency' of the 'psychological' opposites – such as the dark/evil and feminine – so vividly as individuation. On the contrary, the individuation process mobilises this potency within the whole spectrum of the unconscious polarities and dynamics towards constructive paths of psychic development.

Notes

1. Commenting on this principle, Capra remarks that 'the scientist cannot play the role of a detached objective observer, but becomes involved in the world he observes to the extent that he influences the properties of the observed objects' (Capra 1975: 153).
2. Einstein's *relativity theory* has clearly proved the relativity of time: the perception of time, absolutely crucial for most physical phenomena, is different when the observatory position changes, namely dependent on the observer's motion. Lightman (2000: 143, fig. III-9) illustrates an experiment in which an observer 1 is on a moving train, whereas an observer 2 is sitting on a bench and watches the train from outside. After examining the differences of how the two observers perceive the same phenomenon, the conclusion is reached that 'what were simultaneous events to the person on the train were not simultaneous to the person on the bench, contrary to common sense' (*ibid.:* 145). This experiment becomes more challenging when the speed reaches that of light, that is, beyond the boundaries of perceptible dimensions.
3. Karl Popper challenges this view by arguing that the task-role of the observer is merely to 'test the theory' (1982: 35ff) and not to have an impact on the theory itself.
4. Andrew Samuels discusses further these dualities in the context of the archetypal mother (see 1985: 151).
5. See also *L.Asc., CCSG* 40: 33–5 and Paul's epistle to *Romans* 12, 21.
6. Clement also uses metaphors from medical practice: 'Just as our body needs a physician when it is sick, so, too, when we are weak, our soul needs the Educator to cure its passions . . .' (*Paedagogus* 3, 1: *SC* 70, 112).
7. *B Corinthians* 13, 4.
8. *Hebrews* 2, 14.
9. The reader may recall at this point the discussion on the feminine aspect in Chapter 7.

9

CONCLUSION

A 'trans-disciplinary paradigm' of psychic development

Reaching this final point of this comparative study between Jung's and Maximus' developmental models, namely between *individuation* and *deification,* an overlapping while diverging discourse emerges. The overlaps and diversions may give rise to a partial complementarity: 'partial' because there are elements entirely different in each theory due to the dissimilar ontological and epistemological underpinnings. These overlaps, however, permit considering a compound view of both psychological and spiritual development within the suggested framework of the five ontological levels. The reservoir of the external and the internal factors that are essential for development should be sought within this framework. In fact, the Jungian and Maximian systems address numerous potentialities spanning the psychosomatic, the socio-cultural, and the metaphysical levels. In this respect, the two models, as seen together, could establish an intriguing dialogue among psychology, philosophy, and theology, a dialogue that also engages certain ideas and methodologies from modern sociology and physics (as previously discussed in various points of this book). It is thus a broader *trans-disciplinary* framework within which the Jungian and Maximian models unfold and reveal their 'strong' and 'weak' points while simultaneously complementing each other.

Jung's and Maximus' models: dissimilar foundations towards complementary dynamics

It is important to recall once more the vast distance that separates Maximus' and Jung's eras in terms of socio-cultural constructs. Maximus' theory is grounded in an early Christian world, almost entirely reliant on the 'will of God', which, by Jung's time, had gradually reached an era being governed by the 'will of man': it was characterised 'by the progressive crossing-out of God and an accelerating emphasis on instrumental rationality' (Hauke 2000: 32). In fact, Maximus develops his ideas in an epoch in which the church was more than merely a system of doctrines and sacraments, being profoundly involved in the socio-cultural dynamics and political debates. The church was therefore able to provide a philosophical system and a new 'spiritual culture' as a broadly adopted lifestyle. In other words, we refer to an era in which 'the Eastern Christian was eager to enter into the state of grace, the right relationship to God, here and now' (Runciman 1933: 129), a commitment far different from all the priorities of modernity. On the other hand, this 'here and now', although in a different sense, is the *sine qua non* reality for modern man, within his indispensable engagement in fulfilling social and cultural activities. Instead, during Maximus' epoch, the Christians in the East 'had been formed in a spiritual culture' of a 'profoundly different world' (Brown 1988: 323). These striking differences emphasize the contrast between 'a spiritual culture-as-religion' and a 'modern culture-out-of-no-religion' and epitomize the inadequacy of the former to respond to the diversity and the complexity of the contemporary socio-cultural challenges of the latter.

Despite the fact that Maximus' model emerges from the context of the early Christian church (almost five centuries before the schism between the Eastern and Western churches), his ontological and experiential claims are not all dictated or inspired by an 'institutional' church – as it might be the case with regard to the 'ontological argument' and pertinent inquiries in modernity. In fact, Maximus opposed the official church when he realised that their positions on dogmatic issues at bottom depended on emperors' policies. In addition, contrary to the silence of Jung's father on religious questions (i.e. 'one ought not to think, just believe'; *MDR*: 43), Maximus is exceptionally eloquent when articulating a considerably 'modern' psychic model – as both the medium/apparatus and locus of the meeting point between the psychological and the divine. To Jung's fundamental position that 'only through the psyche . . . we can establish that God acts upon us, but we are unable to distinguish whether these actions emanate from God or from the unconscious' (1952a: para. 757), Maximus suggests God the Logos, who is united hypostatically with man and through man with the whole creation. The Logos can be experienced through his principles/*logoi,* intentions, and proposals to all the beings, which determine both their essence and development.

Jung challenged contemporary religion(s) by three 'psychological' standpoints, which in turn can also be challenged by comparison to Maximus' philosophical and theological positions. We can epitomize this dialogue as it unfolds throughout this study (especially in Chapters 5 to 8), stressing both the divergent and the complementary viewpoints of the two thinkers. Furthermore, this discourse also addresses the complementary perspectives on development by Jung and Maximus. Jung's first standpoint on religion in fact calls for a robust 'psychological' dimension of religious doctrines and narratives. This apparent psychological 'reduction', while departing from the accuracy of ontological/doctrinal assumptions, affirms a phenomenological understanding and experience of religious beliefs. Whereas Jung considers the ontological question – of what is real – 'outside of the competence of all psychology' (1945/1948: para. 528), on the other hand he applies a phenomenological approach to God/religion, which remains within an 'ontology and epistemology of ambiguity, by exploring the existential tensions between the revealed and the concealed' (Brooke 1991: 245). Maximus responds to Jung's inclination to remain with the confines of psychology and applies both ontological (apophatic) and phenomenological (cataphatic or experiential) methods by expanding ideas of his Greek precursors (Plato, Plotinus, Origen) and ecclesiastical writers. Maximus' ontology is grounded in a traditional affirmation of a God as creator, an ontology which nevertheless is sturdily supported by the conscious capability of the psyche to 'know by grace', to experience the words, spiritual qualities, and actions, namely the *logoi,* of such a God.

Jung was compelled to strongly oppose such an ability of the psyche to know 'by grace', because he is, or rather he wanted to be, a genuine Kantian. Later in his life, Kant placed limitations on what the reason can conceive in his *Critique of Pure Reason,* although earlier he was a devotee of Leibniz, whose *monads* – the 'eternal particles' of all beings – echo Maximus' *logoi* of beings. The Kantian method, by synthesising empiricism and rationalism in a 'manifold' of perception (mediated by the senses, understanding/reason and imagination), sets limits to the perception of objects. Jung similarly articulates his key notion of the archetypes within the psychic boundaries *alone* – while leaving ambiguous the potential of the archetypes towards the Kantian 'thing-in-itself'.

Jung extensively utilises these archetypes, such as the God-image, the hero, and the Great Mother, to describe what religious doctrines narrate. However, neither Kant nor Jung avoided dabbling with what is 'beyond' human perception, the ontological realm, since they both mobilise ideas of the 'noumenal' world, reflected in Jung's concepts of *psychoid* and *synchronicity* that engage metapsychological dimensions. Jung was in fact taken not only back to pre–Kantian approaches but also into the post–Kantian tenets of German idealism and romanticism (see Bishop 2000: 192). This inconsistency over the limitations of psychic perception and the potential of the archetypes (as extensively discussed in Chapter 4) can be understood as the inevitable outcome of Jung's reduction of the spiritual to the psychological, akin to Freud's reduction of the psychological to the biological realm.

Jung's reductive approach results, accordingly, in both a departure from a 'theological' accuracy and an affirmation to psychological processes that now can convincingly narrate the remote-from-human-experience 'divine' doctrines and beliefs. Central to this approach is Jung's emphasis on the 'natural religiosity' of the psyche and the Self. The Self is the centralising principle towards wholeness, 'intimately related to the religious function' (Stein 2004: 206). But such a *religious function,* in an interplay with the *transcendent function* (Jung 1916/1957), shapes psychic development but not spiritual progress in Maximus' sense. In order to fill this lacuna of a higher/spiritual dimension – and because the archetypes are not linked with metaphysics – Jung draws upon Gnostic and alchemical equivalents (*pleroma, hierosgamos, lapis*). In this respect, the central archetype of the Self/God-image, a 'borderline concept', ultimately bears a spiritual-religious function, insofar as the Self could act as 'a church within . . . a system of values and moral arbiter' (*CDJA*: 61). But this also means that the Self meets intrinsic difficulties to be confined within the psychic boundaries alone. Individuation, as a process of development towards manifold perspectives, in fact embraces a pluralistic set of potentialities, spiritual or religious included: insofar as individuation is 'equivalent to the search for a relationship with God' (Stein 1990: 16), it robustly indicates that psychological development overlaps with a progress in a spiritual dimension, too; and although Jung opts for primarily psychic equivalents of the spiritual, he ultimately does not escape from the necessity to tentatively address – although ambiguously – its ontological character beyond the boundaries of psychology.

Maximus challenges this position by both the *cataphatic* and *apophatic* methods, whereby he synthesises an understanding, namely a 'psychological' experience, of the divine. The inner antinomy that archetypes bear – a God-image not purely psychological, not metaphysical, due to the Kantian limitations – is resolved in Maximus by relating the God-image ontologically to God-likeness, God as such. The processes of spiritual development, of deification, are described at three stages, similarly to the individuation process (Chapter 5). The *telos* of this process, that is God the 'Logos in many *logoi*', is clearly indicated. Jung narrates psychological development through the encounter with certain archetypes (shadow, persona, anima, animus, wise man, etc.) and indicates the *telos* of this development to be the multifaceted Self. Whilst individuation is a process open to different religious traditions and can be experienced by non–Christians, it acquires a specific potential in Christian contexts: it is here that the 'ever present archetype of wholeness' might be considered a counterpart of the 'image of Christ', which can then lead to 'an integration, a bridging of the split . . . caused by the instincts' (Jung 1951/1959: para. 73). In this fashion, Jung's God-image could be potentially a parallel to Maximus' Logos-Christ as a reciprocal goal.

It can now be understood how the first point, the psychological reduction, gives place to the more important issue of psychological experience, the second of the Jungian concerns on religion. Jung strongly recommends that '"legitimate" faith must always rest on experience' (1911/1956: para. 345). Although Jung emphasizes psychological experience, little discussion is provided for spiritual experience (as discussed in Chapter 6). The Jungian typology, the psychic model comprising four functions, primarily addresses the psychic functions that characterize each personality – the *psychological type* – and not processes of spiritual progress. Certain aspects of active imagination, by conveying unconscious material, might trigger a spiritual dimension, but for Jung this is not the sought target. Maximus, instead, draws a sharp distinction between *relative knowledge*, the ordinary reasoning within human thinking (directly compared to Jung's *thinking* and *active imagination*), and '*truly authentic knowledge*, gained only by actual [spiritual] experience, not merely reason and ideas, which provides a total perception of the known object through a participation by grace' (*Q.Thal.* 60: 77, italics mine). There is therefore a huge difference between Jung's active imagination, through which the ego encounters unconscious dynamics and aims the inner Self, and Maximus' compound psychic function that is able to directly experience the divine through prayer and spiritual contemplation. In Maximus, spiritual experience means knowledge of a personal God as a result of co-operation between the all-inclusive will (expressed by the functions of the *aesthesis, reason-logos, nous*) and the *logoi*-as-virtues, the agents that act as 'mediators' between man and God the Logos.

Jung's position at this point is that the ego gradually integrates unconscious elements in a synthesis, 'a mediatory product' (Samuels 1985: 90), towards the Self. But this 'Self' is principally confined within the psychological dimension alone. Instead, Maximus attributes to Christ the Logos, as both God and human (θεάνθρωπος), the centralising principle that integrates everything beyond the psychological world: in fact, Logos acts as 'the centre of radii', but at the same time 'he circumscribes their extension in a circle and brings back to himself the distinctive elements of beings, which himself brought into existence' (*Myst.* 1: 668A). Is it not surprising then that Jung, thirteen centuries later, speaks of the Self as 'not only the centre, but also the whole circumference which embraces both conscious and unconscious' (1944: para. 44)? However, the ground of such embracing is only 'natural', whereas in Maximus the Logos is the *uncreated* Creator to whom everything owes its *genesis* and *telos.*

Despite the fact that the centralising principle of the Self 'embraces' and 'circumscribes' all psychic potentialities, Jung's individuation process ultimately remains a 'biological process' and not a transformation towards the 'face-to-face communion' with the Logos-Christ. This critical difference is apparent when considering the different *telos* of the two models in spite of their comparable teleological processes. Jung, while pointing out the critical absence of an experiential dimension in modern religion, does not nevertheless describe the exact psychic or spiritual processes, as Maximus does, through which the missing experiential perspective of contemporary religious constructs could be attained.

These conclusions bring us to the third and most challenging position of Jung's theory on religious/spiritual dimension, which ultimately also concerns psychological development: it is the 'fourth element', the body, the feminine, and the dark/evil side, which are the missing element(s) of the classical Trinitarian God-as-wholeness. The cultural dimension here is critical: the 'cultural unconscious' and the emergence from it, the 'cultural complexes', as the 'blocks' of our inner sociology (Singer 2010: 234), decisively shape the development of the psyche, insofar as they determine the critically important, for individuation, interplay between inner and outer world.

Yet, whilst in Jung the process towards the Self unfolds in culture, in real time and space, and 'culture expresses the depth of the self and is an avenue to those depths' (Bockus 1990: 43), and whereas the psychic energy flows only through the pre-formatted channels of the riverbeds/archetypes – determining the limits and potentialities of human life – spiritual struggle, according to Maximus, rather pushes these limits to the extremes to overcome these archetypal polarities by implementing the virtues. In this respect, spiritual struggle might deprive individuals of essential experiences through encountering 'objects' and their tangible realities – and thus 'halt' processes of purely psychological development as individuation implies – for instance, the encounter with the anima/animus or the dark/evil side. In principle, spiritual development is not directed towards socio-cultural constructs like individuation but towards the metaphysical qualities of an all-embracing and loving God. Maximus defines spiritual development eschatologically, as an initial potential 'encrypted' in man's *heart* that unfolds thoroughly in eternity, beyond the natural, and, of course, psychic, boundaries.

Maximus' model aims at a metaphysical God, within a process which, whatever the adjustments that one could envisage regarding the different epochs (a 'spiritual culture-as-religion' *versus* a 'culture-out-of-no-religion'), is clearly shown to be less interested in the actual engagement of socio-cultural dynamics through myths, images, art, and symbols. Jung's model *needs* to engage with the social and cultural constructs in order to advance and thoroughly unfold the capabilities of the psyche in its quest towards the depths of psychic wholeness. According to Jung, *active imagination* towards an active cultural engagement is absolutely essential for an individuated life. This is a perspective that Maximus does not discuss directly, insofar as he strongly advocates *renunciation,* a kind of detachment from 'objects', which is critical to avoid the negative psychic qualities, the *passions.* In addition, Maximian *logoi of beings* (the archetypal but uncreated principles beyond nature and space-time) do not suggest an encounter with the parental or interpersonal 'other' – especially via the mother/father complexes – or other objects in the way that Jung wants his Self to act, namely as an integrating principle. These points are conclusive towards an understanding of the socio-cultural as the main realm that individuation engages, whereas deification attempts to overcome it, inasmuch as it targets at the metaphysical sphere.

These divergent directions can be attributed to the different 'third agents' that are activated by the two theoretical models: the *archetypes* versus the *logoi*-as-virtues, respectively. According to Maximus, the highest point of development is the transformation of psychic functions/will into God's virtues, particularly into divine 'love', through the membership in Christ's body and the sacramental communion. Individuation, on the other hand, is governed by the archetypal dynamics between opposites, grounded in the cultural context and its symbols along with one's personal history. Instead, spiritual progress finds its most vigorous expression in the ascetic struggle to encounter and accomplish the virtues. Accordingly, deification does not emphasize dominant cultural aspects, the feminine and bodily included, but incorporates the personal characteristics into the relationship with God. Ultimately, deification does not address what individuation aspires to attain, namely a multifaceted Self that incorporates the 'incalculable potency' of the body/matter, the feminine, and dark/evil. Instead, Maximus highlights the *transfiguration* of these elements eschatologically, when man attains the highest levels of spiritual perfection. The emphasis therefore is laid on superseding the archetypal polarities, projections, and dualities within which Jung views God, his images, and in particular his 'dark side', the key feature in *Answer to Job.*

It is apparent that there exists a crucial distance between Jung's idea of God-image as an archetype of the collective unconscious subjected to dualities, polarities, and projections within space-time and Maximus' principle of God as such, whose image-towards-likeness is inherent in the human psyche. Maximus' God is beyond the limits of both space-time and psychic imagination; however, God can be experienced in space-time via his *logoi*-as-virtues, of which love is the supreme, through the psychic functions that have been educated and illumined in the depths of the human *heart*. Maximus views God the Logos as the beginning and the end of human existence and not, like Jung, as a required – due to God's 'imperfection' – rebirth and 'compensation' of the idea of God within human consciousness. The Logos-Christ recapitulates all the ontological divisions of the universe, male-female, earth-heaven included: he does not 'need' man for his rebirth as a compensating 'enhanced' version of an initially unfair God the Father (masking his evil side) who tortured Job, in Jung's narration, but wants man to constantly share with him a creative, although not without 'toil', experience of his own endless life-in-love.

Spiritual progress towards deification/*theosis* is an attainment of eschatological dimensions or, more precisely, within an 'eschatological economy': it is the 'time' of a limitless realm where 'the hospitality of God' (Knight 2006) acts mercifully upon man, in which 'evil' vanishes by the light of an unconditional and ultra-cosmic love. By contrast, when Jung applies the term 'eschatological' (1952a: para. 647) and implies transcendence of time while interpreting *synchronicity*, his actual viewpoint of time is 'chronological'. Jung's version of 'eschatology' does not claim any metaphysical dimension: it results in a treatment of 'evil' and its implications within a time-space historical continuum. Maximus considers eschatology as the only true 'ontology', which starts from the-not-yet-revealed *telos* of the beings. As Loudovikos puts it, '[t]he end is the ontological beginning; it is a new ontology which is personal and eschatological' (2010: 205). This 'end' of course presupposes a different conception of time, the 'eternal time', which is at odds with the Kantian – and also Jungian – dichotomy of presence and appearance, 'that makes us prisoners of a spacious present' (Knight 2006: 22). Eschatology, definitely being in *antinomy* with the 'relative knowledge' and the 'natural' process of individuation, is, however, a profound hope and a challenge to experience a yet unforeseen existential perspective in an *apocalyptic* dimension – which *theosis* provides as a possibility open to all humanity.

Having recapitulated the main divergences and convergences of Jung's and Maximus' models, it can be understood that the two systems, while establishing different priorities and directions of development, due to their different foundations, both serve towards an understanding of development within a trans-disciplinary framework that embraces all potentialities of human life and progress. The main features of the two discussed models could be tabulated in Table 9.1.

Beyond spiritual 'one-sidedness' and psychological 'wholeness'

Individuation and deification determine those developmental 'paths' and potentialities into which psychic energy can be channelled. The totality of these paths/directions comprises a *trans-disciplinary paradigm of development* that expands beyond psychology, namely towards sociological, philosophical, and theological

Table 9.1 A concise comparison of Jungian and Maximian theories and concepts

Process	Psychic development individuation	Spiritual progress towards deification
Psychic model	Based on fourfold *opposites*, archetypal dualities, targeting the union of conscious-unconscious	Based on three psychic functions and the *logoi*, targeting unification with the Logos-Christ
Ontology and phenomenology	Ignorance of a God as such; however, the Self/*God-image* is to be ultimately experienced	God as such in three persons; Logos-Christ incarnate and hypostatically united with man
Epistemology	Kantianism: limitations of human perception, God unknown: Socratic ignorance (Papadopoulos, 2006)	Distinction between knowledge within the human mind, and knowledge as a spiritual experience of the divine
Stages of development	a. Containment/nurturance stage (dominant figure of the mother) b. Adapting/adjusting stage (the father) c. Centring/integrating stage (hero, Self/God-image) (Stein, 2006)	a. Praxis (fight against passions): the *logos* to guide the *aesthesis* b. Natural contemplation: the *nous* to guide the *logos* c. Mystical theology: the *nous* unites the psyche with God
Dynamics of psychic functions	The *inferior function* must develop and bring unconscious material to the consciousness. *Active imagination* and *transcendent function*	Hierarchical: The logical function/*logos* dominates the *aesthesis*, whereas the *nous* integrates the *logos* and the *aesthesis* within the *all-embracing will.*
External agents developmental directions	Symbols, archetypes, cultural complex(es) principally at the socio-cultural level	The spiritual principles (*logoi*-as-virtues) primarily at the metaphysical level
Psychic energy and transformation	Psychic energy encounters with archetypal imagery and flows through the archetypes-as-riverbeds (persona, shadow, anima/us, hero)	Encounter with the metaphysical *logoi*-as-virtues via psychic functions and the membership in Christ's body (the sacraments)
The final goal	*A multifaceted Self/God-image* Dark-evil and the feminine incorporated, in alchemical or Gnostic transformations: *lapis, coniunctio, unus mundus*	*Man deified to God's 'likeness'* 'The Logos in many *logoi*' Psychic functions attain God's love. Dark/evil and feminine transfigured by the membership in Christ's body

realms. Individuation rather corresponds to a 'horizontal' development, which merges interpersonal and socio-cultural perspectives, while spiritual development/ deification to a primarily 'vertical' development towards metaphysics, insofar as deification in Maximus does not engage factors and elements from the 'horizontal' socio-cultural realm – as opposed to individuation (see Figure 9.1). In both models, the psychic energy is teleologically converged and integrated into higher principles/concepts, such as the Self in Jung and spiritual 'love' in Maximus. We can discuss further this teleological process.

In Maximus, the goal of spiritual development is to unite the psychic functions with the *logoi*-as-virtues that converge to the divine (*Amb.* 21: 1248A–49C). This objective is attained through the co-operation, the *synergy,* between man and God. Man undertakes a mediatory work, following the 'archetypal' Christ's work by his incarnation, crucifixion, and ascension into heaven, to unify the five divisions of the cosmos:

> In order to bring about the union of everything with God as its cause, the human person begins first of all with its own division [male-female], and then, ascending through the intermediate steps by order and rank [*ekoumenê*-paradise, earth-heaven], it reaches the end of this high ascent [angelic world], which passes through all things in search of unity [created-uncreated world], to God, in whom there is no division.
>
> (*Amb.* 41, 1305C, trans. Louth)

Despite the fact that the human person is the physical bond for that 'great mystery of divine purpose' (ibid.: 1305B), the energy/power for such an accomplishment is not provided by the psyche alone. It is a gift granted by God's intervention, who 'knows' the creatures as 'portions' of His existence and who awaits these creatures, even before their creation, to freely 'move according to the Logos' (*Amb.* 7: 1080C). This synergic action via an external agent (*logoi*) in fact functions as a genuine 'Archimedean' point, from which one can acquire his/her development beyond the psyche: it is a unique transfiguration via God's words and his virtues/love.

Jung strongly refutes it: 'I do not imagine for a moment that I can stand above or beyond the psyche . . . from some transcendental Archimedean point "outside" . . .' (1951: para. 254). The psychic energy (libido) is treated through its 'transformation' – but different from a spiritual *transfiguration* – as it flows in various channels (Jung 1912: para. 258ff). Jung borrows from physics the principle of the conservation of energy, formulated as *principle of equivalence:* 'the disappearance of a given quantum of libido is followed by the appearance of an equivalent value in another form' (1928b: para. 35). In this sense, Jung's four functions may relate and transform into archetypal figures (hero/heroine, father/mother, anima/animus, puer/puella; see Beebe 2006) without losing any of their initial energy. All these functions and archetypes alongside the principles of *logos* and *eros* (see Chapter 5) gradually integrate, through the *transcendent function,* into the central principle of individuation, the teleological Self.

Yet, as has been discussed, the transcendent function shares aspects of the four functions, too: Jung writes: 'aesthetic formulation needs understanding of the meaning, and understanding needs aesthetic formulation. The two supplement each other to form the transcendent function' (1916/1957: para. 177). It is an interplay between 'thinking' as an activation of the 'intellectual interpretation' and 'sensation' of the 'artistic interpretation', where Maximian and Jungian functions do overlap. An interface between the two teleologically functioning models arises in the following scheme: it is an advance from the psychosomatic towards either the cultural (the archetypes and its principles) or the metaphysical level (God or the equivalent Self.)

Central principle: Teleology towards Self/God-image or God-likeness (in Maximus)

Partial principles and archetypes: (*Logos, Eros, Hero,* and *virtues/love*)

Main Functions: (Jung's *transcendent function,* Maximus' *gnomic will*)

Secondary Functions: (*Sensation/aesthesis, intuition/nous,* etc.)

Biological factors (primary processes, instincts)

Despite the fact that the Self is the ultimate union of all opposites and potentialities, including the spiritual dimension of a 'hero' – whose 'most approximate human form is the priest' (*CDJA*: 66) – Jung's vision of psychic transformation remains within the psyche. Due to the *principle of equivalence,* psychic transformations to alchemical or Gnostic counterparts could indicate a change that retains its primarily psychological character in a 'substitute formation':

> For instance, when a child begins to separate himself subjectively from his parents, fantasies of substitute parents arise, and these fantasies are almost always transferred to real people. . . . Another field rich in striking examples is the psychology of Christianity, where the repression of instincts (i.e. of primitive instinctuality) leads to religious substitute formations, such as the medieval *Gottesminne,* 'love of God', the sexual character of which only the blind could fail to see.
>
> (Jung 1928b: para. 36)

By treating 'love of God' as a transformed libidinal material, Jung is not at all aware of what is the precise impact of such a 'love' on Maximus: it is 'the inward universal relationship to the first good connected with the universal purpose of our natural kind' (*Ep.* 2, 401D); and this is because love 'has gathered together in itself all good things that are recounted by the *logos* of truth in the form of virtue' (ibid.: 393B). It is thus the universal principle of 'love' that 'unites' – and not 'love' as a psychological shield of repressed desires. When psychic energy unites with the virtues, which are conveyed by love of the *Logos in many logoi* (*Amb.* 21: 1248A–49C), it acquires *ontological* dimensions of a divine love.[1] This dimension is absent in Jung's vision of the all-uniting Self, which is therefore deprived of the ontological qualities it might merit.

But aside from the different, although overlapping, final goals, there exists another critical difference: it is the problem of one-sidedness that Jung's 'wholeness' wishes to address and resolve. In opposition to Maximus' principle of 'love', which is 'a genuine disposition of voluntary goodwill towards one's neighbour' (*Ep.* 2: 401D), Jung's theory on development signifies what appears that spiritual development towards 'love' fails to address. The characteristics of Maximus' 'love', the qualities that will assure a passage to this goal, are: 'love of humankind . . . love of the poor, compassion, mercy, humility, meekness . . . patience, freedom from anger, longsuffering, perseverance, kindness, forbearance, goodwill, peace towards all' (ibid.: 405A). Despite the plurality of features that describe such love, the problem of an *imbalanced* development arises here, aligned with Jung's emphasis on psychic 'one-sidedness'.

Jung specifically emphasizes the problem of psychic one-sidedness of an undeveloped personality, indicating accordingly the significance of a balanced development via the employment of all functions (Jung 1921/1971; Ekstrom 1988). Erikson's eight developmental stages also signify a similar dialectical interaction between 'basic strengths' and basic *antipathies,* for example love/exclusivity, care/rejectivity, or wisdom/disdain in the three latest stages (Erikson 1982: 32–33). These 'basic strengths' are partially equivalent with qualities-as-virtues. Indeed, Wulff does not hesitate to call them 'virtues' (see Wulff 1997: 401). In Erikson's three last stages, 'love' is combined with 'care' and 'wisdom', which cover the opposite attitudes of exclusivity, rejectivity, and disdain. It is questionable, however, whether the development towards these spiritual virtues, such as 'love', necessarily implies an equal psychic maturity that is attained by encountering these basic antipathies – an equivalent to Jung's dark/evil side. The core of this problem in fact addresses the extent to which the *logoi*-as-virtues would trigger an engagement with the 'antipathies', particularly through archetypal polarities and forces (e.g. mother/father imagery and complexes, social norms, or cultural complexes). The degree of such an engagement is critical when appraising spiritual development in individuals involved in religious or spiritual contexts, including priests and other spiritual leaders.

Hence, there is no accident when Erikson endeavours to explore the personalities of the leaders like Luther and Gandhi by relating their spiritual development towards the virtues/strengths and the corresponding antipathies (see Wulff 1997: 397ff; Erikson 1982). Contemporary incidents of a distorted love (paedophilia) in religious circles may fall within such problematic and imbalanced spiritual development. This seems to be the case when a significant amount of psychic energy still functions beneath the *persona's* masks of an allegedly 'spiritual love', while, in fact, it is being entrapped or repressed into unconscious unresolved tensions between archetypal libidinal eros and acutely fixated complexes. In analogous cases, the possibly dreadful implications of a controversial 'detachment' from objects (renunciation) become apparent – a 'detachment' which ultimately blocks vital processes of psychic maturation through the confrontation with complexes, images, and the object-as-other at early stages of psychic life, generating precariously unsettled attitudes.

It is on these socio-cultural applications of 'love' that Jungian views of the Self/ wholeness and of a balanced development can be of significant value and reinforce the argument that spiritual development, in a Christian sense, does not entirely correspond to psychological maturity/wholeness. Although spiritual development does struggle against the psychic *passions,* psychological 'wholeness' principally provides a much deeper picture and understanding of the entrapped psychic/libidinal energy and calls for appraisal of all kinds of unconscious structures, instincts and impulses included.

On the other hand, Jung's vision of psychological development sets certain limitations regarding the 'amount' of psychic energy that can be transformed from one level or direction to another. This phenomenon metaphorically demonstrates the notion of *entropy* in physics: in close systems, like the biological, transformation occurs from levels of lower complexity/randomness to levels of higher complexity/entropy; it is here that entropy never decreases.[2] Discussing Jung's views of transformation (1951/59: para. 358ff, 391), Tyng espouses the idea that transformation goes beyond the limits of the notion of entropy: '[a]lthough entropy is predicted as probable, laws of probability predict both the probable and improbable (causal and synchronistic)' (1990: 104); in this respect, 'the law of entropy combines with laws of probability that predicts a proportion of the improbable' (ibid.: 105). Psychic functions can pass through the probable towards the improbable at the state of higher qualities or virtues by engaging energy from an external or internal source, that is the unconscious or God.

At this point, Maximus stresses those functions that need to be released from their attachment to material things by the Holy Spirit and to be 'restored to the original place': it is because our 'intelligence [*nous*] . . . confined to the superficial aspects of sensible things . . . acquired no understanding of what lies beyond the senses' (*Cap.* IV, 18: 1309C–12A). By approaching 'objects' only with the senses, through fragmented – and not integrated by the Spirit – psychic functions, one can be trapped in an understanding of objects that is within the 'passions', far from the genuine spiritual dimensions that 'lie beyond the senses', namely the *logoi* as the spiritual meanings of the beings. Although Jung affirms an understanding as well as an experience of objects via both the senses and archetypal images, he also recognises a degree of renunciation when the Self may 'force on us something that our human limitation cannot endure. . .'; it is the point at which one may experience that, '[b]ecoming conscious means continual renunciation' (Jung 1976: 120). After all this, it is apparent that psychic transformation presupposes a certain 'detachment' from the ego's norms, too. Hence, whatever the degree of a renunciation or detachment, it is understood that experiencing the 'virtues' as positive psychic qualities is the ultimate 'stake' of any developmental, either psychological or spiritual, process. As Jung puts it, what matters more is what we are able to *experience*: 'No one can know what the ultimate things are . . . if such experience helps to make life healthier, more beautiful, more complete and more satisfactory . . . you may safely say: "This was the grace of God".' (1938/1940: para. 167).

It is thus apparent from all these explored dimensions of psychic development that although psychological development, in a Jungian sense, and spiritual progress, in Maximus' view, perform as distinct facets of a broader phenomenon, they are paradoxically connected teleologically and function as complementary counterparts to each other: the psychological wholeness needs spiritual-as-experience progress in order to integrate with and experience the full – metaphysical included – potential of the inner Self. In turn, spiritual-as-experience progress needs psychological wholeness to avoid an imbalanced psychological development that leads to a treacherous one-sidedness.

Having so far explored the main developmental perspectives of the two theories, and despite the fact that schemes might conceal more than reveal, it would be challenging to portray the two models of development in a comparative and overlapping perspective (see analogous scheme in Kelsey 1991: 183). Figure 9.1 demonstrates a *trans-disciplinary paradigm of development* within distinct ontological levels, as they have been analysed in Chapter 2, as well as the primary

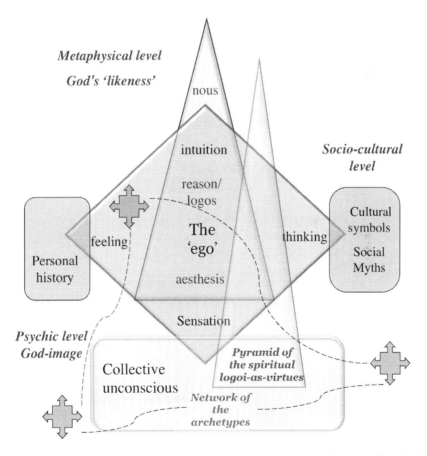

Figure 9.1 A trans-disciplinary paradigm of development: balancing the vertical/spiritual progress with the horizontal development/equilibrium between opposites

horizontal perspective of Jungian individuation combined with the vertical dimension of Maximian deification.

Implementing a new perspective to each model
within a trans-disciplinary context

The 'trans-disciplinary paradigm of development' clearly suggests the directions of development that each of the two models has not sufficiently addressed. It also indicates that there is still 'space' for both models to improve in terms of developmental perspectives and accordingly to potentially acquire wholeness at all levels. More specifically, Jung's understanding of the spiritual dimension in fact is confined within the psychological level in the state of God-image(s): it is *spiritual-as-psychological,* at the lower area of the spiritual continuum. In Jung's system, the dynamics of one's personal psychological history along with the socio-cultural background – within the network of the archetypes – determine psychic development. However, such a development does not address one's potential to attain higher stages of the spiritual continuum beyond the psychological, such as at the metaphysical level.

By contrast, Maximus' understanding of development is based on the divine *logoi,* which convey God's spiritual 'calls' to all creatures. Inasmuch as deification progresses through the synergy of man's will with theses *logoi*-as-virtues, it bears an ontological dimension towards the encounter with the Other-God. However, Maximus' model is not specified and exemplified through parental or other archetypal images, social norms, or cultural symbols (key factors in individuation), which all are imperative for psychic development. Despite the theoretical perspectives of the *logoi* as principles of development, Maximus does not exemplify these perspectives in one's bodily, psychic, or interpersonal reality: accordingly, in Maximus the spiritual is *spiritual-beyond-psychological,* or *spiritual-as-metaphysical* at the ultraviolet/higher area of the spiritual continuum.

The emerging complementarity between the two models provides the ground to understand that psychological 'wholeness' should give more *space* towards the spiritual or metaphysical dimension. In turn, spiritual progress must consider the potentialities of development in purely psychological terms, such as the interpersonal or parental archetypal dynamics. As a result, both models, while challenging each other's priorities (the Self vs. God's love), depend on each other for accomplishing the whole spectrum of the developmental perspectives spanning the five ontological levels (the bodily, psychic, social, cultural, metaphysical) and their parameters (e.g. personal complexes/characteristics, collective archetypal patterns, cultural symbols, and *logoi*-as-virtues). It is then apparent that the theoretical ending point of the one system could be a starting point for the other and vice versa. Such paradoxical connections, as a call for a 'new space' to enter, is a theme that could be found illustrated in modern arts enigmatically, for example, in Barnett Newman's sculpture of 'broken obelisk'.[3] This is a metaphorical establishment of an interaction of two different realms, which, while being attached to each other through a tenuous meeting point – in a delicate but constructive co-existence – both appear to constantly call for more 'space' whereby the one may 'enter' into the other.

Spiritual development towards *theosis* implies a primarily mono-dimensional spiritual development towards God through detachment from objects – a detachment that might deprive the individual of crucial interactions and 'psychological' experiences essential for psychic 'wholeness'. On the contrary, individuation suggests a multi-dimensional development that may complement the less developed areas in the process of spiritual development. In this respect, the spiritual-beyond-psychological requires certain 'embodiments' at the psychic and socio-cultural levels in order to fully disclose its contents (otherwise it remains rather impenetrable); and in turn, the spiritual-as-psychological needs the metaphysical perspective to fulfil its fuller immanent archetypal potential. In this reciprocal and complementary process, the archetypes could function as those psychic 'receptors' that encounter and embody the spiritual *logoi*-as-virtues in order to release their own full potential – that is, the God-image towards 'likeness'. Jung's preference to lay emphasis alone on the psychic dimension of the spiritual experience, opting to 'protect' this experience from merely projections of unapproachable God(s) – by reducing God to its mere images – results in absence of precisely 'what' such an experience of God *ontologically* engages. This is a point at which Jung's positions can extensively be restored by Maximus' insights.

In this respect, when referring to Christian religious contexts, Jung's spiritual-as-psychological is challenged to encounter the other side of the coin, which is the spiritual-as-metaphysical, as a manifestation of the evolving God-image towards God's likeness. It is here that Jung's version of the spiritual requires a more versatile psychic model such as the Maximian one, in which all the functions cooperate with the spiritual meanings of all the things, the *logoi*-as-virtues, to synergistically generate spiritual experience. With regard to non-religious contexts, Jung's pluralistic equivalents of wholeness, such as the *lapis*, *coniunctio*, and *unus mundus*, need further clarification as to the specific ways in which they can be 'experienced' as fulfilling spiritual concepts.

After all these, it can be understood that deification/*theosis* indicates an attainment of highly differentiated *spiritual senses* (such as the *intelligible aesthesis* and *nous*) within an invisible 'spiritual body'. This 'body', however, obtains less developed 'arms' and 'legs' (that is, the Jungian archetypal images, e.g. the parental) through which 'objects' can be physically accessed and experienced. Indeed, regarding Maximus' theory on development, there is very little said about the role of archetypal/parental figures – and especially of the mother, which Jung elevated to the Great Mother – as important factors that trigger processes of development. It is obvious that the theory of spiritual progress lacks the clarity and perspectives of the analysis over the father and mother archetypal imagery as well as their impact on psychological maturation that psychoanalysis and analytical psychology explored in detail.

Contrary to the 'spiritual body', individuation stands for a 'psychological body' with fully developed physical senses, arms, and other organs, while lacking 'spiritual senses' to attain purely spiritual experience. It thus appears that there must be an ever-present antinomy between advantageous perspectives of development: that is, between the 'vertical' accomplishments of spiritual experience in theosis versus the 'horizontal' development of individuation towards the archetypal imagery and the socio-cultural dynamics – which in turn can be understood as a 'regression' or 'reduction to the psychological' from Maximus' viewpoint. This antinomy also appears to lie in the ontological as well as phenomenological/experiential divergences between active imagination and prayer (see Chapter 6). It also appears to determine the different background of such practices as analysis and confession, which are applied by the two theories.

The cultural level is decisively vital for bridging and integrating the psychological level with the *spiritual-as-metaphysical*: it is because culture relates to both and provides that necessary ground in which the psychological might be extended to the spiritual – by engaging cultural, artistic, or metaphysical characteristics – spanning all the levels of the spiritual continuum. The cultural dimension can therefore be the critical 'bridge' to overcome the innate antinomy between the two models. Jung's model of development indispensably engages the interpersonal and socio-cultural dimension as a source of imagery, patterns, and symbols to advance and express the God-image(s) that trigger psychic wholeness. However, given that Jung's understanding of spiritual experience is non-specified within a specific cultural or religious context, the socio-cultural engagement suggests that the spiritual experience might be crucially different in certain contexts, for example, between Eastern and Western cultures. This plurality of diverse spiritual manifestations therefore is not without repercussions in terms of a consistent paradigm of individuation as well as of psychological maturity that is able to engage in spiritual experience in general and Christian ideas in particular.

On the other hand, Maximus understands religious/spiritual experience as a deep 'knowledge' of a loving God beyond any culture. The 'distance' that the Maximian spiritual system appears to maintain from contemporary culture(s) is not without implications, too. Despite the fact that the divine can be experienced through an ongoing spiritual education of all the psychic functions and the synergistic intervention of God, in Maximus' view, such an experience nonetheless might not include the broader spectrum of the archetypal and cultural dynamics that individuation implies. Should the spiritual-as-metaphysical within the current Christian context aspire to be experienced by modern man, it must constantly be able to be incarnate in inspiring contemporary cultural symbols and constructs that will convey the 'divine' in an understandable manner. Whether these intrinsic antinomies between the psychological and the spiritual/metaphysical will be addressed and overcome through an experiential dimension and inspirational cultural incarnations should be the crucial question to be answered by all contemporary spiritual and religious systems or beliefs.

Due to these antinomies, a balanced development towards all directions appears rather a theoretical attainment than a feasible one in practical terms. However, it is the question of *choice* that is of crucial importance here, along with the complex sum of numerous individualistic parameters, from interpersonal history to cultural context and complexes. Viewed together, both modes of development could illustrate the scheme of the Cross, which for Jung denotes 'the union of opposites (vertical and horizontal)' (1958: para. 762) as well as 'a form of suffering [which] expresses psychic reality' together with the 'wholeness and . . . the passion' of one's struggle in life (Jung 1946: para. 523). It is Jung's ambition for a new world which could recover its religious roots through an inner psychological dimension, leading modern man towards the underlying world of an *anima mundi,* which can function as the union of all potentialities of psychic energy. However, for such a union to be accomplished, an authentic experience is essential (that is Maximus' *truly authentic knowledge*) in the realms beyond the psyche, through the struggle of man's *heart* to learn, contemplate, and experience all the *logoi*-words and potentialities of a loving God.

> If God incarnates in the empirical man, man is confronted with the divine problem . . . Christ is the model for the human answers and his symbol is the *cross,* the union of opposites. This will be the fate of man, and this he must understand, if he is to survive at all. We are threatened with universal genocide if we cannot work out the way of salvation by a symbolic death.
>
> (1958/1959: para. 1661)

Maximus, as already shown, grounds this 'way of salvation' in the synergy between God's *logoi*/virtues-as-love and man's *will,* the fully fledged and all-inclusive psychic function. The full-conscious and integrated will in Maximus' understanding is the intellectual, rational, and emotional means whereby one reaches God and his willingness to share his life, knowledge, and love with man in a revelation of his abysmal dimensions. But the distance that separates Maximus' view of spiritual development and revelation/salvation from our epoch inevitably generates 'limitations'. As Jung puts it, '[a]n epoch is like an individual: it has its own limitations of conscious outlook, and therefore requires a compensatory adjustment' (1930/1950: para. 153).

Should the process of spiritual development towards *theosis* need an 'adjustment' to fully address 'the divine problem' of modern man's heart, this is the avoidance of imbalanced psychological development: it is precisely what individuation calls for by unveiling aspects of personality that might be hidden behind masks and personas in the 'current' world 'here and now' while also revealing potentialities of feminine and bodily character, grounded in one's socio-cultural context – which theosis ultimately has to fully confront, too, through the spiritual 'love' that transfigures all psychic aspects. Further, the concepts and challenging positions of analytical psychology may indicate the spiritual stake that Christian philosophy and theology have to fully address, which is the 'death' of the personal God in modern psychic reality. This 'God's death', a predominant notion since the emergence of modernity, in fact is the psychological 'death' and the annihilation of a fulfilling and rewarding spiritual experience of a loving *God* – which Jung strongly criticised, particularly in the Western culture. Maximian theology provides at this point rich material for an experiential perspective that fulfils current expectations for a loving and not punishing God/Father.

On the other hand, the 'adjustment' that analytical psychology needs is the implementation of a deeper epistemology addressing clearly metaphysical/ontological considerations, as well as the application of an efficacious psychic model wholly engaged in spiritual experience via its functions. By understanding and acknowledging the deeper meaning and significance of the spiritual experience, individuation might expand towards *meta*-psychological perspectives, alongside the interpersonal and socio-cultural, in God's 'likeness', attaining thus the fullness of potentialities – one of which is the spiritual progress towards deification. It is a personal journey towards an 'exclusive' spiritual attainment through the reciprocal relationship with a person-as-Other rather than a merely theoretical exploration of a spiritual system enriched by clinical or other professional experience.

Is a constructive synthesis of psychological and spiritual development feasible, one in which the cost of psychic or spiritual one-sidedness could be avoided? The answer is, to a certain extent, positive, inasmuch as 'depth psychology, politics and religion all share, at some level, in what . . . [has been defined] as the fantasy of providing therapy for the world' (Samuels 1993: 337). Both psychological development and spiritual progress, rooted in an experience of one's deeper 'Self' or 'heart', could stand as a challenge of an unfathomable magnitude to all contemporary institutions and trends in the painful quest for a meaningful life, for a 'spiritual therapy' primarily based on personal *experience-as-knowledge* and *knowledge-as-experience,* which ultimately stems from an emerging loving Other-God, beyond symbols and images.

Notes

1. Following Maximus, Gregory Palamas (14th century) emphasizes the importance of prayer as a means of psychic integration while also stressing the potentialities of psychic functions towards the experience of God. The key in this process is 'the return of the intellect [*nous*] to itself and its concentration on itself. Or . . . the convergence of all psychic functions in the intellect . . . and the attaining of the state in which both intellect and God work together . . . restored to their original state and assimilated to their Archetype'. See Gregory Palamas, *To Xenia,* in *Philokalia. The Complete Text.* Compiled by St Nikodimus of the Holy Mountain and St Makarios of Corinth. Vol. IV: 319, trans. G. E. H. Palmer, P. Sherrard and K. Ware (1995), London: Faber & Faber.
2. See *Oxford Dictionary of Sciences,* Oxford University Press, 2005; also, Lightman 2000: 98ff.
3. Museum of Modern Arts (MoMA), New York.

BIBLIOGRAPHY

Abraham, W.J. (2008) 'Eschatology and Epistemology', in J.L. Walls (ed.), *The Oxford Handbook of Eschatology,* Oxford: Oxford University Press.

Adler, A. and Jahn, E. (1933) *Religion und Individualpsychologie,* Frankfurt: Fischer.

Adler, G. (1979) *Dynamics of the Self,* London: Coventure Ltd.

Allport, G.W. (1950) *The Individual and His Religion: A Psychological Interpretation,* New York: MacMillan.

———. (1959) 'Religion and Prejudice', *Crane Review* 2: 1–10.

Aristotle (1933–1989) *Aristotle in 23 Volumes,* trans. Hugh Tredennick, Cambridge, MA: Harvard University Press; London: William Heinemann Ltd.

Armstrong, A.H. (1940) *The Architecture of the Intelligible Universe in the Philosophy of Plotinus. An analytical and Historical Study,* Cambridge: Cambridge University Press.

———. (1947) *An Introduction to Ancient Philosophy,* London: Methuen & Co. Ltd.

———. (ed.) (1967) *The Cambridge History of Later Greek and Early Medieval Philosophy,* Cambridge: Cambridge University Press.

Aziz, R. (2007) *The Syndetic Paradigm. The Untrodden Path Beyond Freud and Jung,* Albany, NY: State University of New York Press.

Bair, D. (2004) *Jung. A Biography,* New York and London: Little Brown and Company.

Balthasar, H.U. (1947) *Liturgie cosmique: Maxime le Confesseur,* trans. L. Lhaumet and H.A. Prentout, Paris: Aubier.

———. (1988; 2nd edn 2003) *Cosmic Liturgy: The Universe According to Maximus the Confessor,* trans. B.E. Daley, San Francisco: Ignatius Press.

Bathrellos, D. (2004) *The Byzantine Christ. Person, Nature and Will in the Christology of St Maximus the Confessor,* Oxford: Oxford University Press.

Beck, H.G. (1959) *Kirch und Theologische Literatur im Byzantinischen Reich,* Münich: C.H. Beck.

Becker, K.L. (2001) *Unlikely Companions: C.G. Jung on the Spiritual Exercises of Ignatius of Loyola,* Herefordshire, Gracewing, and Surrey, UK: Inigo Enterprises.

Beebe, J. (2004) 'Understanding Consciousness through the Theory of Psychological Types', in Joseph Cambray and Linda Carter (eds.), *Analytical Psychology. Contemporary Perspectives in Jungian Analysis,* Hove and New York: Brunner-Routledge.

———. (2006) 'Psychological Types', in *HJP* [see abbreviations].

Belzen, J.A. (ed.) (2012) *Psychology of Religion. Autobiographical Accounts,* New York, Dordrecht, Heidelberg, London: Springer.

Bernard, R.H. (2006) *Research Methods in Anthropology. Qualitative and Quantitative Approaches,* Lanham, New York, Toronto, Oxford: Altamira Press.

Berthold, G. (1982) 'The Cappadocian Roots of Maximus the Confessor', in F. Heinzer and C. von Schönborn (eds.), *Maximus Confessor: Actes du Symposium sur Maxime le Confesseur, Fribourg 2–5 Septembre 1980,* Fribourg: Editions Universitaires Fribourg Suisse.

———. (1985) *Maximus Confessor: Selected Writings,* introd. Jaroslav Pelikan, trans. George Berthold (The Classics of Western Spirituality), Mahwah, NJ: Paulist Press [translations of *Mystagogia* and other Maximus' texts].

Bishop, P. (1996) 'The Use of Kant in Jung's Early Psychological works', *Journal of European Studies,* 26: 107–40.

———. (2000) *Synchronicity and Intellectual Intuition in Kant, Swedenborg, and Jung.* Problems in Contemporary Philosophy, Vol. 46, Lampeter: The Edwin Mellen Press.

———. (2002) *Jung's Answer to Job: A Commentary,* Hove and New York: Brunner-Routledge.

Black, D. (2005) 'The Challenge of Evolution and the Place of Sympathy', in Nathan Field (ed.), *Ten Lectures on Psychotherapy and Spirituality,* London, New York: Karnac.

———. (ed.) (2006) *Psychoanalysis and Religion in the 21st Century. Competitors or Collaborators?* The New Library of Psychoanalysis, London and New York: Routledge.

Blowers, P.M. (1991) *Exegesis and Spiritual Pedagogy in Maximus the Confessor: An Investigation of the 'Quaestiones ad Thalassium'.* Christianity and Judaism in Antiquity Vol. 7, Notre Dame, IN: University of Notre Dame Press.

———. (1992) 'Maximus the Confessor, Gregory of Nyssa, and the Concept of "Perpetual Progress"', *Vigiliae Christianae* 46: 151–71.

———. (1995) 'The Anagogical Imagination: Maximus the Confessor and the Legacy of Origenian Hermeneutics', *Origeniana Sexta* (Leuven): 639–54.

———. (1996) 'Gentiles of the Soul: Maximus the Confessor on the Substructure and Transformation of the Human Passions', *Journal of Early Christian Studies* 4: 57–85.

Blowers, P.M. and Wilken, R.L. (2003) *On the Cosmic Mystery of Jesus Christ. Selected writings from St Maximus the Confessor,* Crestwood, New York: St. Vladimir's Seminary Press. [translations of *Amb.* 7, 8, 42, *Q.Thal.* 1, 2, 6, 17, 22, 42, 60, 61, 64, and *Opusc.* 6].

Bockus, F.M. (1990) 'The Archetypal Self: Theological Values in Jung's Psychology', in R.L. Moore and D.J. Meckel (eds.), *Jung and Christianity in Dialogue: Faith, Feminism and Hermeneutics,* New York: Paulist Press.

Britton, R. (2006) 'Emancipation from the Super-Ego: A Clinical Study of the Book of Job', in David Black (ed.), *Psychoanalysis and Religion in the 21st Century. Competitors or Collaborators?* London and New York: Routledge.

Brock, S.P. (1973) 'An Early Syriac Life of Maximus the Confessor', *Analecta Bollandiana* 91: 299–346.

Brooke, R. (1991, 2nd edn 2009) *Jung and Phenomenology,* Pittsburgh, PA: Trivium Publications.

Brown, P. (1988) *The Body and Society. Men, Women and Sexual Renunciation in Early Christianity,* New York: Columbia University Press.

Buchdahl, G. (1992) *Kant and the Dynamics of Reason. Essays on the Structure of Kant's Philosophy,* Oxford, UK, and Cambridge, MA: Blackwell Publishing.

Butler, C. (2002) *Postmodernism. A Very Short Introduction,* Oxford: Oxford University Press.

Capek, M. (1961) *The Philosophical Impact of Contemporary Physics,* Princeton, NJ: D. Van Nostrand Reinhold Company.

Capra, F. (1975) *The Tao of Physics. An Exploration of the Parallels between Modern Physics and Eastern Mysticism,* London: Flamingo 1983.

Carr, D. (1994) *Phenomenology and the Problem of History. A Study of Husserl's Transcendental Philosophy*, Evanston, IL: Northwestern University Press.

Chodorow, J. (2006) 'Active Imagination', in *HJP.*

Clarke, J.J. (1992) *In Search of Jung. Historical and Philosophical Enquires*, London and New York: Routledge.

———. (1995) *Jung on the East*, London: Routledge.

Clarke, T.E. (1988) 'Jungian Types and Forms of Prayer', in Robert Moore (ed.), *Carl Jung and Christian Spirituality*, New York: Paulist Press.

Clendenen, A. (2009) *Experiencing Hildegard. Jungian Perspectives*, Wilmette, IL: Chiron Publications.

Colman, W. (2000) 'Models of the Self', in Elphis Christopher and Hester McFarland Solomon (eds.), *Jungian Thought in the Modern World*, London, New York: Free Association Books.

Cooper, A.G. (2005) *The Body in St Maximus the Confessor: Holy Flesh, Wholly Deified*, Oxford: Oxford University Press.

Corbett, L. (1996) *The Religious Function of the Psyche*, London and New York: Routledge.

Craig, W.L. (2008) 'Time, Eternity, and Eschatology', in J.L. Walls (ed.), *The Oxford Handbook of Eschatology*, Oxford: Oxford University Press.

Crowley, V. (2003) *Wicca, New Edition: A Comprehensive Guide to the Old Religion in the Modern World*, Rockport, MA: Element Books Ltd.

D'Andrade, R. (2006) 'Moral Models in Anthropology', in H.L. Moore and T. Sanders (eds.), *Anthropology in Theory. Issues in Epistemology*, Malden, MA: Blackwell Publishing. (Original work published 1995)

Davie, G. (2007) *The Sociology of Religion*, Los Angeles, London: Sage Publications.

DeHoff, S.L. (1998) 'In Search of a Paradigm for Psychological and Spiritual Growth: Implications for Psychotherapy and Spiritual Direction', *Pastoral Psychology* 46, 5: 333–46.

Dionysius the Areopagite. (1990) *Corpus Dionysiacum I, De Divinis Nominibus, (DN)*, B.R. Suchla (ed.), in *PTS* 33, Berlin: Walter de Gruyter.

———. (1991) *De Coelesti Hierarchia, De Ecclesiastica Hierarchia, (EH), De Mystica Theologia, (MT), Epistulae*, G. Heil and A.M. Ritter (eds.), *PTS* 36, Berlin: Walter de Gruyter.

Dourley, J.P. (2008) *Paul Tillich, Carl Jung, and the Recovery of Religion*, London and New York: Routledge.

Durkheim, E. (1895) 'Rules of the Explanation of Social Facts' in George E.G. Catlin (ed.), *The Rules of Sociological Method*, 8th edn, trans. Sarah A. Solovay and John H. Mueller, New York: The Free Press. (Reprinted in Moore, H.L., Sanders, T. (eds.) (2006) *Anthropology in Theory. Issues in Epistemology*, Malden, MA: Blackwell Publishing.)

Eckman, B. (1986) 'Jung, Hegel, and the 'Subjective Universe'', *Spring* 1986: 88–99.

Edinger, E.F. (1972/1992) *Ego and Archetype: Individuation and the Religious Function of the Psyche*, Boston and London: Shambhala.

Eigen, M. (2001) 'Mysticism and Psychoanalysis', *Psychoanalytic Review* 88, 3: 455–81.

Ekstrom, S.R. (1988) 'Jung's Typology and DSM-III Personality Disorders: A Comparison of Two Systems of Classification', *Journal of Analytical Psychology* 33, 4: 329–44.

Elkins, D.N. (2001) 'Beyond Religion: Toward a Humanistic Spirituality', in K.J. Schneider, J.T. Bugental, and J.F. Pierson (eds.), *The Handbook of Humanistic Psychology: Leading Edges in Theory, Research, and Practice*, Thousand Oaks, CA: Sage.

Ellenberger, H. (1970) *The Discovery of the Unconscious: The History and Evolution of Dynamic Psychiatry*, London: Allen Lane, The Penguin Press.

Emmons, R.A. and Paloutzian, R.F. (2003) 'The Psychology of Religion', *Annual Review of Psychology* 54: 377–402.

Erikson, E.H. (1982) *The Life Cycle Completed,* New York, London: W.W. Norton & Company.

Evdokimov, P. (1998) *Ages of the Spiritual Life,* trans. Sister Gertrude, S.P., rev. Michael Plekon and Alexis Vinogradov, Crestwood, NY: St Vladimir's Seminary Press.

Farrell, J.P. (1989) *Free Choice in St Maximus the Confessor,* South Canaan, PA: St Tikhon's Seminary Press.

Festugière, A.J. (1967) *Contemplation et vie contemplative selon Platon,* 3rd edn, Paris: J. Vrin.

Ffytche, M. (2012) *The Foundation of the Unconscious. Schelling, Freud and the Birth of the Modern Psyche,* Cambridge: Cambridge University Press.

Field, N. (ed.) (2005) *Ten Lectures on Psychotherapy and Spirituality,* London: Carnac.

Florovsky, G. (1931) *The Byzantine Fathers of the Sixth to Eighth Century.* Collected Works of G. Florovsky Vol. 10, trans. Raymond Miller *et al.* (1987), Vaduz: Buchervertriebsanstalt.

Fordham, M. (1957) *Children as Individuals,* London: Hodder and Stoughton.

———. (1985) *Explorations into the Self,* London: Academic Press.

———. (1995) *Freud, Jung, Klein – the Fenceless Field. Essays on Psychoanalysis and Analytical Psychology,* ed. Roger Hobdell, London and New York: Routledge.

Foucault, M. (1981) *The History of Sexuality. An Introduction,* Vol. 1, Harmondsworth: Penguin.

Freud, S. (1923) 'The Ego and the Id', in *The Standard Edition of the Complete Psychological Works of Sigmund Freud (S.E.) Volume XIX* (1961), London: The Hogarth Press.

———. (1927) 'The Future of an Illusion', in *S.E. Volume XXI* (2001), London: Vintage.

———. (1930) 'The Civilisation and Its Discontents', in *S.E. Volume XXI* (2001), London: Vintage.

Friedman, M. (1985) *The Healing Dialogue in Psychotherapy,* New York: Jason Aronson.

Gadamer, H.G. (1975; 2nd edn 2006) *Truth and Method,* trans. Joel Weinsheimer and Donald G. Marshall, London, New York: Continuum.

Gaist, B.J. (2010) *Creative Suffering and the Wounded Healer: Analytical Psychology and Orthodox Christian Theology,* Rollinsford, NH: Orthodox Research Institute.

Garrigues, J.M. (1976) *Maxime le Confesseur: la charité, avenir divin de l'homme.* Théologie historique Vol. 38, Paris: Editions Beauchesne.

Gauthier, R.A. (1954) 'Saint Maxime le Confesseur et la psychologie de l'acte humain', *Recherches de Théologie Ancienne et Médiévale* (Louvain) 21: 51–100.

Geanakoplos, D.J. (1969) 'Some Aspects of the Influence of the Byzantine Maximos the Confessor on the Theology of East and West', *Church History* 38: 150–63.

Giddens, A. (1991) *Modernity and Self-Identity. Self and Society in the Late Modern Age,* Stanford, CA: Stanford University Press.

———. (1993) *The Constitution of Society. Outline of the Theory of Structuration,* Cambridge: Cambridge University Press.

Giegerich, W. (2011) 'The Disenchantment Complex: C.G. Jung and the Modern World', *International Journal of Jungian Studies* 4, 1: 4–20.

Gould, C.C. (1983) 'Beyond Causality in the Social Sciences: Reciprocity as a Model of Non-Exploitative Social Relations', in R.S. Cohen and M. Wartofsky (eds.), *Epistemology, Methodology, and the Social Sciences,* London: D. Reidel Publishing Company.

Grondin, J. (1999) 'Understanding as Dialogue: Gadamer', in *The Edinburgh Encyclopedia of Continental Philosophy*, Edinburgh: Edinburgh University Press.

———. (2003) *The Philosophy of Gadamer*, trans. Kathryn Plant, Montreal & Kingston, Ithaca: McGill, Queen's University Press.

Guthrie, W.K.C. (1967) *The Greek Philosophers. From Thales to Aristotle*, London: Methuen & Co Ltd.

Hann, C. and Goltz, H. (eds.) (2010) *Eastern Christians in Anthropological Perspectives*, Berkley, Los Angeles, London: University of California Press.

Hauke, C. (2000) *Jung and the Postmodern. The Interpretation of Realities*, Hove and New York: Brunner-Routledge.

Heelas, P. and Woodhead, L. (2005) *The Spiritual Revolution. Why Religion Is Giving Way to Spirituality*, Malden, MA: Blackwell Publishing.

Hegel, G.W.F. (1807; 2nd edn 1931) *The Phenomenology of Mind*, trans. J.B. Baillie, London: George Allen and Unwin Ltd.; New York: The Macmillan Co.

———. (1807/1977) *Phenomenology of Spirit*, trans. A.V. Miller, foreword J.N. Findlay, Oxford: Oxford University Press.

———. (1985) 'Lectures on the Philosophy of Religion' in P.C. Hodgson (ed.), *Hegel's Lectures On the Philosophy on Religion*. Vol. III: *The Consummate Religion*, trans. R.F. Brown, P.C. Hodgson and J.M. Steward, Berkley: University of California Press.

Heidegger, M. (1927/1962) *Being and Time*, trans. J. Macquarrie and E. Robinson, Oxford: Basil Blackwell.

———. (1994) *Hegel's Phenomenology of Spirit*, trans. Parvis Emad and Kenneth Maly, Bloomington & Indianapolis: Indiana University Press.

Heidemann, D.H. (2008) 'Substance, Subject, System: The Justification of Science in Hegel's Phenomenology of Spirit', in Dean Moyar and Michael Quante (eds.), *Hegel's Phenomenology of Spirit. A Critical Guide*, Cambridge: Cambridge University Press.

Heil, J. (2004) *Philosophy of Mind. A Contemporary Introduction*, 2nd edn, New York and London: Routledge.

Heisig, J. (1979) *Imago Dei: A Study of C.G. Jung's Psychology of Religion*, Lewisburg, PA: Bucknell University Press.

Henderson, J. (1990) *Shadow and Self: Selected Papers in Analytical Psychology*, Wilmette, IL: Chiror Publications.

Hill, P.C., Pargament, K.I., Wood, R.W., McCullough, M.E. Jr., Swyers, J.P., Larson, D.B. and Zinnbauer, B.J. (2000) 'Conceptualizing Religion and Spirituality: Points of Commonality, Points of Departure', *Journal for the Theory of Social Behaviour* 30, 1: 51–77.

Hillman, J. (1980) *Egalitarian Typologies versus the Perception of the Unique*, Eranos Lectures, Series 4, Dallas: Spring Publications.

———. (1983) *Archetypal Psychology: A Brief Account*, Woodstock, CT: Spring Publications.

Hoffman, M.T. (2011) *Toward Mutual Recognition. Relational Psychoanalysis and the Christian Narrative*, New York, London: Routledge.

Hogenson, G.B. (2004) 'Archetypes: Emergence and the Psyche's Deep Structure', in Joseph Cambray and Linda Carter (eds.), *Analytical Psychology. Contemporary Perspectives in Jungian Analysis*, Hove and New York: Brunner-Routledge.

Homans, P. (1990) 'C.G. Jung: Christian or Post–Christian Psychologist?', in Robert L. and Daniel J. Meckel (eds.), *Jung and Christianity in Dialogue: Faith, Feminism and Hermeneutics*, New York: Paulist Press.

Horstmann, R.P. (2008) 'The *Phenomenology of Spirit* as a "Transcendentalistic" Argument for a Monistic Ontology', in Dean Moyar and Michael Quante (eds.), *Hegel's Phenomenology of Spirit. A Critical Guide,* Cambridge: Cambridge University Press.

Huskinson, L. (2004) *Nietzsche and Jung. The Whole Self in the Union of Opposites,* Hove and New York: Brunner-Routledge.

Jacoby, M. (1990) *Individuation and Narcissism. The Psychology of Self in Jung and Kohut,* trans. Myron Gubitz, Françoise O'Kane, Hove and New York: Routledge.

Jaeger, W. (1947) *The Theology of the Early Greek Philosophers. The Gifford Lectures 1936,* Oxford: Clarendon Press.

James, W. (1902/2002) *The Varieties of Religious Experience. A Study in Human Nature,* Mineola, NY: Dover Publications.

———. (1909) *A Pluralistic Universe. Hibber Lectures at Manchester College on the Present Situation in Philosophy,* New York, London: Longmans, Green and Co.

Jarrett, J.L. (1979) 'The Logic of Psychological Opposition – or How Opposite Is Opposite?' *Journal of Analytical Psychology* 24: 318–25.

———. (1981) 'Schopenhauer and Jung', *Spring* 195: 201.

Jonte-Pace, J. and Parsons, W.B. (eds.) (2001) *Religion and Psychology: Mapping the Terrain. Contemporary Dialogues, Future Prospects,* London, New York: Routledge.

Jugler, P. (1990) 'The Unconscious in a Postmodern Depth Psychology', in Karnin Barnaby and Pelegrino D'Acierno (eds.), *C.G. Jung and the Humanities: Toward a Hermeneutics of Culture,* London: Routledge.

Jung, C.G. [unless otherwise stated] (1953–1983) *The Collective Works of C.G. Jung* (*CW*), Sir H. Read, M. Fordham, G. Adler, W. McGuire (eds.), trans. R.F.C. Hull, London: Routledge & Kegan Paul.

———. (1909/1949) *The Significance of the Father in the Destiny of the Individual. CW* 5.

———. (1911/1956) *Symbols of Transformation. CW* 5.

———. (1912) *Concerning Psychoanalysis. CW* 4.

———. (1916/1957) *The Transcendent Function. CW* 8.

———. (1917/1943) *On the Psychology of the Unconscious. CW* 7.

———. (1918) *The Role of the Unconscious. CW* 10.

———. (1921/1971) *Psychological Types. CW* 6.

———. (1926) *Spirit and Life. CW* 8.

———. (1928a) *The Relations between the Ego and the Unconscious. CW* 7.

———. (1928b) *On Psychic Energy. CW* 8.

———. (1928/1931a) *The Spiritual Problem of Modern Man. CW* 10.

———. (1928/1931b) *Analytical Psychology and Weltanschauung. CW* 8.

———. (1929) *Commentary on 'The Secret of the Golden Flower'. CW* 13.

———. (1930/1950) *Psychology and Literature. CW* 15.

———. (1934a) *The Development of Personality. CW* 17.

———. (1934b) *A Review of the Complex Theory. CW* 8.

———. (1934/1950) *A Study in the Process of Individuation. CW* 9i.

———. (1934/1954) *Archetypes of the Collective Unconscious. CW* 9i.

———. (1934/1976) *The Vision Seminars Vol. 2.* New York: Spring Publications.

———. (1935) *Principles of Practical Psychotherapy. CW* 16.

———. (1935/1953) *On the Tibetan Book of the Dead. CW* 11.

———. (1936) *Wotan. CW* 10.

———. (1937a) *Psychological Factors Determining Human Behaviour. CW* 8.

———. (1937b) *Religious Ideas in Alchemy. CW* 12.

———. (1938/1940) *Psychology and Religion* (The Terry Lectures). *CW* 11.

———. (1938/1954) *Psychological Aspects of the Mother Archetype*. *CW* 9i.

———. (1939a) *Conscious, Unconscious and Individuation*. *CW* 9i.

———. (1939b) *Psychological Commentary on 'The Tibetan Book of the Great Liberation'. CW* 11.

———. (1940) *The Psychology of the Child Archetype. CW* 9i.

———. (1940/1950) *Concerning Rebirth. CW* 9i.

———. (1942/1948) *A Psychological Approach to the Dogma of the Trinity. CW* 11.

———. (1942/1954) *Transformation Symbolism in the Mass. CW* 11.

———. (1943/1948) *The Spirit Mercurius. CW* 13.

———. (1944) *Psychology and Alchemy. CW* 12.

———. (1945) *After the Catastrophe. CW* 10.

———. (1945/1948) *On the Nature of Dreams. CW* 8.

———. (1945/1954) *The Philosophical Tree. CW* 13.

———. (1946) *The Psychology of the Transference. CW* 16.

———. (1947/1954) *On the Nature of the Psyche. CW* 8.

———. (1951) *Fundamental Questions of Psychotherapy. CW* 16.

———. (1951/1959) *Aion: Researches into the Phenomenology of the Self. CW* 9ii.

———. (1952a) *Answer to Job. CW* 11.

———. (1952b) *Synchronicity: An Acausal Connecting Principle. CW* 8.

———. (1952c) *Foreword to White's 'God and the Unconscious' and Werblowsky's 'Lucifer and Prometheus'. CW* 11.

———. (1954) *Archetypes of the Collective Unconscious. CW* 9i.

———. (1955/1956) *Mysterium Coniunctionis. CW* 14.

———. (1957) *The Undiscovered Self (Present and Future). CW* 10.

———. (1958) *Flying Saucers: a Modern Myth of Things Seen in the Skies. CW* 10.

———. (1958/1959) *Jung and Religious Belief. CW* 18.

———. (1959) *Good and Evil in Analytical Psychology. CW* 10.

———. (1973) *Letters* Vol I: 1906–1950, G. Adler and A. Jaffé (eds.), London: Routledge & Kegan Paul.

———. (1976) *Letters* Vol II: 1951–1961, G. Adler and A. Jaffé (eds.), London: Routledge & Kegan Paul.

———. (2009) *The Red Book,* Sonu Shamdasani (ed.), New York, London: W.W. Norton.

Kant, I. (1781/1998) *Critique of Pure Reason,* eds. and trans. Paul Guyer and Allen Wood, The Cambridge Edition of the Works of Immanuel Kant, Cambridge: Cambridge University Press.

———. (1793) *Religion within the Boundaries of Mere Reason and other Writings,* eds. and trans. Allen Wood, George Di Giovanni (1998), Cambridge Texts in History of Philosophy. Cambridge: Cambridge University.

Kelly, S.M. (1993) *Individuation and the Absolute. Hegel, Jung, and the Path Toward Wholeness,* New York: Paulist Press.

Kelsey, M.T. (1991) 'Jung as Philosopher and Theologian', in R. Papadopoulos and G. Saayman (eds.), *Jung in Modern Perspective,* Dorset, UK: Prism Press.

Kerr, J. (1993) *A Most Dangerous Method: The Story of Jung, Freud and Sabina Spielrein,* New York: Alfred A. Knopf.

Kirk, G.S. and Raven, J.E. (1960) *The Pre–Socratic Philosophers. A Critical History With a Selection of Texts,* Cambridge: Cambridge University Press.

Klein, M. (1997) *Envy and Gratitude and Other Works 1946–1963,* London: Vintage.

Knight, D.H. (2006) *The Eschatological Economy. Time and the Hospitality of God,* Grand Rapids, MI, Cambridge, UK: William B. Eerdmans Publishing Company.

Knox, J. (2003) *Archetype, Attachment, Analysis. Jungian Psychology and the Emergent Mind,* Hove and New York: Brunner-Routledge.

Kohut, H. (1977) *The Restoration of the Self,* New York: International Universities Press.

Konstantinovsky, J. (2009) *Evagrius Ponticus. The Making of a Gnostic,* Surrey, UK, and Burlington, VT: Ashgate.

Kornarakis, I. (1958) *Ἡ Συμβολὴ τῆς Ψυχολογίας τοῦ Κάρλ Γιούνγκ ἐν τῇ Ποιμαντικῇ Ψυχολογίᾳ* [*The Contribution of Carl Jung's Psychology to Pastoral Psychology*], Athens.

Kugler, P. (2008) 'Psychic Imaging: A Bridge between Subject and Object', in Polly Young-Eisendrath and Terence Dawson (eds.), *The Cambridge Companion to Jung,* Cambridge: Cambridge University Press.

Kuhn, T. (1970) *The Structure of Scientific Revolution,* 2nd edn, Chicago: University of Chicago Press.

———. (1977) *The Essential Tension: Selected Studies in Scientific Tradition and Change,* Chicago: University of Chicago Press.

Ladner, G.B. (1995) *God, Cosmos and Humankind. The World of Early Christian Symbolism,* trans. Thomas Dunlap, Berkley, Los Angeles, London: University of California Press.

Laing, R.D. (1960) *The Divided Self: An Existential Study in Sanity and Madness,* Harmondsworth: Penguin.

Lammers, A.C. and Cunningham, A. (eds.) (2007) *The Jung–White Letters,* London: Routledge.

Levinas, E. (1991/2006) *Entre Nous. Thinking-of-the-Other.* trans. Michael B. Smith and Barbara Harshav, London and New York: Continuum.

Lévy-Bruhl, L. (1965) *The 'Soul' of the Primitive,* trans. Lilian A. Clare, London: George Allen and Unwin Ltd.

Lightman, A. (2000) *Great Ideas in Physics,* New York, London, Tokyo: McGraw-Hill.

Lossky, V. (1957) *The Mystical Theology of the Eastern Church,* trans. the Fellowship of St Albans and St Sergius, Cambridge and London: James Clarke & Co. Ltd.

———. (1978) *Orthodox Theology: An Introduction,* Crestwood, NY: St Vladimir's Seminary Press.

Lothane, Z. (1996) 'In Defense of Sabina Spielrein', *International Forum of Psychoanalysis* 5: 203–17.

Loudovikos, N. (2003) 'Towards a Theology of Psychotherapy' [Summary in English], in *Ψυχανάλυση καὶ Ὀρθόδοξη Θεολογία,* Athens: Armos.

———. (2010) *A Eucharistic Ontology. Maximus the Confessor's Eschatological Ontology of Being as Dialogical Reciprocity,* trans. Elizabeth Theokritoff, Brookline, MA: Holy Cross Orthodox Press.

Louth, A. (1981; 2nd edn 2007) *The Origins of the Christian Mystical Tradition. From Plato to Denys,* Oxford: Oxford University Press.

———. (1993) 'St Denys the Areopagite and St Maximus the Confessor: A Question of Influence', *Studia Patristica* 27: 166–74.

———. (1996) *Maximus the Confessor,* London and New York: Routledge. [translations of *Ep.* 2, *Amb.* 1, 5, 10, 41, 71, and *Opusc.* 3, 7].

———. (1997) 'St. Maximus the Confessor between East and West', *Studia Patristica* 32: 332–45.

———. (2008) 'Eastern Orthodox Eschatology', in Jerry L. Walls (ed.), *The Oxford Handbook of Eschatology,* Oxford: Oxford University Press.

———. (2009) 'The Reception of Dionysius in the Byzantine World: Maximus to Palamas', in Sarah Coakley and Charles M. Stang (eds.), *Re-Thinking Dionysious the Areopagite*, West Sussex: Wiley-Blackwell.

Main, R. (ed.) (1997) *Jung on Synchronicity and the Paranormal*, London: Brunner-Routledge.

———. (2004) *The Rupture of Time. Synchronicity and Jung's Critique of Modern Western
Culture*, Hove and New York: Brunner-Routledge.

———. (2006) 'Religion', in *HJP*.

Malinowsky, B. (1944) *A Scientific Theory of Culture*, Chapel Hill, NC: University of
North Carolina.

Mantzaridis, G. (1984) *The Deification of Man. St Gregory Palamas and the Orthodox
Tradition*, trans. Liadain Sherrad, Crestwood, NY: St Vladimir's Seminary Press.

Matthews, G. (2000) 'Internalist Reasoning in Augustine for Mind–Body Dualism', in
John P. Wright and Paul Potter (eds.), *Psyche and Soma. Physicians and Metaphysicians
on the Mind–Body Problem from Antiquity to Enlightenment*, Oxford: Clarendon Press.

Maximus, the Confessor (unless otherwise stated) (1895) *Patrologia Cursus Completus
(PG) Series Graeca* Vols. 90–91. J.P. Minge (ed.), Paris. [Reprint of the *Opera Omnia*,
by Francis Combefis and Francis Oehler, Halle, 1857)].

———. (1980) (*Maximi Confessoris) Quaestiones ad Thalassium* I, (Quaestiones I–LV),
with a Latin translation by John Scotus Eriugena, Carl Laga and Carlos Steel (eds.),
Corpus Christianorum Series Craeca Vol. 7, Leuven University Press, Turnhout: Brepols
(*CCSG* 7).

———. (1981) (*Various Works by Maximus*), in *The Philokalia: The Complete Text. Volume II*. Compiled by St Nikodimus of the Holy Mountain and St Makarios of Corinth,
ed. and trans. G.E.H. Palmer, P. Sherrard, K. Ware, London: Faber & Faber.

———. (1982) (*Maximi Confessoris) Quaestiones et Dubia*, José H. Declerck (ed.), Turnhout: Brepols (*CCSG* 10).

———. (1988) (*Maximi Confessoris) Ambigua ad Iohannem*, a translation into Latin by
John Scotus Eriugena, C. Laga (ed.), Turnhout: Brepols (*CCSG* 18).

———. (1990) (*Maximi Confessoris) Quaestiones ad Thalassium* II, (Quaestiones LVI–
LXV), with a Latin translation by John Scotus Eriugena, Carl Laga and Carlos Steel
(eds.), Leuven University Press, Turnhout: Brepols (*CCSG* 22).

———. (1991) (*Maximi Confessoris) Opuscula exegetica duo*, Peter Van Deun (ed.),
Turnhout: Brepols (*CCSG* 23).

———. (1993) *Mystagogia*, S. Soteropoulos (ed.) [Σ. Σωτηρόπουλος, Ἡ Μυσταγωγία τοῦ
Ἁγίου Μαξίμου τοῦ Ὁμολογητοῦ], 2nd edn, Athens.

———. (1999) (*Maximi Confessoris) Scripta saeculi viivitam Maximi Confessoris illus-
trantia*, with a Latin translation by Anastasius Bibliothecarius, Pauline Allen and Bron-
wen Neil (eds.), Turnhout: Brepols (*CCSG* 39).

———. (2000) (*Maximi Confessoris) Liber asceticus*, (with early Latin translation)
S. Gysens, Peter Van Deun (eds.), Turnhout: Brepols (*CCSG* 40).

———. (2002) (*Maximi Confessoris) Ambigua ad Thomam una cum epistula secunda ad
eundem*. B. Janssens (ed.), Turnhout: Brepols (*CCSG* 48).

McGuire, W. and Hull, R.F.C. (1977) *C.G. Jung Speaking: Interviews and Encounters*,
London: Thames and Hudson.

Meckel, D. and Moore, R. (eds.) (1990) *Self and Liberation: The Jung–Buddhism Dialogue*, New York: Paulist Press.

Meier, C.A. (1977) *Personality. The Individuation Process in the Light of C.G. Jung's
Typology*, trans. David N. Roscoe, Einsiedeln: Daimon.

Melissaris, A.G. (2002) *Personhood Re-Examined: Current Perspectives from Orthodox Anthropology and Archetypal Psychology. A Comparison of John Zizioulas and James Hillman,* Katerini, Greece: Epektasis Publications.

Michael, E. (2000) 'Renaissance Theories of Body, Soul, and Mind', in John P. Wright and Paul Potter (eds.), *Psyche and Soma. Physicians and Metaphysicians on the Mind–Body Problem from Antiquity to Enlightenment,* Oxford: Clarendon Press.

Miller, J.C. (2004) *The Transcendent Function: Jung's Model of Psychological Growth through Dialogue with the Unconscious,* Albany, NY: State University of New York Press.

Mills, J. (2013) 'Jung's Metaphysics', *International Journal of Jungian Studies* 5, 1: 19–43.

Moore, H.L. and Sanders, T. (eds.) (2006) *Anthropology in Theory. Issues in Epistemology,* Malden, MA: Blackwell Publishing.

Moore, R. (ed.) (1988) *Carl Jung and Christian Spirituality,* New York: Paulist Press.

Moore, R.L. and Meckel, D.J. (eds.) (1990) *Jung and Christianity in Dialogue: Faith, Feminism and Hermeneutics,* New York: Paulist Press.

Moran, J. (2000) 'Orthodoxy and Modern Depth Psychology', in Andrew Walker and Costas Carras (eds.), *Living Orthodoxy in the Modern World, Orthodoxy Christianity and Society,* Crestwood, NY: St Vladimir's Seminary Press.

Mulhall, S. (2005) *Heidegger and Being and Time* (Routledge Philosophy GuideBook to), 2nd edn, London and New York: Routledge.

Myers, I. and Myers, P. (1980) *Gifts Differing: Understanding Personality Type,* Palo Alto, CA: Consulting Psychological Press.

Nagel, E. (1968) *The Structure of Science,* London: Routledge.

Nagy, M. (1991) *Philosophical Issues in the Psychology of C.G. Jung,* New York, Albany, NY: State University of New York Press.

Narby, J. (2006) *Intelligence in Nature. An Inquiry into Knowledge,* New York: Penguin Group.

Nellas, P. (1997) *Deification in Christ: The Nature of the Human Person,* trans. Norman Russell, Crestwood, New York: St Vladimir's Seminary Press.

Nemesius (Nemesii Emeseni). (1988) *De Natura Hominis,* Moreno Morani (ed.), *De Natura Hominis,* Leipzig: BSB B.G. Teubner Verlagsgesellschaft.

Neumann, E. (1954) *The Origins and History of Consciousness,* trans. R.F.C. Hull, Bollinger Series XLII (1993), Princeton, NJ: Princeton University Press.

———. (1955) *The Great Mother. An Analysis of the Archetype,* trans. Ralph Manheim, Bollinger Series XLVII (1991) Princeton, NJ: Princeton University Press.

Nichols, A. (1993) *The Byzantine Gospel: Maximus the Confessor in Modern Scholarship,* Edinburgh: T & T Clark.

Nicolaus, G. (2011) *C.G. Jung and Nikolai Berdyaev: Individuation and the Person. A Critical Comparison,* London and New York: Routledge.

Nicolescu, B. (2002) *Manifesto of Transdisciplinarity,* Albany, NY: State University of New York Press.

———. (2010) 'Methodology of Transdisciplinarity – Levels of Reality, Logic of the Included Middle and Complexity', *Transdisciplinary Journal of Engineering and Science* 1 (1): 19–38.

Nietzsche, F. (1886) *Beyond Good and Evil. Prelude to a Philosophy of the Future,* trans. R.J. Hollingdale (1974), Penguin Books.

Noll, Richard (1996). *The Jung Cult: Origins of a Charismatic Movement,* London: Fontana Press.

Norman, R. (1976) *Hegel's Phenomenology. A Philosophical Introduction,* Sussex: Sussex University Press.

Otto, R. (1917/1950) *The Idea of the Holy,* trans. John W. Harvey, London, Oxford, New York: Oxford University Press.

Palmer, M. (1997) *Freud and Jung on Religion,* London and New York: Routledge.

Paloutzian, R.F. (1996) *Invitation to Psychology of Religion,* 2nd edn, Needham Heights, MA: Allyn & Bacon.

Paloutzian, R.F. and Park, C.L. (eds.) (2005) *Handbook of the Psychology of Religion and Spirituality,* New York: The Guilford Press.

Papadopoulos, R. (1980) 'The Dialectic of the Other in the Psychology of C.G. Jung: A Metatheoritical Investigation', unpublished PhD thesis, University of Cape Town.

———. (1991) 'Jung and the Concept of the Other', in R. Papadopoulos and G. Saayman (eds.), *Jung in Modern Perspective,* Dorset, UK: Prism Press.

———. (2006) 'Jung's Epistemology and Methodology', in *HJP.*

Plass, P. (1980) 'Transcendent Time in Maximus the Confessor', *The Thomist* 1980: 259–77.

Plato (1925ff) *Plato in Twelve Volumes,* trans. Harold N. Fowler, Cambridge, MA: Harvard University Press.

Plotinus (1991) *The Enneads,* trans. Stephen MacKenna, Penguin Books.

Popper, K. (1982) *Quantum Theory and the Schism in Physics,* London: Hutchinson & Co. Ltd.

———. (1994) *Knowledge and the Body–Mind Problem. In Defence of Interaction,* London and New York: Routledge.

Pound, E. (1948) *The Cantos of Ezra Pound,* New York: New Directions.

Preston, E. (1990) 'Mind and Matter in Myth', in Karnin Barnaby and Pelegrino D'Acierno (eds.), *C.G. Jung and the Humanities: Toward a Hermeneutics of Culture,* London: Routledge.

Quinodoz, J.M. (2006) *Reading Freud. A Chronological Exploration of Freud's Writings,* trans. David Alcorn, London and New York: Routledge.

Repicky, R.A. (1988) 'Jungian Typology and Christian Spirituality', in Robert Moore (ed.), *Carl Jung and Christian Spirituality,* New York: Paulist Press.

Ricoeur, P. (1967) *The Symbolism of Evil,* Boston: Beacon Press.

Rilke, R.M. (2005) *The Poet's Guide to Life. The Wisdom of Rilke,* ed. and trans. Ulrich Baer, New York: The Modern Library.

Romanyshyn, R.D. (2000) 'Alchemy and the Subtle Body of Metaphor. Soul and Cosmos', in Roger Brooke (ed.), *Pathways into the Jungian World: Phenomenology and Analytical Psychology,* London and New York: Routledge & Kegan Paul.

Rorem, P. (1993) *Pseudo-Dionysius. A Commentary on the Texts and an Introduction to Their Influence,* New York, Oxford: Oxford University Press.

Rosenberg, A. (2008) *Philosophy of Social Science,* 3rd edn, Boulder, CO: Westview Press.

Rosenzweig, S. (1992) *Freud, Jung and Hall the King-Maker: The Historic Expedition to America, 1909, with G. Stanley Hall as Host and William James as Guest,* St. Louis: Hogrefe & Huber.

Rossum, J.V. (1993) 'The Logoi of Creation and the Divine "Energies" in Maximus the Confessor and Gregory Palamas', *Studia Patristica* 27: 213–17.

Rowland, S. (2002) *Jung. A Feminist Revision,* Cambridge: Polity Press.

Runciman, S. (1933) *Byzantine Civilisation,* London: Edward Arnold & Co.

Russell, N. (2004) *The Doctrine of Deification in the Greek Patristic Tradition,* Oxford: Oxford University Press.

Rychlak, J.F. (1991) 'Jung as Dialectician and Teleologist', in R. Papadopoulos and G. Saayman (eds.), *Jung in Modern Perspective,* Dorset, UK: Prism Press.

Sakharov, N.V. (2002) *I Love, Therefore I am. The Theological Legacy of Archimandrite Sophrony,* New York: St Vladimir's Seminary Press.

Sakharov, S. (Archim. Sophrony) (1988) *We Shall See Him as He Is,* Essex: Stavropegic Monastery of St. John the Baptist.

Salman, S. (2008) 'The Creative Psyche: Jung's Major Contributions', in Polly Young-Eisendrath and Terence Dawson (eds.), *The Cambridge Companion to Jung,* Cambridge: Cambridge University Press.

Samuels, A. (1985) *Jung and the Post–Jungians,* London and New York: Routledge and Kegan Paul.

———. (1989) *The Plural Psyche,* London and New York: Routledge.

———. (1990) 'Beyond the Feminine Principle', in Karnin Barnaby and Pelegrino D'Acierno (eds.), *C.G. Jung and the Humanities: Toward a Hermeneutics of Culture,* London: Routledge.

———. (1993) *The Political Psyche,* London and New York: Routledge.

———. (2005) 'A New Anatomy of Spirituality', in Nathan Field (ed.), *Ten Lectures on Psychotherapy and Spirituality,* London, New York: Karnac.

Schlauch, C.R. (2007) 'Being-There-With-and-For: Contemporary Psychoanalysis Characterizes Notions of Being Religious', *Pastoral Psychology* 56: 199–221.

Schopenhauer, A. (1819/1995) *The World as Will and Idea,* trans. Jill Berman, London: Everyman.

Schubart, W. (1944) *Religion und Eros,* München: C.H. Beck; reprinted in Greek, trans. M.Z. Kopidakis and A. Skliri (1993), Athens: Olkos.

Schwartz-Salant, N. (1989) *The Borderline Personality. Vision and Healing,* Wilmette, IL: Chiron Publications.

Segal, R.A. (1992) *The Gnostic Jung,* Princeton, NJ: Princeton University Press.

Shamdasani, S. (1999) 'In Statu Nascendi', *Journal of Analytical Psychology* 44: 539–46.

Sherwood, P. (1955) *The Earlier Ambigua of Saint Maximus the Confessor and his Refutation of Origenism,* Studia Anselmiana 36, Rome: Orbis Catholicus, Herber.

———. (1995) *Saint Maximus the Confessor. The Ascetic Life. The Four Centuries on Charity.* Ancient Christian Writers (*ACW*) 21, New York: The Newman Press.

Shilling, C. (2005) *The Body in Culture, Technology and Society,* London: Sage Publications.

Singer, T. (2010) 'The Transcendent Function and Cultural Complexes: A Working Hypothesis', *Journal of Analytical Psychology* 55, 234–41.

Singer, T. and Kimbles, S.L. (2004) 'The Emerging Theory of Cultural Complexes', in Joseph Cambray and Linda Carter (eds.), *Analytical Psychology. Contemporary Perspectives in Jungian Analysis,* Hove and New York: Brunner-Routledge.

Smith, M.C. (1997) *Jung and Shamanism in Dialogue: Retrieving the Soul, Retrieving the Sacred,* New York: Paulist Press.

Snell, B. (1960) *The Discovery of the Mind. The Greek Origins of European Thought,* trans. T.G. Rosenmeyer, New York and Evanston: Harper and Row Publishers (originally published by the Harvard University Press in 1953).

Solomon, H.M. (2000) 'The Ethical Self', in Elphis Christopher and Hester McFarland Solomon (eds.), *Jungian Thought in the Modern World.* London, New York: Free Association Books.

Spoto, A. (1995) *Jung's Typology in Perspective,* Wilmette, IL: Chiron Publications.

Squire, A.K. (1966) 'The Idea of the Soul as Virgin and Mother in Maximus the Confessor', *Studia Patristica* 8: 456–61.

Staniloae, D. (1978) 'Image, Likeness and Deification in the Human Person', in *Orthodox Dogmatic Theology,* trans. Ioan Ionita and Robert Barringer, Vol. I: 388–408 (Bucharest).

——. (1990) *Φιλοσοφικὰ καὶ Θεολογικὰ Ἐρωτήματα. [Introduction to Maximus' Philosophical and Theological Questions],* Athens: Apostolic Diakonia.

Stauropoulos, A. (2000) *Κλινική και Θεραπευτική Ποιμαντική Θεολογία στη σχέση της με την Ψυχοπαθολογία και την Ψυχοθεραπεία. [Clinical and Therapeutic Pastoral Theology in its relationship with Psychopathology and Psychotherapy],* Athens.

Stein, M. (1985) *Jung's Treatment of Christianity. The Psychotherapy of a Religious Tradition,* Wilmette, IL: Chiron Publications.

——. (1990) 'C.G. Jung, Psychologist and Theologian', in Robert L. Moore and Daniel J. Meckel (eds.), *Jung and Christianity in Dialogue: Faith, Feminism and Hermeneutics.* New York: Paulist Press.

——. (2004) 'Spiritual and Religious Aspects of Modern Analysis', in Joseph Cambrey and Carter (eds.), *Analytical Psychology. Contemporary Perspectives in Jungian Analysis,* Hove and New York: Brunner-Routledge.

——. (2006) 'Individuation', in *HJP.*

Stein, S.M. and Black, D.M. (eds.) (1999) *Beyond Belief: Psychotherapy and Religion.* London: Karnac Books.

Stevens, A. (1982) *Archetype: A Natural History of the Self,* London: Routledge and Kegan Paul, New York: William Morrow.

——. (2006) 'The Archetypes', in *HJP.*

Storr, A. (1973) *Jung,* London: Fontana Press.

Thatcher, A. (1987) 'Christian Theism and the Concept of a Person', in Arthur Peacocke and Grant Gillett (eds.), *Persons and Personality. A Contemporary Inquiry.* Ian Ramsey Centre Publication 1: Oxford: Basil Blackwell.

Thermos, V. (1999) 'Toward a Theological Understanding of Psychopathology and Therapy', in *Theology and Psychiatry in Dialogue,* Athens: Apostolic Diakonia.

Thunberg, L. (1985) *Man and Cosmos: The Vision of St Maximus the Confessor,* New York, Crestwood: St Vladimir's Seminary Press.

——. (1995) *Microcosm and Mediator: The Theological Anthropology of Maximus the Confessor,* 2nd edn, Chicago: Open Court Publishing.

Törönen, M. (2007) *Union and Distinction in the Thought of St Maximus the Confessor.* Oxford Early Christian Studies: Oxford: Oxford University Press.

Torrance, R.M. (1994) *The Spiritual Quest. Transcendence in Myth, Religion, and Science,* Berkley, Los Angeles, London: University of California Press.

Turner, B.S. (2008) *The Body and Society. Explorations in Social Theory,* London: Sage.

Tyng, A.G. (1990) 'Individuation and Entropy as a Creative Cycle in Architecture', in Karnin Barnaby and Pelegrino D'Acierno (eds.), *C.G. Jung and the Humanities: Toward a Hermeneutics of Culture,* London: Routledge.

Ulanov, A.B. (1999) *Religion and the Spiritual in Carl Jung,* New York: Paulist Press.

Urban, E. (2005) 'Fordham, Jung and the Self: A Re-Examination of Fordham's Contribution to Jung's Conceptualization of the Self', *Journal of Analytical Psychology* 50: 571–94.

Varvatsioulias, G. (2002) *Neurosis According to Caren Horney and the Anthropological Aspects of St Maximus the Confessor. A comparative study,* PhD thesis, University of Durham. Online. Available <http://thesis.ekt.gr/10342> (accessed 4.4.2012).

von-Franz, M.L. (1964) 'The Process of Individuation', in Carl Jung (1964) *Man and His Symbols,* New York: Dell Publishing.

———. (1971) 'The Inferior Function', in *Jung's Typology,* New York: Spring.

von-Franz, M.L. and Hillman, J. (1971) *Lectures on Jung's Typology,* Zurich: Spring Publications.

Wallace, E.R. (1984) 'Freud and Religion: A History and Reappraisal', *Psychoanalytic Study of Society* 10: 115–61.

Ware, K. (1967) 'The Transfiguration of the Body', in A.M. Allchin (ed.), *Sacraments and Image: Essays in the Christian Understanding of Man,* London: The Fellowship of St. Alban and St. Sergius.

———. (1987) 'The Unity of the Human Person According to the Greek Fathers', in Arthur Peacocke and Grant Gillett (eds.), *Persons and Personality. A Contemporary Inquiry.* Ian Ramsey Centre Publication 1: Oxford: Basil Blackwell.

———. (1997) '"My Helper and My Enemy": The Body in Greek Christianity', in Sara Coakley (ed.), *Religion and the Body,* Cambridge: Cambridge University Press.

Weber, M. (1949) *The Methodology of the Social Sciences,* New York: Free Press.

White, V. (1952) *God and the Unconscious,* London: The Harvill Press.

———. (1960) *Soul and Psyche,* London: Collins.

Wiggins, D. (1987) 'The Person as Object of Science, as Subject of Experience and as Locus of Value', in Arthur Peacocke and Grant Gillett (eds.), *Persons and Personality. A Contemporary Inquiry,* Oxford: Basil Blackwell.

Wilber, K. (2000) *Sex, Ecology, Spirituality,* Boston, MA: Shambhala Publications.

Winnicott, D.W. (1989) *Psycho-Analytic Explorations,* London: Karnac Books.

Wright, K. (1998) 'Gadamer, Hans-Georg', in *Routledge Encyclopedia of Philosophy,* Edward Craig (ed.), London and New York: Routledge.

Wulff, D.M. (1997) *Psychology of Religion. Classic and Contemporary,* New York: John Wiley & Sons, Inc.

Yiannaras, C. (2003) 'Psychoanalysis and Orthodox Anthropology', *Theologia* A: 51–60.

Zahle, J. (2007) 'Holism and Supervenience', in Stephen P. Turner and Mark W. Risjord (eds.), *Philosophy of Anthropology and Sociology,* Handbook of the Philosophy of Sciences, Amsterdam: Elsevier.

Zizioulas, J. (1985) *Being as Communion. Studies in Personhood and the Church,* Crestwood, New York: St Vladimir's Seminary Press.

———. (2006) *Communion and Otherness,* New York and London: T&T Clark.

———. (2008) *Lectures in Christian Dogmatics,* Douglas Knight (ed.), London: T&T Clark.

INDEX

Abraham, J. 158
active imagination 103, 116, 124, 126, 166, 168, 178; functioning as the *transcendent function* 125, 170; as integration of all functions 115–16; and prayer 116; 'translates emotions into images' 124
Adler, A. 6, 18
Adler, G. 41, 54, 130
alchemy 26, 55, 86, 107, 135–6, 170; Adam, 'original hylic-psychic man' 133; alchemical equivalents 132, 143, 147, 165, 172; alchemical Mercurius 48, 86, 135–6; *coniunctio (oppositorum)* 9, 12, 26, 133, 135, 170, 177; *hierosgamos* 135–6, 165; *lapis philosophorum* 8, 9, 135; *mandala* 33, 43, 49, 136; *maternal uroborus* 133; *pleroma* 165; 'pneumatic man' 133; *prima materia* 84, 93, 96, 104, 132, 134
Allport, W. 18
Anaxagoras 113
Anaximander 20, 36, 113
anima/animus, see Jung's archetypal theory
anima mundi 179
anthropology 6, 52, 60; apophatic anthropology 59ff, 120; 'negative anthropology' 61
Apocalypses 152
apokatastasis; see Maximus' doctrine of final restoration
archetypes; *see* Jung's archetypal theory
Archimedean point 48, 171
Aristotle 14, 20–1, 24, 112–13, 137; principle of wholeness 3; *dynameis* (faculties of the psyche) 113, 121–2, 127–8; *entelecheia* 20; *nous* (active and passive) 20, 21

Armstrong, A.H. 21, 37, 80
asceticism 45, 89, 96–97, 101–2, 140, 144, 168
Athanasius of Alexandria 137, 140
Augustine 61, 145, 152
Aziz's 'syndetic paradigm' 15

Balthasar, U. 58–9, 63, 65, 123, 139, 141, 156
Bathrellos, D. 121–2
Beebe, J. 94, 109, 117
Belzen, A. 18
Berdyaev, N. 53, 89, 105
Bishop, P. 41, 69, 75, 153, 158, 165
Black, D. 25–6, 48
Blowers, M. 58, 62, 80, 107
Bockus, M. 71, 167
body 3, 11, 16, 19, 29, 120, 130, 132–6, 160, 168, 177; in Aristotle 20; contemplation of 96–7; conveys spiritual meanings 145; deified 14, 144–5; in desert fathers 99, 106; and dualistic Hellenic conceptualization 79, 141; both 'fallible' and 'deified' 144; in Freud 5–6, 41, 52, 98, 134; in Jung 47, 75, 132, 134–6, 145–6; in Maximus 22, 60–4, 100, 136–43; in Plato 36–7; and 'mystic force' 19; as an *organ* of the soul 62; a 'recapitulation' of all sensible things 141; and renunciation 101, 103, 146; 'spiritual' 177; and the spiritual communion of Christ's limbs 141–3; 'subtle' 135, 145
Brooke, R. 73–4, 77, 164
Brown, P. 103, 140, 164
Buber, M. 10, 52

charity; *see* love
Christ 47–8, 58, 62, 64–8, 87–90, 107, 137–8, 140–6, 152, 158, 171; and

nature 22, 45, 53, 61–2, 65–6, 74, 84,
  98–9; divine 58, 64, 88, 140, 151;
  human 21, 22, 37, 60, 89, 107
Nagy, M. 20, 70–2, 74
Nellas, P. 11, 62, 137
Nemesius 119, 121–2
Neoplatonics 21, 57–8, 65, 66, 140–1
Neumann, E. 84, 95, 109, 133
Neurophysiology 3, 23
neurosis 50, 56
New Age 25, 50
Newman, B. 176
Nicolescu, B. 3, 18
Nietzsche 22, 25, 78; *Übermensch* 5
nous (intellect) 24, 96, 101–3, 113, 119,
  123–4, 138–9; *see also* Maximus'
  functions; as 'inner vision' 124;
  trapped to the aesthesis and losing its
  'investigative' aspect 101

Oedipus (complex) 39, 54
ontological security 28–9
ontology 5, 13, 17, 20–2, 60–1, 65, 70, 87,
  108, 137, 144; 'Eucharistic ontology'
  142; a multilevel ontological framework
  28–32; ontological levels 18, 33, 69–71,
  175; ontological potential of beings 22,
  24, 27, 32–5, 52–4, 70–1, 118, 143
opus Christi 148, 152
Origen 8–9, 11, 20, 51, 57–8, 65, 67, 80; and
  Alexandrian school of hermeneutics 62;
  developmental scheme *becoming-rest-
  movement (fall)* 82; *introverted type* 112
Other, the 41–3, 74, 106–8

paedophilia 173
Palmer, M. 8, 49
Paloutzian, R.F. 18, 19; *a multilevel
  interdisciplinary paradigm* 18, 28
Papadopoulos, R. 41, 55, 69, 72, 74, 104,
  136
Parmenides 113
passions 89, 96, 99–104, 107
Pauli's *exclusion principle* 4
Paul's paradigm 155
personhood/personality 60, 84–5,
  92–3, 166; fragmentary 42, 102; as a
  'functional complex' 60; as a *plateau* of
  cultural facts 87
perspectivism 148–9
phantasy 115–16, 128
Phenomenology 22–3, 67, 72–3; of the
  face 108

Philosophy 17–8, 52–3, 60, 65, 69, 83;
  Greek 20–1; of mind 17; modern 22–3,
  73, 77; Neoplatonic 21; of religion 27
Philo 66, 80
Philokalia, the 79, 110, 180
Physics 3–4, 149, 163; *principle of
  equivalence* 171; *entropy* 174
Plato 20–1, 36, 61, 70, 112–13, 137; *bios
  biotos* 113; classification of functions
  into *superior/inferior* 113, 115, 118;
  epistemology 20; eudemonistic ethics
  4; *forms* 20, 36; and psychic functions/
  three parts of the soul 113, 121, 124
Plotinus 21, 61, 65–7, 87
pre/trans fallacy 25, 28, 42
pre-Socratics 20, 61, 79, 113
Popper, K. 29–30, 36, 149
post-Freudians 6, 25
post-Jungians 18, 34, 48–51, 68, 116–18,
  134, 153–4
post-modern/ity 24, 35, 50, 76, 145–6
Pound, Ezra 158
prayer 96, 120, 123–5, 166; bears both
  a 'therapeutic' and a divinising power
  125
privatio boni 152
providence 142, 154–7, 159
psyche, the: *see* Jung's understanding of
  the psyche
psychoid 69, 70, 165
psychological, the 17–19, 25–8, 32
psychology (analytical) 46, 49–51, 113,
  164, 172; archetypal 68; classical 18,
  84; developmental 84; evolutionary
  17; experiential 58; of religion 18,
  (genres of) 25–7

Quantum theory 4
quaternity 46, 85, 117, 131–2, 150

reason 24, 52, 64–5, 88–9, 97, 102, 118;
  see also logos; in Phenomenology 76,
  81; in Stoics 110
reciprocity 31
redemption 11, 47, 152, 154, 160
*reductionism/*reduction 9, 13, 17, 31, 61,
  149; from psychological to somatic 77;
  from spiritual to psychological 13, 71;
  of Trinity to 'man's psychology' 46–7
relativity theory 149, 152
religion; *see also* Jung's theory on religion;
  dimensions of religious commitment
  19; as 'illusion' 17, 26, 39; 'religion

Made in the USA
Columbia, SC
05 November 2019